IMAGES
of America

AFRICAN-AMERICAN LIFE IN SUMNER COUNTY

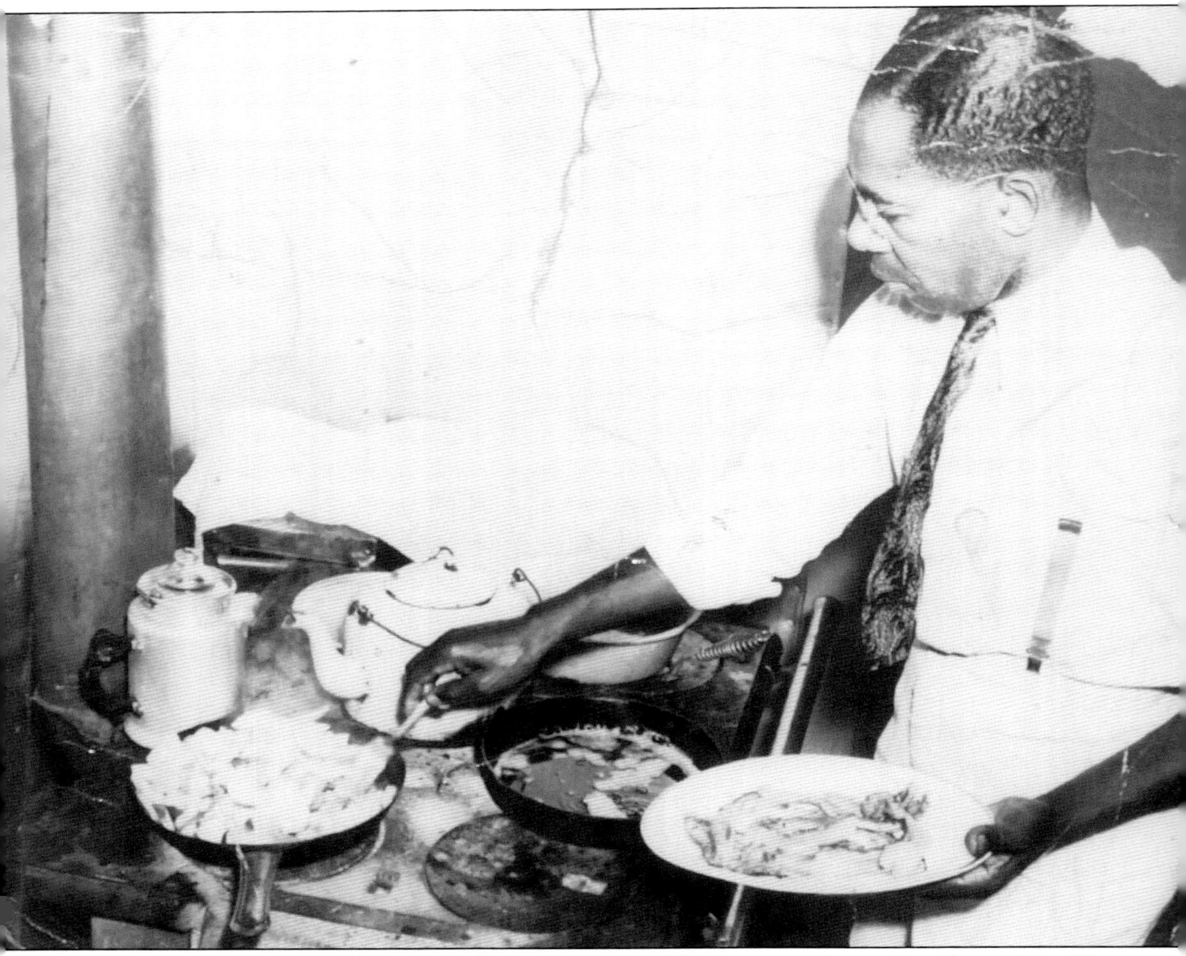

John Hutch Brinkley (1908–1995) was the son of William and Fanny Brinkley of Mt. Olive. When merely a child, his mother died and his father was soon to follow. Despite seemingly insurmountable odds, his desire for an education led him to pack all his worldly goods into a paper sack and walk 10 miles to Gallatin. Hutch found both a job as a cook and a place to live in the H. Frank Dulin home. Mrs. Laura Scott Dulin, H. Frank Dulin's wife, demanded three things of Hutch: (1) never tell a lie; (2) attend church weekly; and (3) stay in school. He graduated from Union High School in 1929 and graduated from Agricultural and Industrial State College in 1951. He then went on to teach school for 43 years at Cairo, Mt. Olive, Hall's Chapel, Macedonia, and Union Elementary Schools. After an honorable discharge from the U.S. Navy on June 26, 1943, he became a licensed funeral director, hospital orderly, notary public, writer of Sunday school literature, trustee of Cairo School, officer of elections at Union Elementary precinct, and director of a WHIN radio broadcast called "Bringing the Church to You."

IMAGES of America

AFRICAN-AMERICAN LIFE IN SUMNER COUNTY

Velma Howell Brinkley with
Mary Huddleston Malone

ARCADIA PUBLISHING

ISBN 978-0-7385-6863-8

Published by Arcadia Publishing
Charleston SC, Chicago IL, Portsmouth NH, San Francisco CA

Printed in the United States of America

Library of Congress Catalog Card Number: 98-85872

For all general information contact Arcadia Publishing at:
Telephone 843-853-2070
Fax 843-853-0044
E-mail sales@arcadiapublishing.com
For customer service and orders:
Toll-Free 1-888-313-2665

Visit us on the Internet at www.arcadiapublishing.com

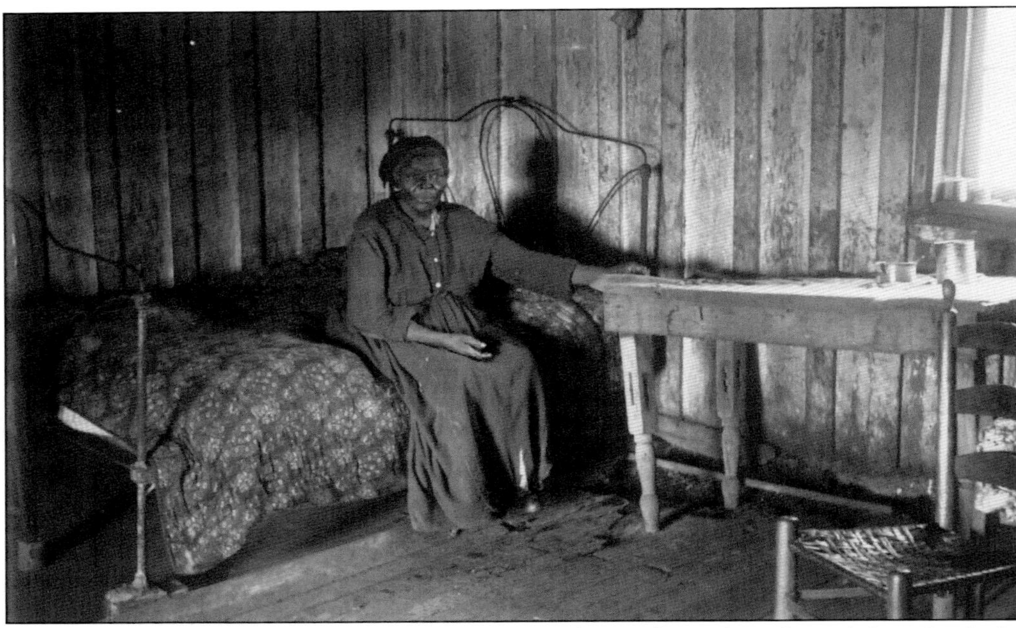

A former slave sits alone in an old slave cabin. Her sun bonnet hangs from the nail above her bed.

On the cover: Members of the Union Elementary eighth grade class of 1955, from left to right, are as follows: (front row) Deannie Parker, Frances Barr, Emma Farley, Katherine Coakley, Katie Goodall, Laura Green, Willie Douglas, Dorothy Allen, and Robert Alexander; (second row) Thomas Drake, Homer Malone, Oscar Crenshaw, Earl Key, Franklin Harper, Irma Baker, Agnes Agnew, and Mattie Austin; (third row) Theola Alexander, Onie Flippen, Frances Drake, Jimmy Gooch, Foster Gooch, Leona Douglas, Lucy Barr, and Mildred Carey; (fourth row) John Link, Bettye Robinson, Laura Franklin, Polly Branham, Joe Dee Austin Jr., Barbara Walker, Leroy Goodall, unidentified, and Clifford Vance; (fifth row) Paul Hall, James Crutcher, Thomas Garrett, Howard McMurray, Sammie Goodrich, Talmadge Wilks, Ernest Johnson, and Leon Adams.

Contents

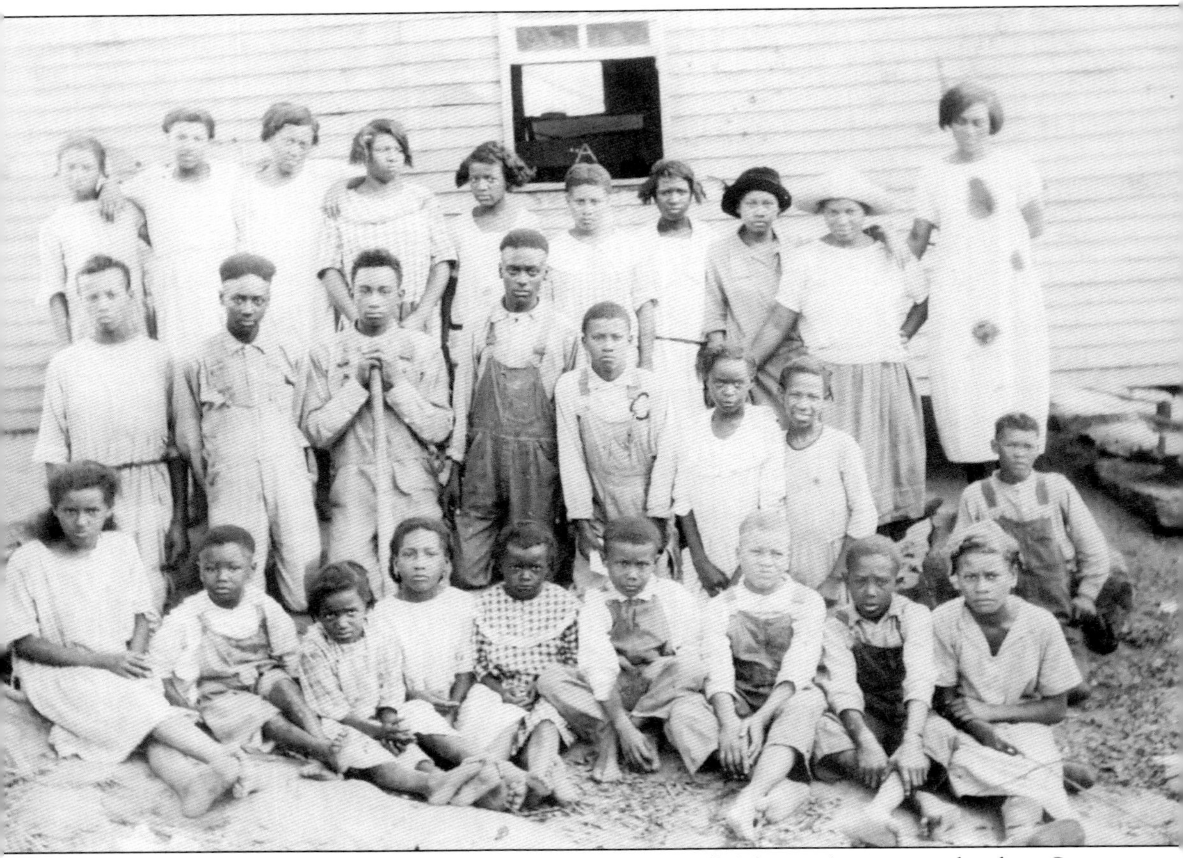

In 1931, this Scattersville School was one of many small African-American schools in Sumner County. Rev. Peter Tyree and Ola Bate (pictured) taught in this one-room school building. Ola, a 1926 graduate of Agricultural and Industrial State College, was the first African-American female from Sumner County to earn a college degree. Her father, Charles Brimage Bate, holds that distinction among African-American males by earning a college degree in 1900 from Roger Williams College. Ola retired in 1968 after 41 years of service as a teacher, and Peter retired in 1946 after 36 years in the classroom.

INTRODUCTION

Sumner County was created by the North Carolina General Assembly on November 17, 1786. It was named in honor of Gen. Jethro Sumner, a North Carolina soldier of the American Revolution. At its creation, Sumner County was bounded on the west by Davidson County, on the north by the Virginia-North Carolina state line, and on the east and south by Native American territories. Sumner and Davidson were the only two counties in existence in what is now known as Middle Tennessee.

Present-day Tennessee had been a part of North Carolina until 1790, when North Carolina gave up her territory west of the mountains to the U.S. government. For the next six years (1790–1796), the territory's official name was the "Territory of the United States of America South of the River Ohio." William Blount (English by birth) of North Carolina was appointed governor of the Southwest Territory by President George Washington.

Slaves entered Sumner County much like they had entered the Jamestown Settlement (1619) many years earlier—in human bondage and chains. The first significant number of slaves reached Sumner County in the late eighteenth century from North Carolina. They came in shackles and chains in the company of their immigrant owners as burden bearers. As agricultural pursuits grew, so did the desire for slave labor. This increased need for slaves was met in one of the following ways: (1) the slave trader; (2) native born, or slaves born in Sumner County; and (3) estate or private sale. Unlike others, who were drawn across the mountains by the promise of freedom, opportunity, and free government land, Africans came in shackles to provide the labor for the founding fathers' dream of a New Republic.

In Sumner County, we have witnessed renewed interest and effort by black people in preserving their recent history and culture, although many of these attempts have gone unnoticed. African Americans and others on a national level have been trying, with varying degrees of success, to preserve black history since the early 1800s when many slave narratives were first being published. Later, in the 1870s, there were communities of free blacks which gave rise to black newspapers and literary societies. Our past teaches us and guides us toward our future. Through the passage of time, however, our historical documents, photographs, and other resources are growing increasingly fragile. We must hasten our preservation efforts despite a lack of resources, neglect, powerlessness, indifference, and other obstacles.

The fact that African Americans lack a thorough knowledge of self continues to take a devastating toll upon the black family. The 13th Amendment, which outlawed slavery, did little to restore one's identity past the plantation experience. The overwhelming majority of black Americans know very little about the land of their ancestors—their tribes, customs, and ways of seeing and doing things—because of the long enslavement experience in the New World.

Historian Dr. John Henrik Clark said, "History is a clock that people use to tell the cultural and political time of day. It is also a compass that people use to find themselves on the map of human geography." Black children need to know that their ancestors created the first civilization and the great cultures of the Nile Valley, Nubia, the Sudan, Ethiopia, Southern Africa, and Mesopotamia. They need to know their genetic connection to a vibrant legacy of perseverance, survival, and triumph. The African American is in peril today, partly because he has not learned his own "true" history, nor has he learned the inherent lessons contained therein. As a result, each generation grapples with issues and problems their forebears resolved and continues making the same mistakes. History is indeed the clock by which we reckon time, place, and contribution within the stream of human existence. African and African American contributions to the tapestry have been great. People of African heritage must learn and embrace them!

We hope this pictorial account will lead the reader to an increased awareness of significant contributions made by local African Americans. Every effort was made to avoid a dry, standardized chronology of name, date, and event; this book deals instead with the uniqueness of each entrant. The main focus, of course, is on the people of Sumner County: people at work, people at play, civic-minded citizens, slaves; the prominent as well as the unknown. In addition, the chapter entitled "Artifacts and Remembrances" presents images which show how black people have evolved from the yoke of slavery to the boardrooms of today. This is not, and was not meant to be, a comprehensive history of a people. It is, instead, the telling of a unique story through pictures.

One

Education

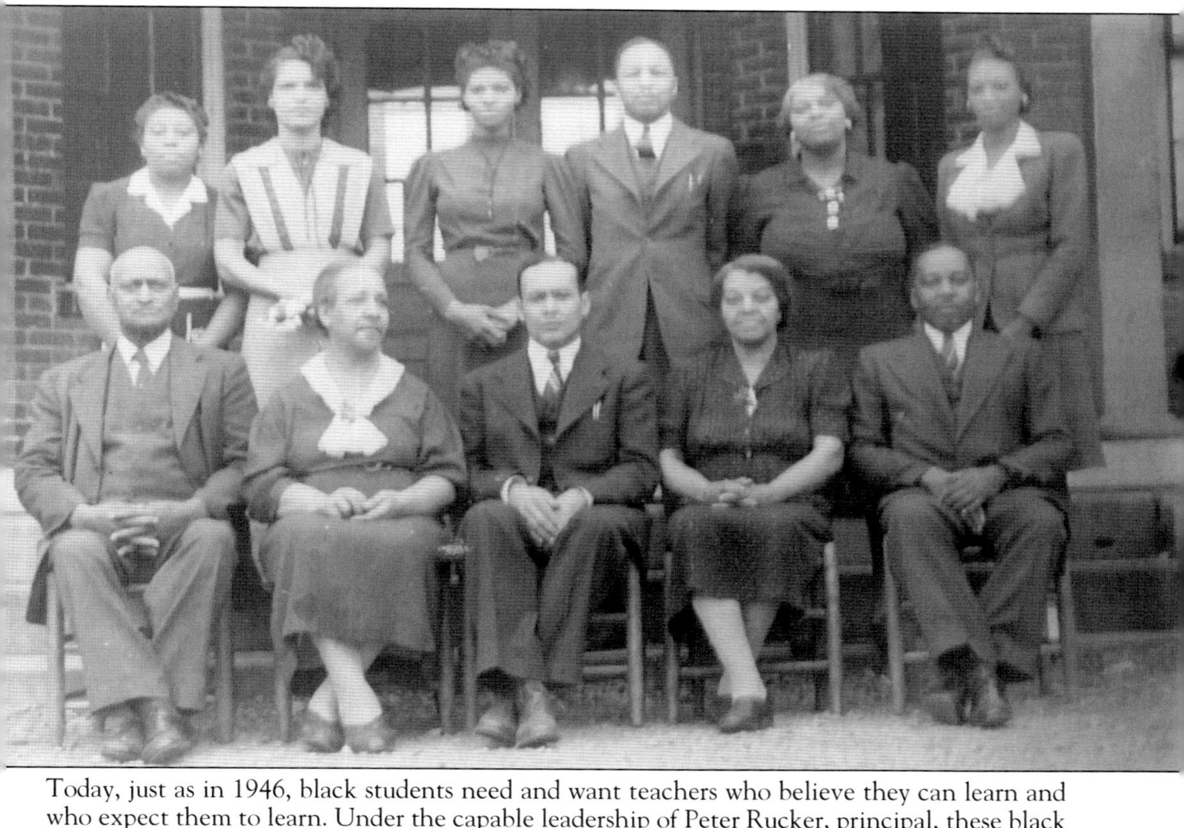

Today, just as in 1946, black students need and want teachers who believe they can learn and who expect them to learn. Under the capable leadership of Peter Rucker, principal, these black educators became bridge builders in the field of education. They are, from left to right, as follows: (front row) Charles Brimage Bate, Diora Wylie Vertrees, Peter Rucker, Nora Turner Bate, and E.A. Gray; (back row) Edna Mae Scott, Everlina Vertrees Rucker, Anna Ligon, Harold Smith, Callie Bell Apple McKissack, and Johnnie Gray.

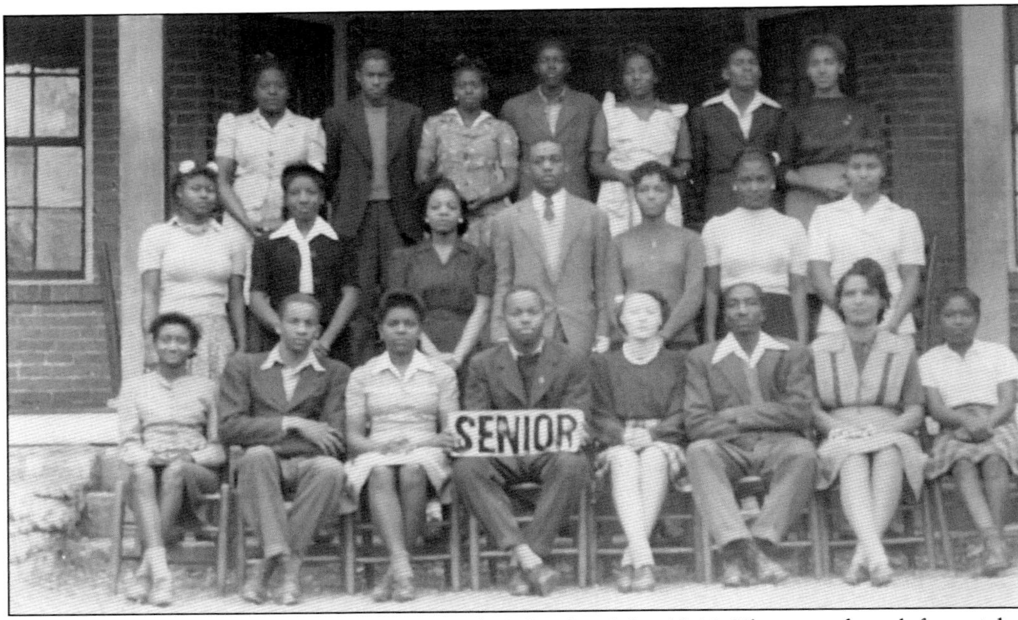

This senior class graduated from Union High School in May 1944. They are, from left to right, as follows: (first row) Odessa Johnson, Tilman Payne, Betty Flippin, James Hudson, Cora Johns, James Dobbins, Everlina Rucker (class advisor), and Sarah Dobbins; (second row) Mattie High, Julia Dobbins, Mattie Wynne, Billy Hogg, Beulah Goodrich, Willow Bonds, and Allen Frances Brewer; (third row) Amanda Wynne, Edward Coakley, Sarah Head, Wallace Turner, Mabel Mills, John Alexander, and Margaret Sadler.

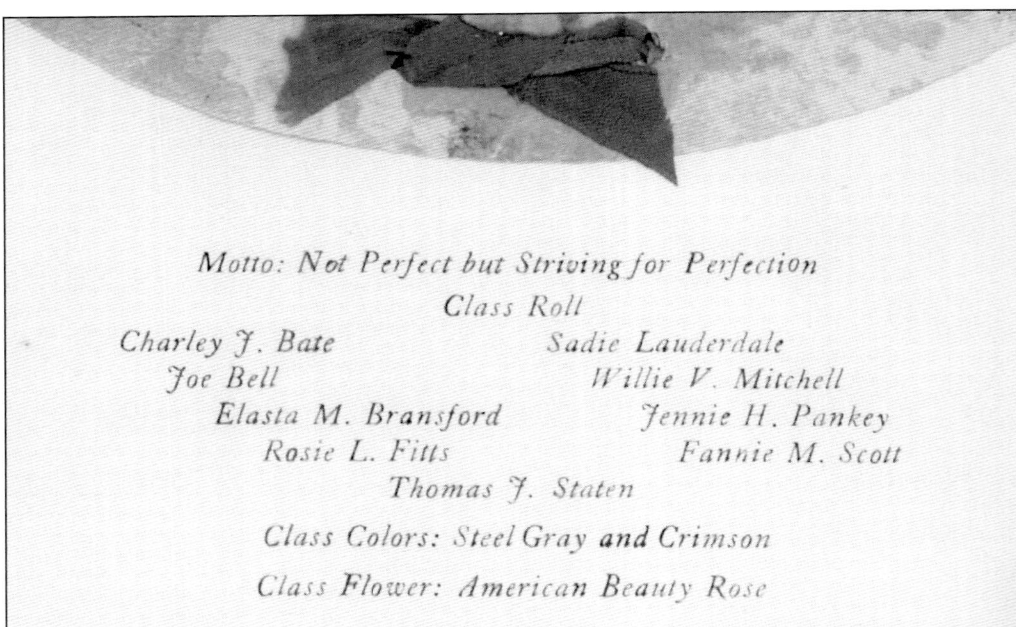

Motto: Not Perfect but Striving for Perfection

Class Roll

Charley J. Bate — *Sadie Lauderdale*
Joe Bell — *Willie V. Mitchell*
Elasta M. Bransford — *Jennie H. Pankey*
Rosie L. Fitts — *Fannie M. Scott*
Thomas J. Staten

Class Colors: Steel Gray and Crimson

Class Flower: American Beauty Rose

This page is from a graduation invitation for the Union High School Class of 1930. The invitation has been preserved in its entirety by class member Elaster Bransford Douglas.

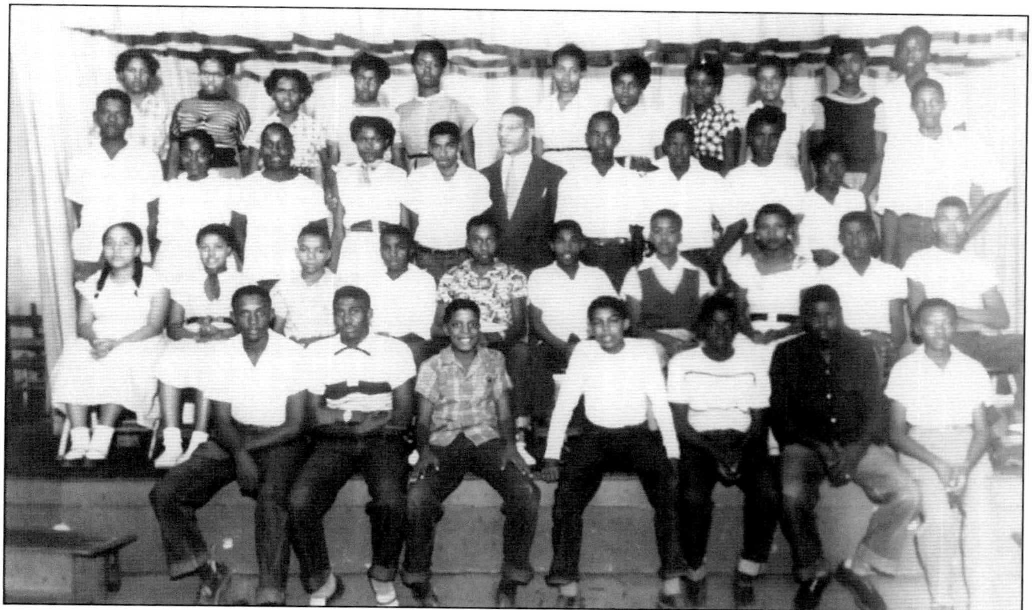

Union Elementary School principal B.J. Hall (third row, six from left) is pictured with a group of students.

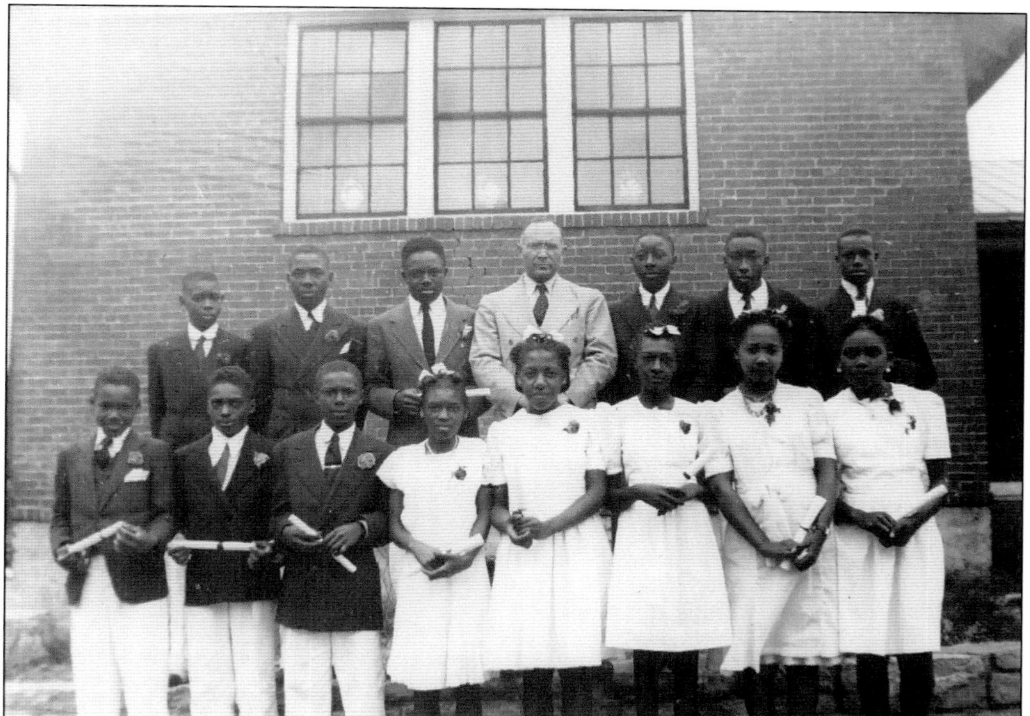

This eighth grade class graduated in May 1942 with Johnnie Gray as teacher. Members of the class, from left to right, are as follows: (front row) James Rippy, Leonard Alexander, four unidentified, Anna Barr, and Ethel Harper; (back row) James McClellan, unidentified, Johnny Carter, Dr. Jonathan Rucker (principal), Sidney Vaughn, H.P. Lyles, and Ward Horsley.

CLOSING EXERCISES

UNION HIGH SCHOOL

SUMNER COUNTY TRAINING SCHOOL

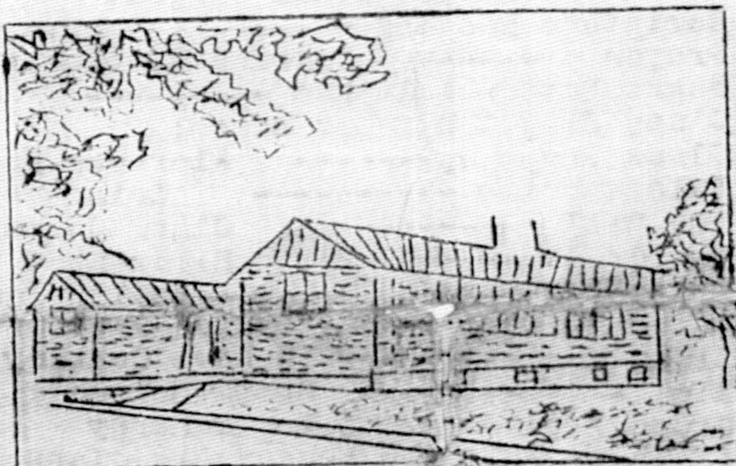

BEGINNING MAY 1[illegible], 7:30 P.M.

ENDING FRIDAY NIGHT MAY 18, 1934

Note that this school program bears two names: Union High School and Sumner County Training School. The last name implies a narrow and limited curriculum, which was used to help gain approval for a new school for African Americans. In the early twentieth century, in order to secure white approval, the name either had to imply or state compliance with the approved Southern agenda for African-American education: mechanical arts, agriculture, and domestic science. Southern whites defended this curriculum as being the only education suited to African Americans' innate capabilities and low social status, according to their beliefs.

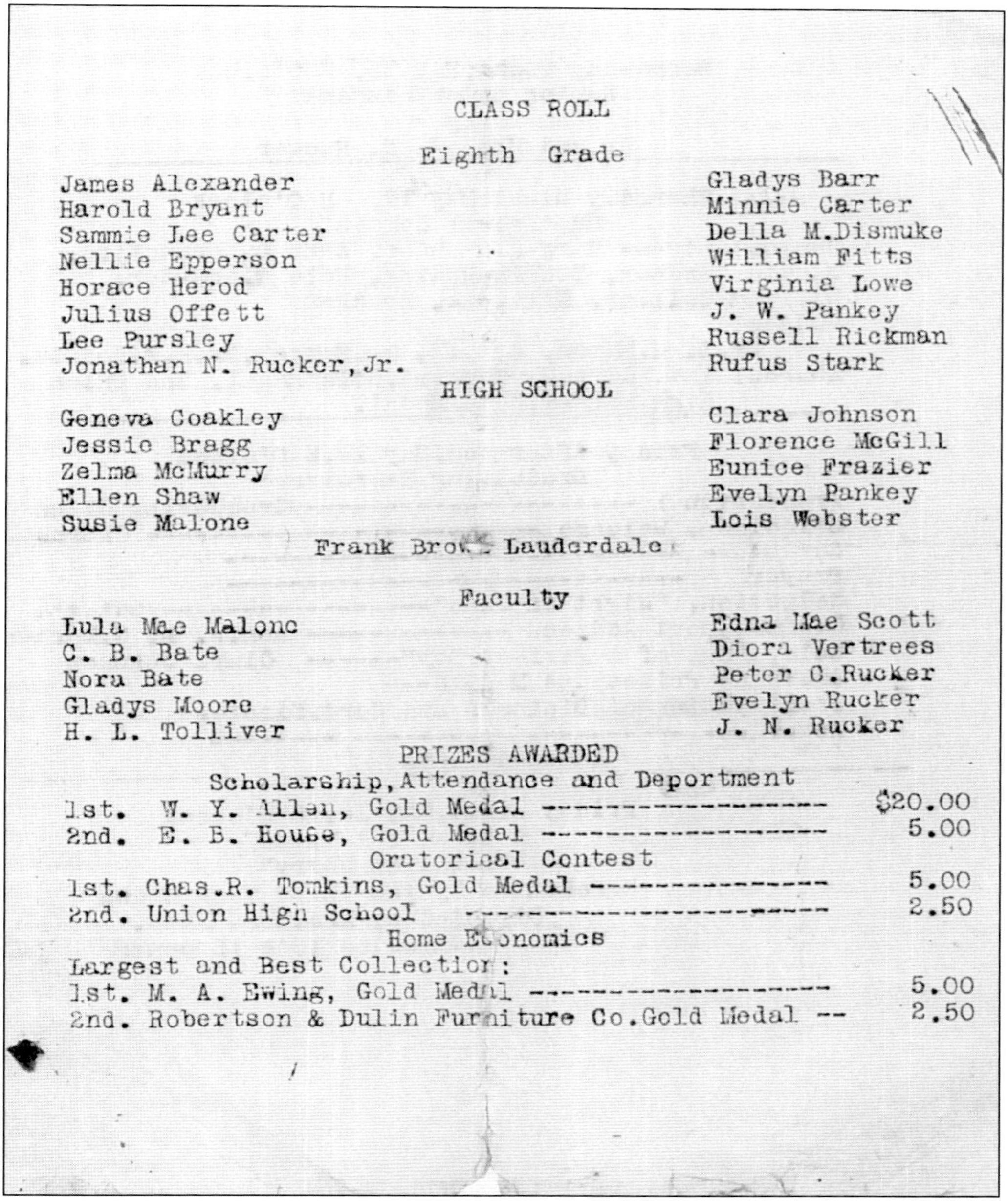

CLASS ROLL

Eighth Grade

James Alexander
Harold Bryant
Sammie Lee Carter
Nellie Epperson
Horace Herod
Julius Offett
Lee Pursley
Jonathan N. Rucker, Jr.
Gladys Barr
Minnie Carter
Della M.Dismuke
William Fitts
Virginia Lowe
J. W. Pankey
Russell Rickman
Rufus Stark

HIGH SCHOOL

Geneva Coakley
Jessie Bragg
Zelma McMurry
Ellen Shaw
Susie Malone
Clara Johnson
Florence McGill
Eunice Frazier
Evelyn Pankey
Lois Webster

Frank Bro[illegible] Lauderdale

Faculty

Lula Mae Malone
C. B. Bate
Nora Bate
Gladys Moore
H. L. Tolliver
Edna Mae Scott
Diora Vertrees
Peter C.Rucker
Evelyn Rucker
J. N. Rucker

PRIZES AWARDED

Scholarship, Attendance and Deportment

1st. W. Y. Allen, Gold Medal ---------------- $20.00
2nd. E. B. House, Gold Medal ---------------- 5.00

Oratorical Contest

1st. Chas.R. Tomkins, Gold Medal ---------------- 5.00
2nd. Union High School ---------------- 2.50

Home Economics

Largest and Best Collection:
1st. M. A. Ewing, Gold Medal ---------------- 5.00
2nd. Robertson & Dulin Furniture Co.Gold Medal -- 2.50

In 1934, graduation was a week-long event that began on May 13. The scheduled events were as follows: baccalaureate sermon (Sunday); senior class program (Monday); a play presented by the home economics department (Tuesday); senior entertainment by Dr. and Mrs. J.N. Rucker (Wednesday); an oratorical contest (Thursday); graduation exercises (Friday afternoon); and a three-act drama (Friday night).

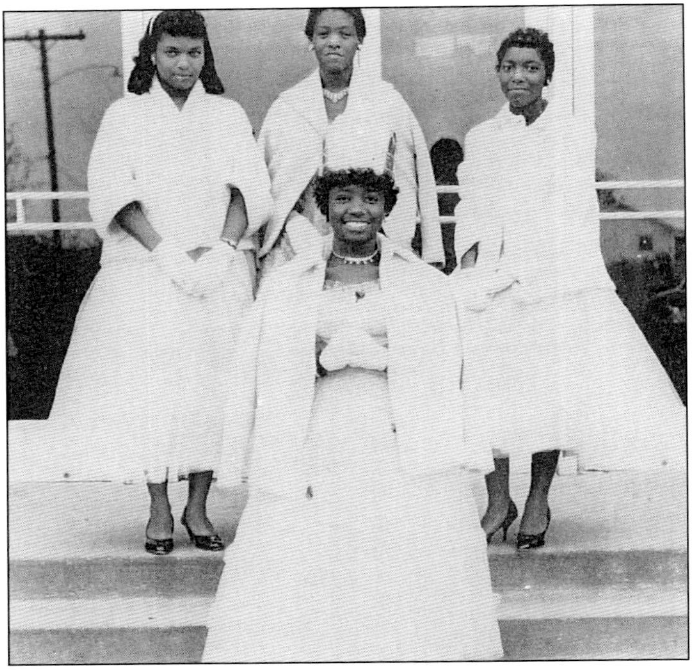

At Union High School, the major fund-raiser was the annual "Queen Contest." This event was a financial contest conducted between classes and individual students. The student who raised the largest amount of money represented her class during the homecoming celebration. This photo shows the 1960 queen, Emma C. Woods, and her attendants. They are, from left to right, as follows: Gloria Douglas, Laura Douglas, and Rosie Ann Stewart.

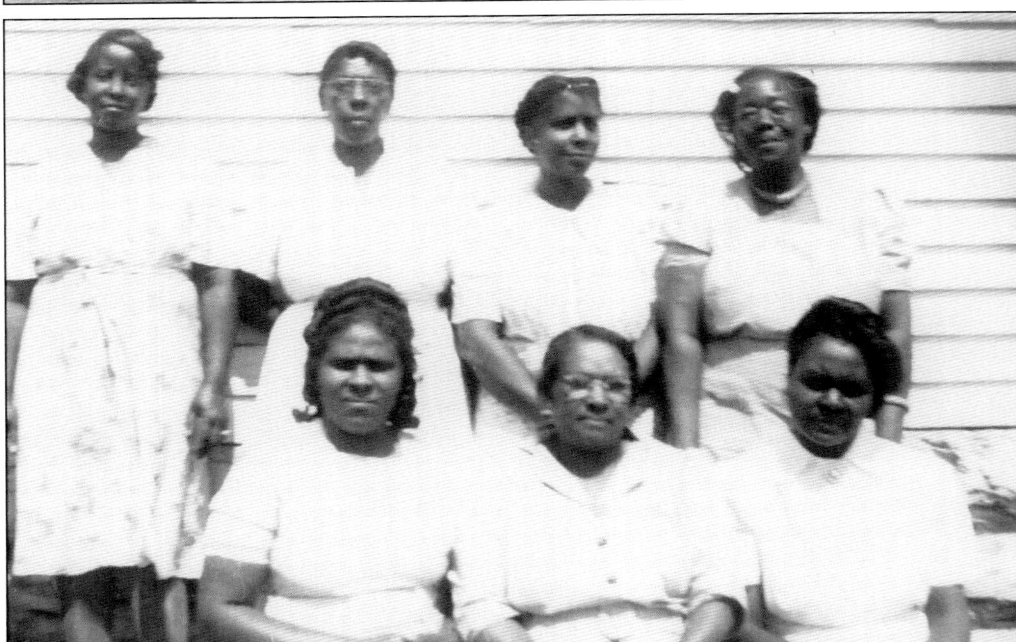

When the PTA was founded in 1897, the goals were straightforward for white organizations: better schools, healthier children, and stronger families. In addition to the more traditional activities, the Cairo PTA provided a lunch program and drinking water, paid the cook, and funded a building program. The 1948 PTA members pictured, from left to right, are as follows: (seated) Mattie D. Fitts, Willie Wilks, and Lillian Lauderdale; (standing) Mary Eliza Hamilton, Ophelia Robb, Alma Wilks, and Mattie Austin.

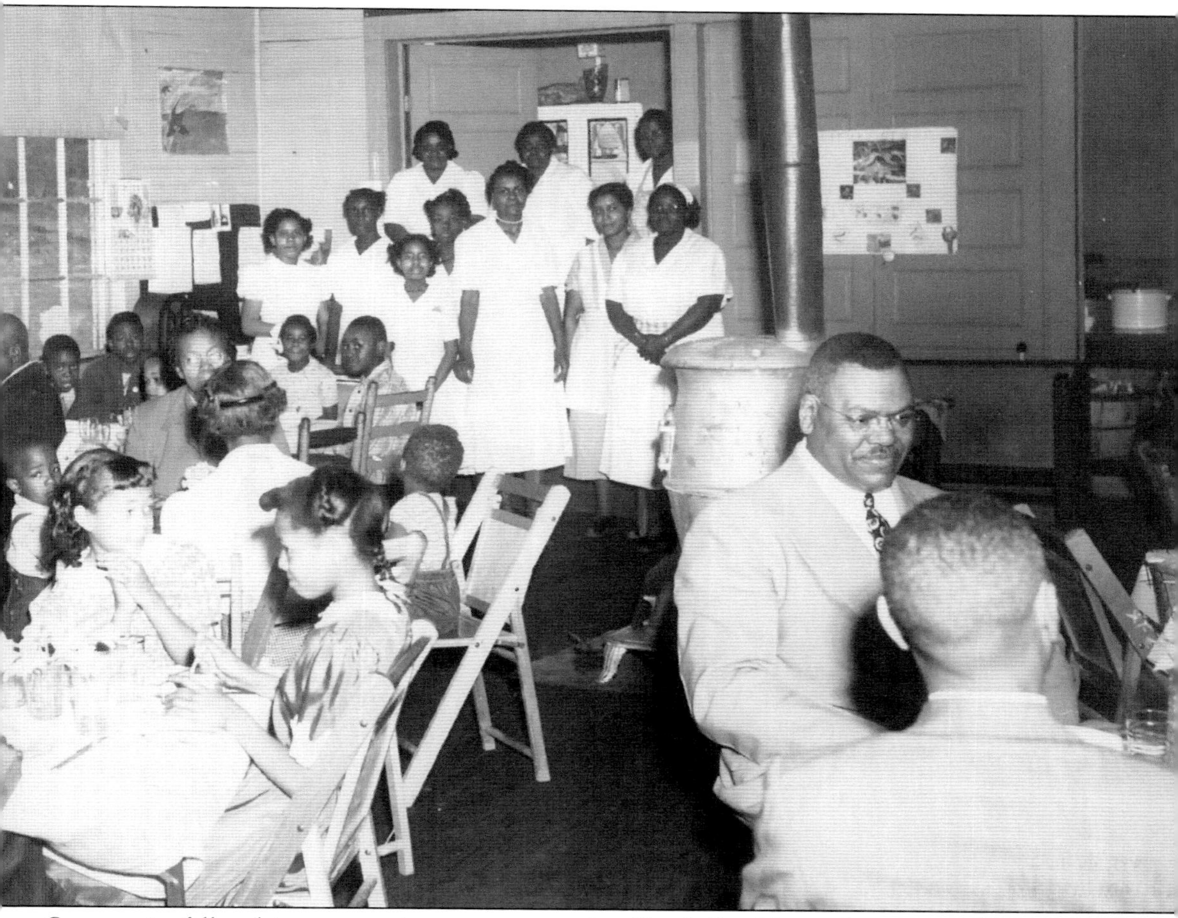

Community fellowship was very important to teacher Hutch Brinkley, so he sponsored events and activities to facilitate the same. This group of parents, teachers, students, and religious leaders gathered for Sunday morning breakfast before attending worship services at their various churches.

Promotional Exercises

of

The Sixth Grade Class

of

Union Elementary School

Class Officers

Gary Lauderdale .... President
Mark Carr .... Vice-President
Billie Staten .... Secretary
Michael Hollerman .... Assistant Secretary
Darlene Branham .... Treasurer
Catherine Walker .... Chaplain
Robert Sweat and Odell Head .... Business Managers

✚

Tuesday Evening, May 27th, 1969

8:00 P. M.

Union Elementary School Auditorium

Mrs. Johnnie Gray and Mr. J. H. Brinkley,
Teachers

Prof. B. J. Hall, Principal

For the sixth grade class of 1969, this promotional event culminated their stay at Union Elementary School on Carson Street. They entered Union High School, which housed grades 7 through 12, in the fall of 1969.

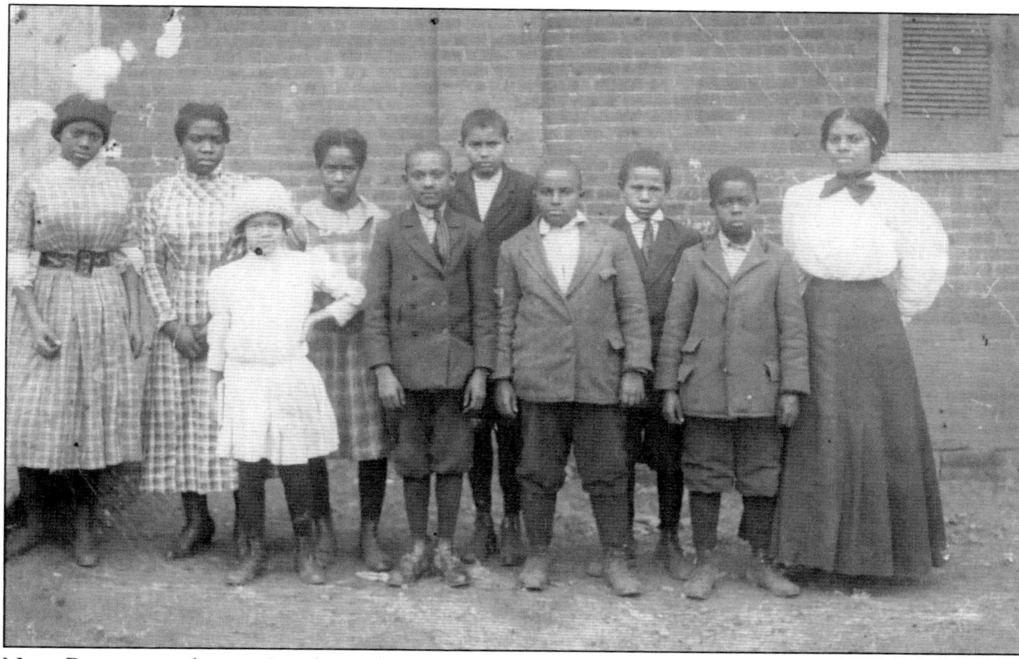

Nora Bate, a teacher at South Gallatin School, stands with her class on Winchester Street for this picture (*c.* 1911).

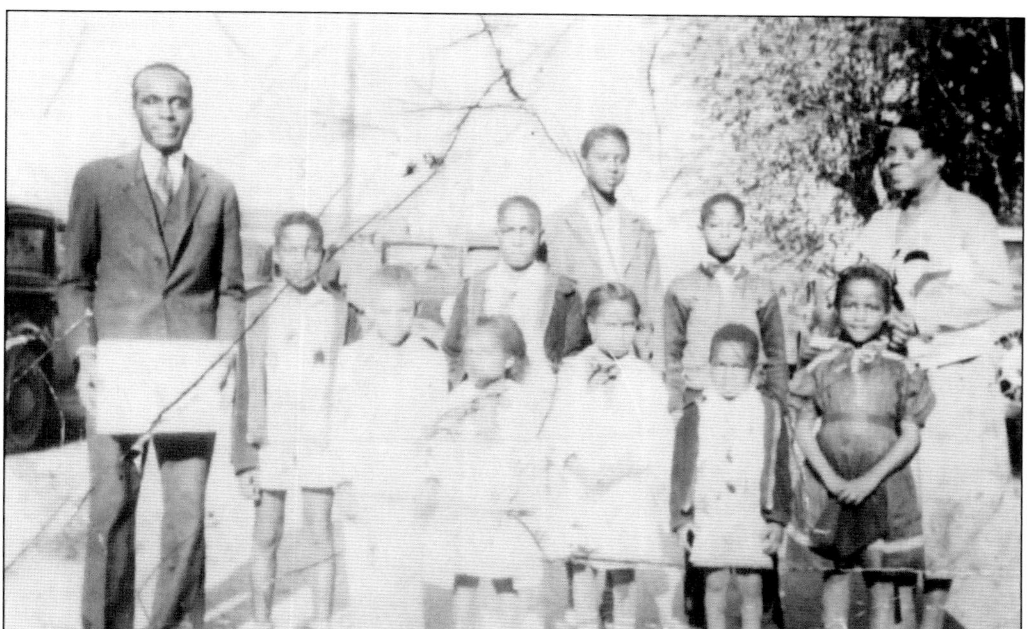

Rev. DeWitt Scott and Jeanes teacher Evelyn P. Hall are pictured with an early school group from Peach Valley School.

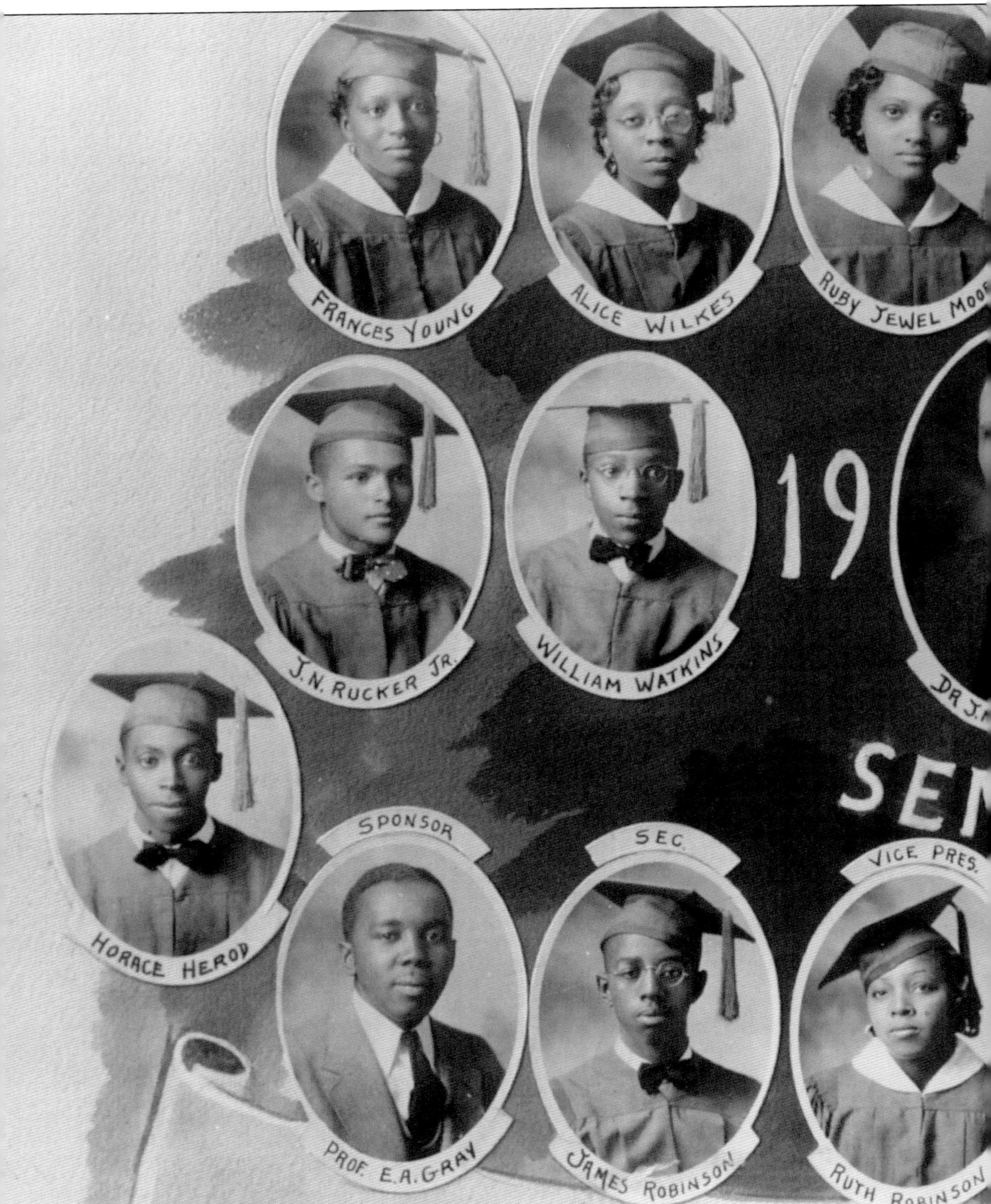

The Class of 1938 was the 14th class to graduate from Sumner County Training School. This group of 17 represented a significant increase over the first graduating class in 1924,

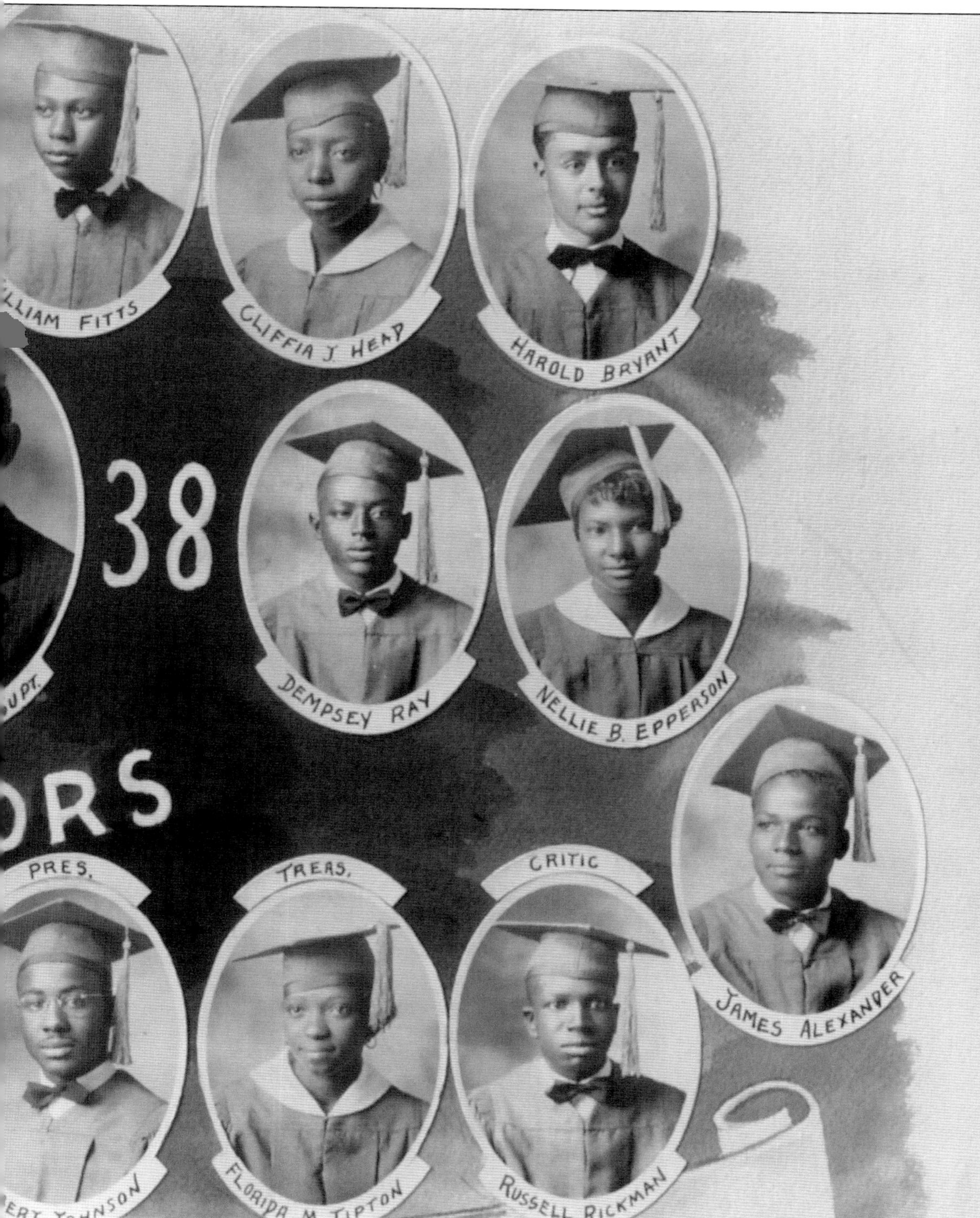

which had 7 members.

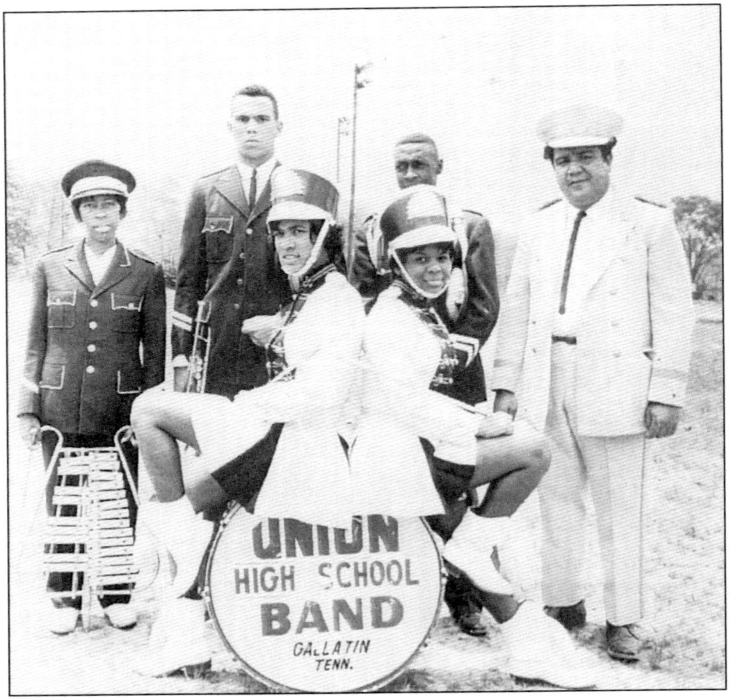

George Randolph Offitt Sr. was the band director at Union High School from 1950 to 1970. Randolph is shown here with the senior band members of the Class of 1965. They are, from left to right, as follows: (sitting) Mary Caroline Carver (head majorette) and Ruth Ann Gurley; (standing) Annie Mae Robb, Randolph Offitt Jr., Wesley Allen Hill, and Randolph Offitt Sr.

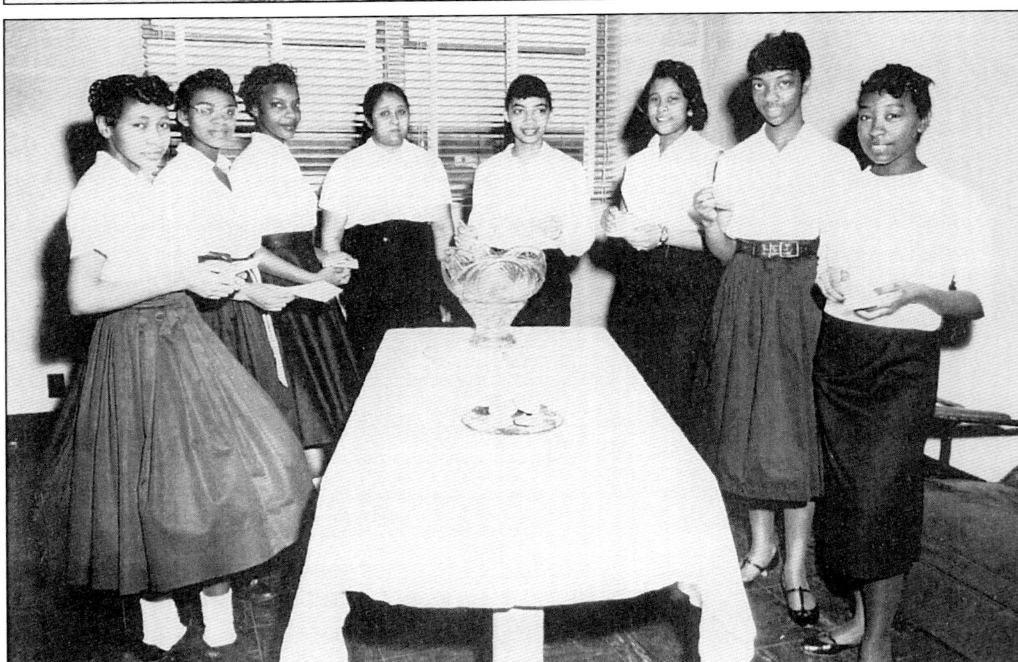

"Better Homes for a Better Nation" was the motto for the New Homemakers of America in 1959. Members of this organization are shown here having refreshments at Union High School. They are, from left to right, as follows: Thelma Flippen, Katherine Randle, Cornella Woods, Ella Lee Dobbins (teacher), Katherine Coakley, Onie J. Flippen, Pervis Barksdale, and Thelma Fentress.

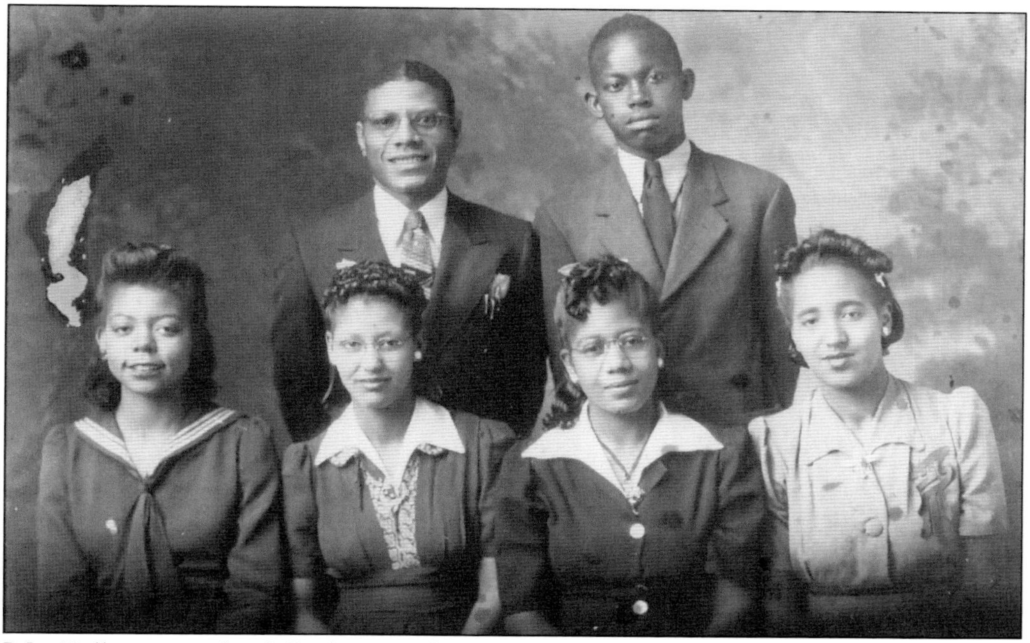

B.J. Hall, principal of Durham's Chapel School, is pictured with the eighth grade graduating class of 1941. The graduates are, from left to right, as follows: (seated) Deotha Malone, Ruby Banks Scott, Sallie Bragg Barr, and Margaret Sadler Bransford; (standing) B.J. Hall and James Hudson.

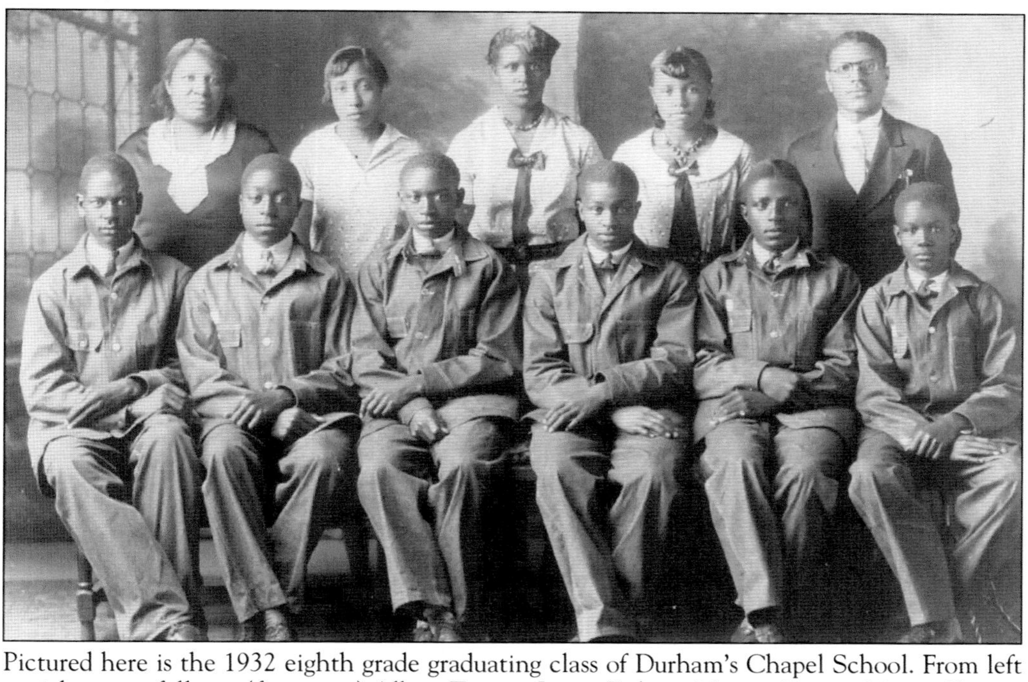

Pictured here is the 1932 eighth grade graduating class of Durham's Chapel School. From left to right are as follows: (front row) Albert Turner, James Debow, Marion Young, Martin Young, Jessie B. Brown, and Overton Chester; (back row) Lucille Bracken (teacher), Lucille Branham, Maggie Lee Malone, Annie Malone, and B.J. Hall (principal).

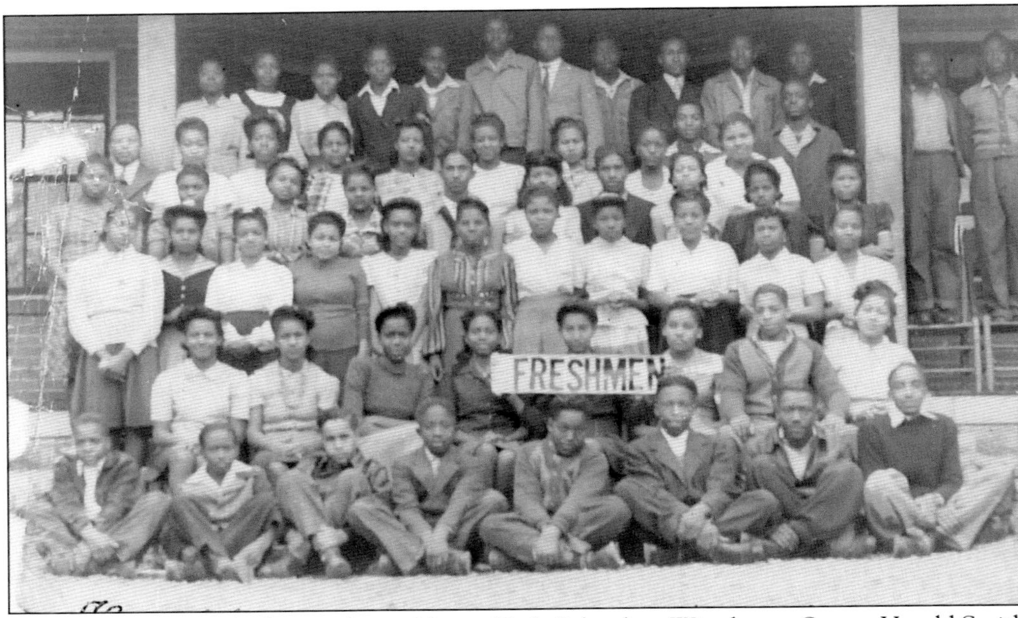

Pictured is the 1945 freshman class at Union High School on Winchester Street. Harold Smith is the homeroom teacher.

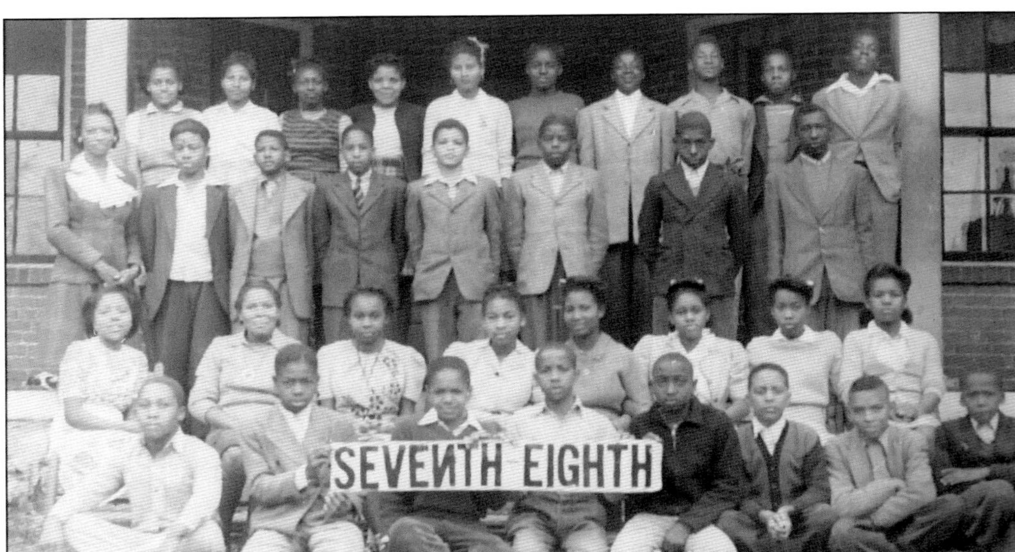

A group of seventh and eighth grade students is shown in this 1945 photograph. They are Johnnie Gray's homeroom students at Union High School on Winchester Street.

These students attended Hall's Chapel School in Rock House Hollow, where J. Hutch Brinkley was the teacher. They are, from left to right, as follows: (first row) Cretdell Adams and Garrett Martin; (second row) Billy Ray and Paul Vaughn; (third row) Bryant Adams and unidentified.

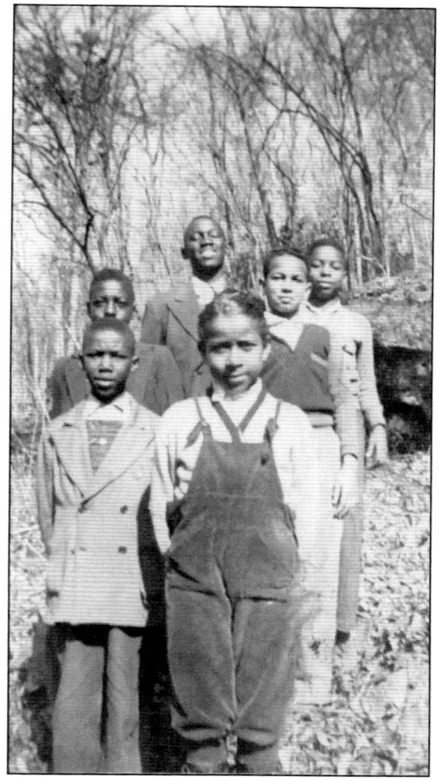

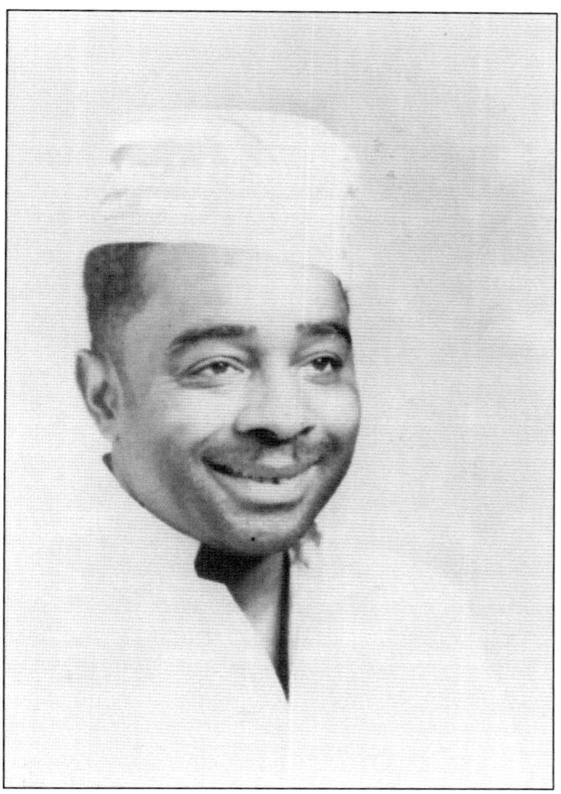

Carter Johnson (1917–1968) was the first African American to be hired by the Gallatin City Fire Department. This picture shows Johnson in his Howard Elementary School cafeteria uniform, a job he held prior to city employment. His wife, the former Katherine Coakley, also worked in the cafeteria. She went for a two-week interim period in 1951 and ended up staying 30 years. Their sons are Charlie and Rev. Bobby Johnson.

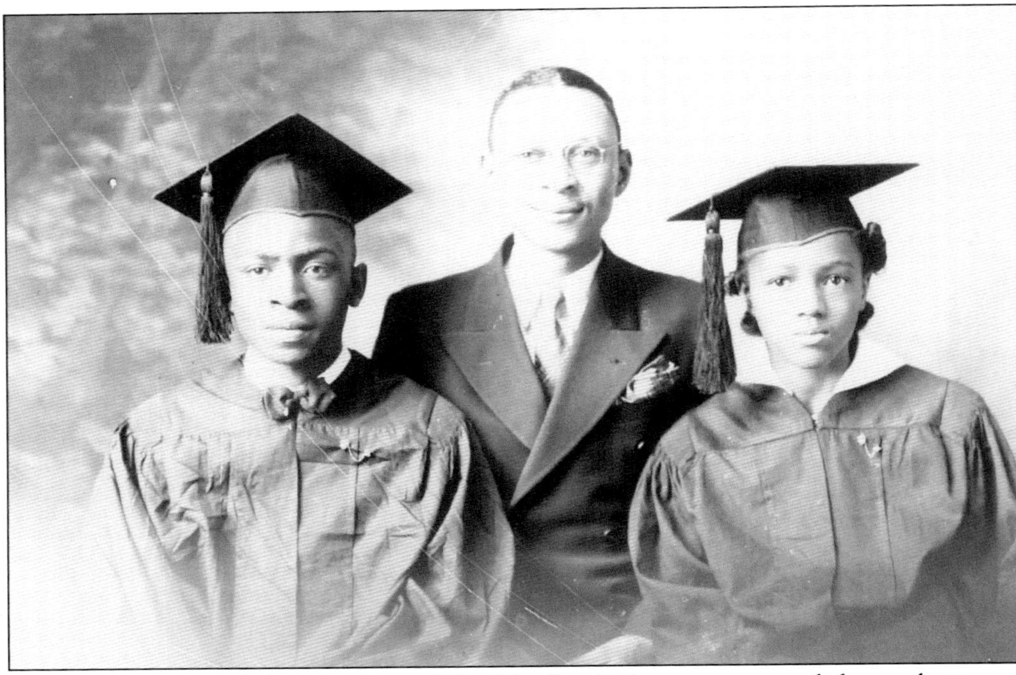

These students, Noel Douglas Jr. and Beulah Goodrich, were prepared for graduation at Avondale School by their teacher John Randle (center).

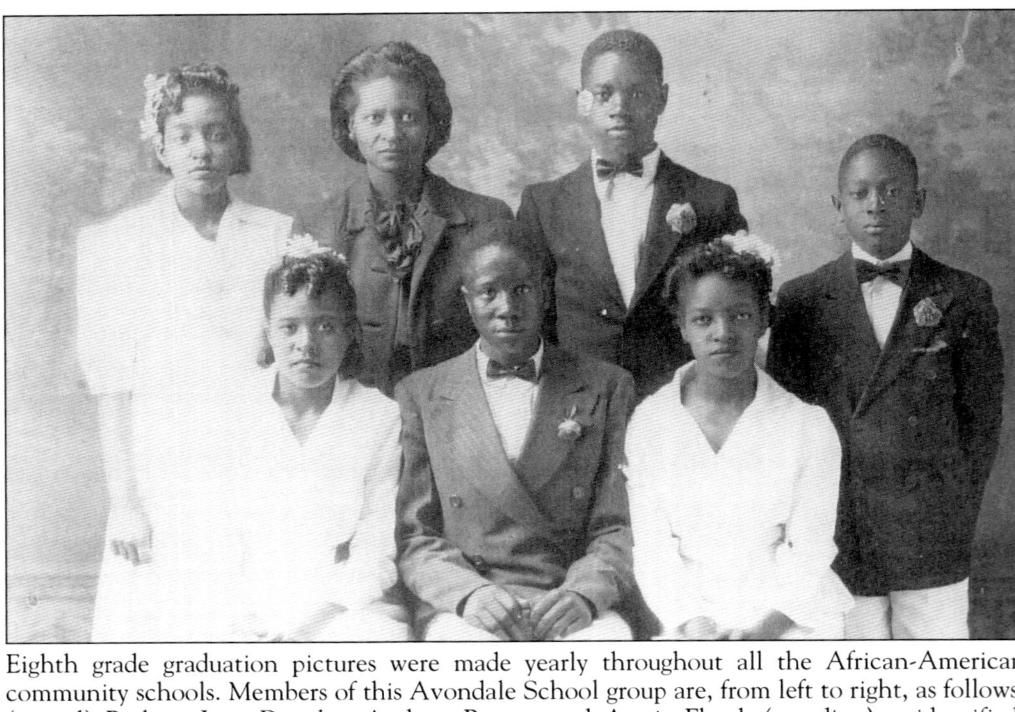

Eighth grade graduation pictures were made yearly throughout all the African-American community schools. Members of this Avondale School group are, from left to right, as follows: (seated) Barbara Jean Douglas, Andrew Boone, and Annie Floyd; (standing) unidentified, Ocenia Bennett (teacher), Miller Bender, and Jimmie Goodrich.

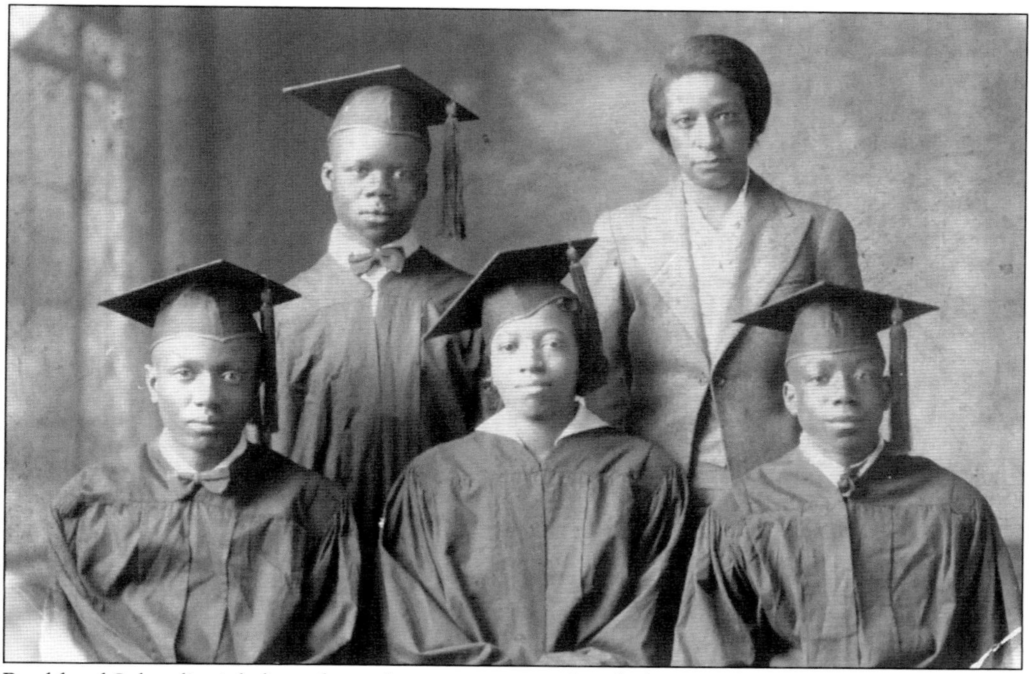

Rockland School's eighth grade graduates are pictured with their teacher, Eva Mayberry Wilson. In addition to being an educator, Eva became the first African American in Sumner County to become a licensed registered nurse in 1922.

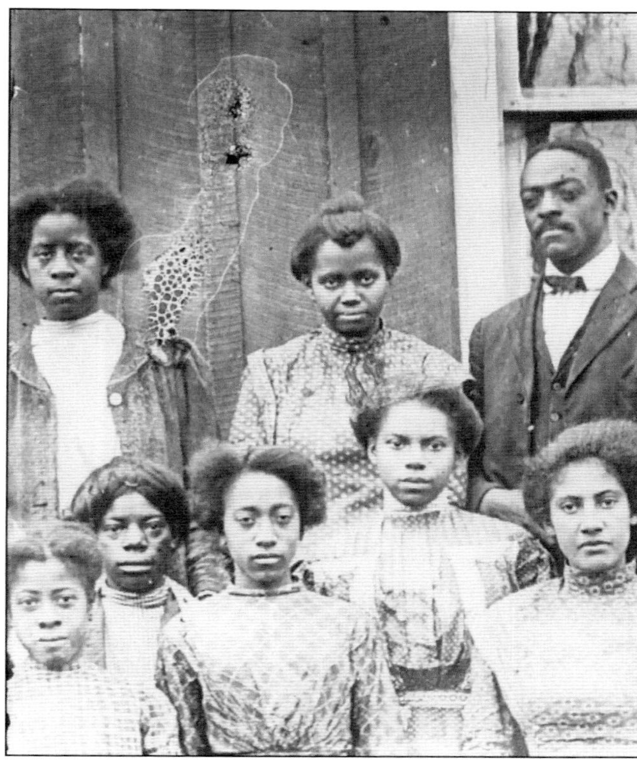

Rev. Henry Tolliver is pictured with a group of his students at Durham's Chapel School.

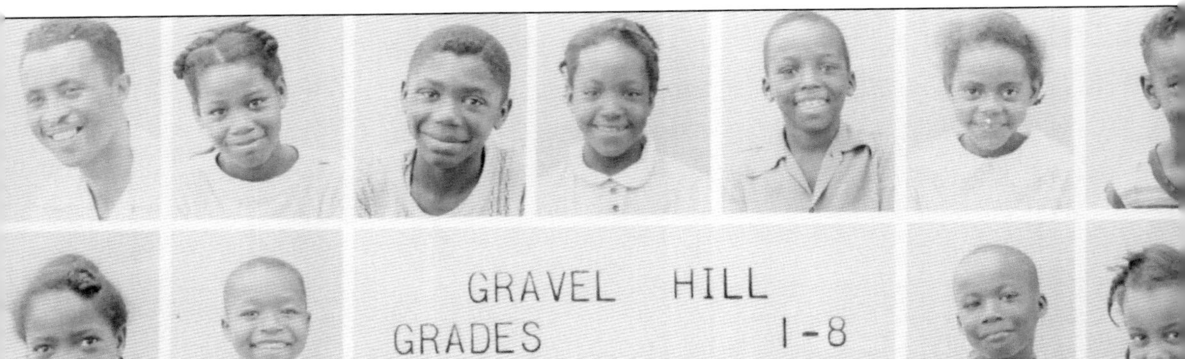

Gravel Hill School had 21 students enrolled for the 1953–54 school year. Joseph Coakley taught each and every subject required for grade levels one through eight.

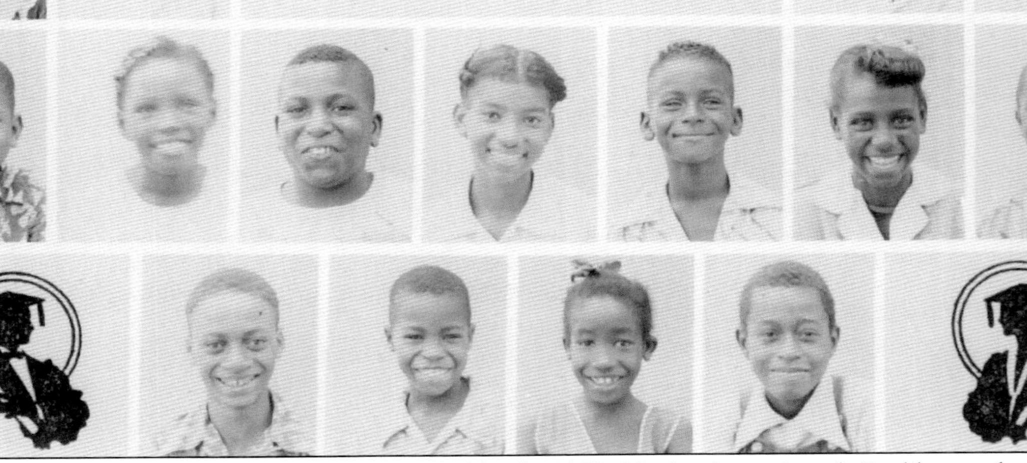

Union Elementary School students boarded the bus for home in March 1957. Some of the early Sumner County School bus drivers included John Frank Horton, Holland Key, Alvis Thurman, Marion Gwynn, Floyd Turner, H.C. Johns, Virgil Coakley, Arthur Lee Hall, and Lee Howard Whiteside.

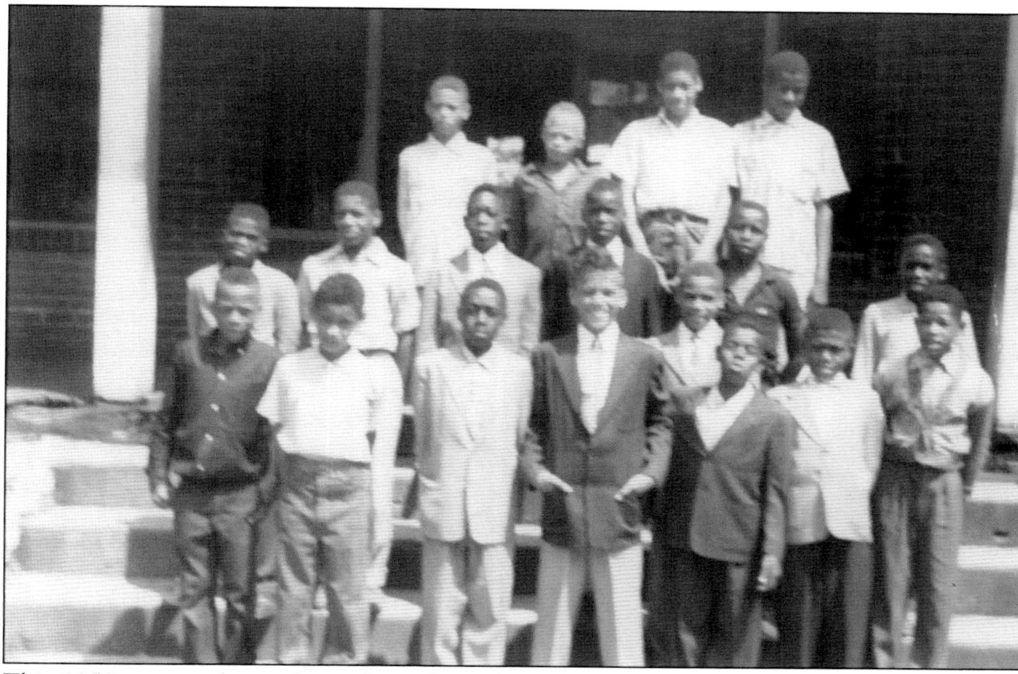

This 1958 picture shows the male students from the sixth grade class at Union Elementary School on Winchester Street. They are, from left to right, as follows: (front row) Charles Burnley, David McCall, Wesley Allen Hill, Randy Offitt, Joseph Alexander, William Terrell, Wilson Woodmore, and Wesley Rutherford; (second row) Robert Allen Walker, Troy Moore, Otis Fentress, Ellis Johnson, Chris Welch, and Tommy Scott; (third row) Floyd Duncan, John D. McMurry, Joe Groves, and Thomas Wayne Carter.

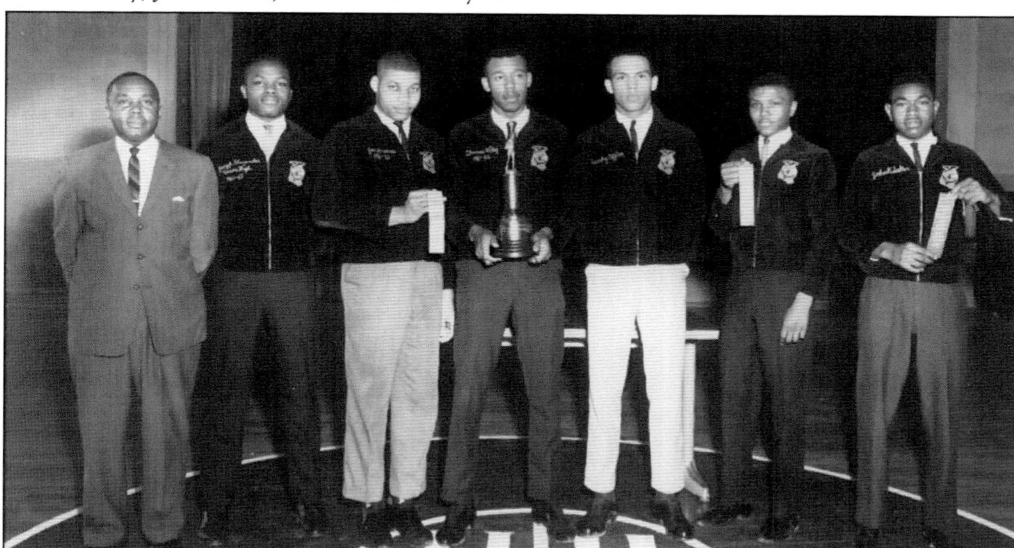

These future Farmers of America at Union High School have just attended a state competition at Tennessee State University and are bringing home a trophy and ribbons of achievement. From left to right are as follows: E.A. Gray (teacher), Samuel Jackson, Joe Groves, Thomas Wiley, Randy Offitt, Wilson Woodmore, and James Brinkley.

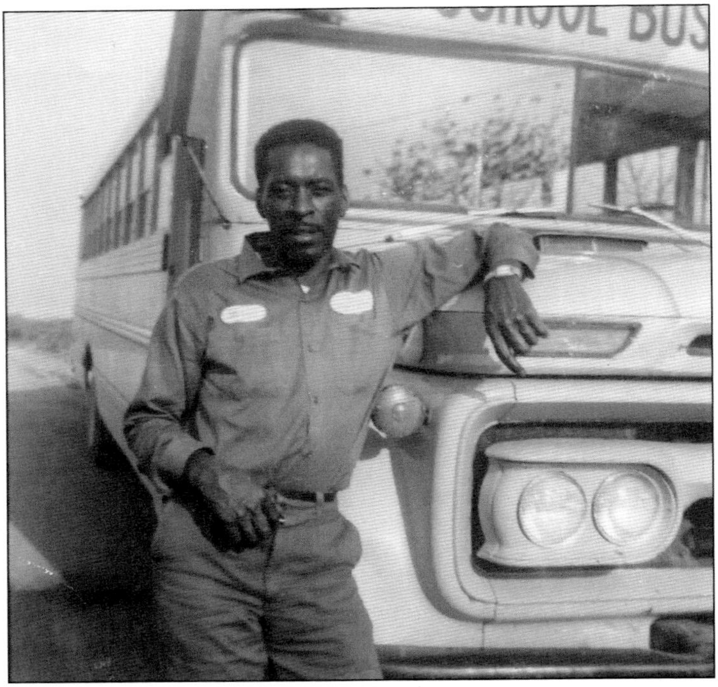

Lee Howard Whiteside (1928–1983) was a 20-year employee of the Sumner County Board of Education, having worked 16 years as a school bus driver. There was mutual respect and love shared by Lee and his passengers. He was noted for making liberal use of the school bus horn, and his small charges knew the meaning of each sound. His last position was with General Electric in Hendersonville.

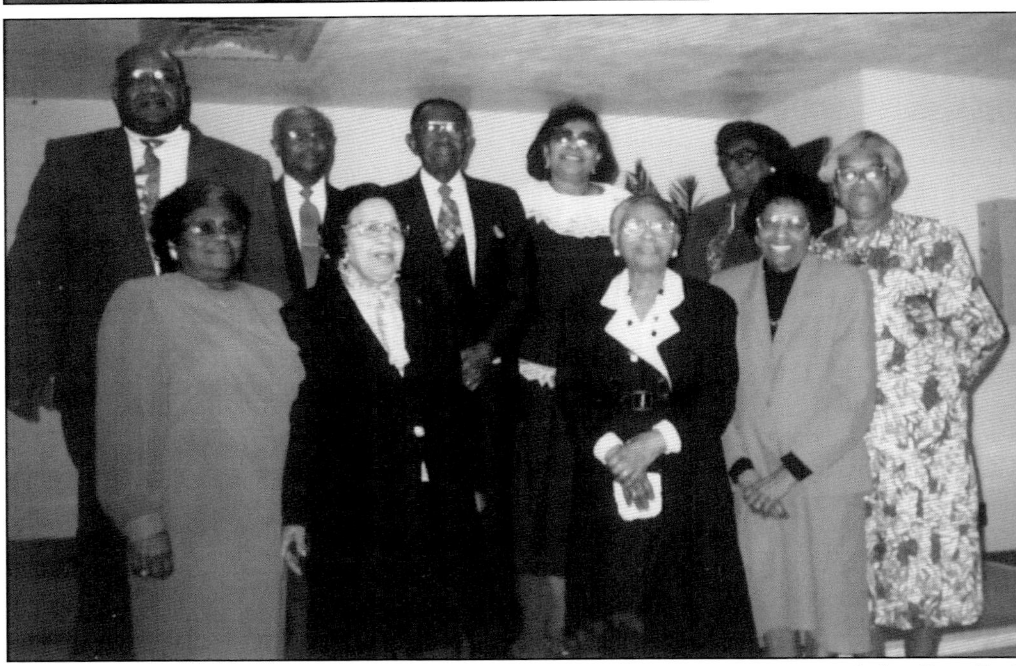

In November 1994, the Business and Professional Women's Committee of the East Fork District Association sponsored the first Golden Apple Awards Banquet. This benefit was given in honor of retired educators for the purpose of funding a scholarship. Some of the retired teachers in attendance are, from left to right, as follows: (front row) Allie Bell, Mary Stewart, Ola Roberson, Dorothy Jordon, and Anna Ligon; (back row) James Epperson, John Carter, Hutch Brinkley, Hazel Murehead, and Johnnie Gray.

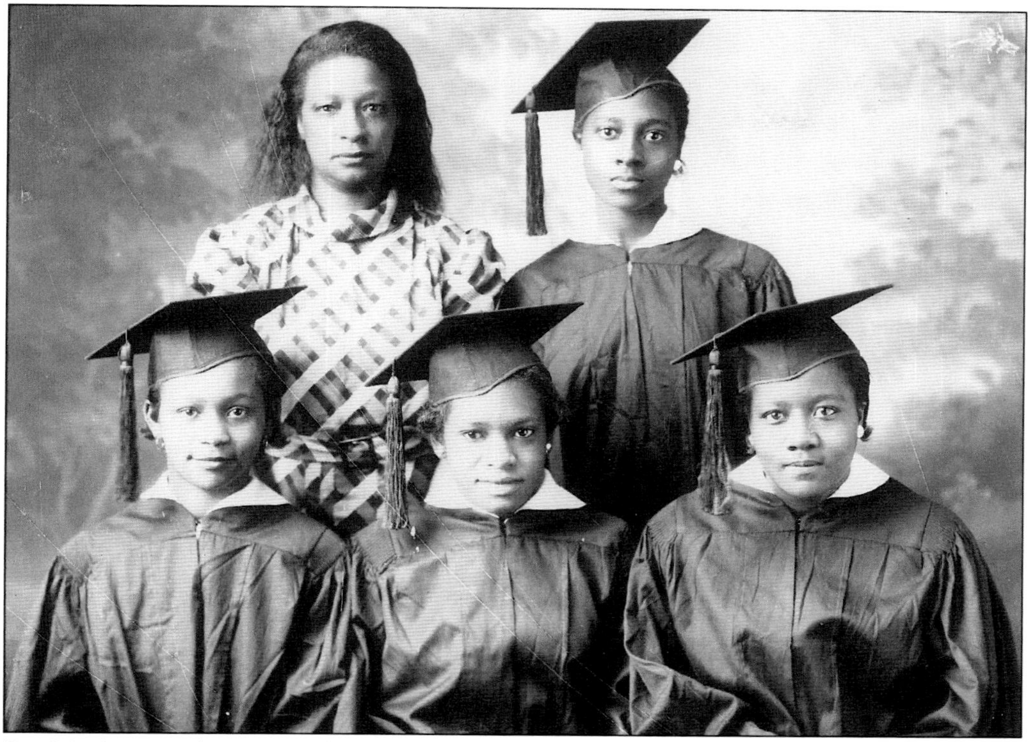

Eva Mayberry Wilson, a teacher at Avondale School in Hendersonville, is pictured with an early graduating class.

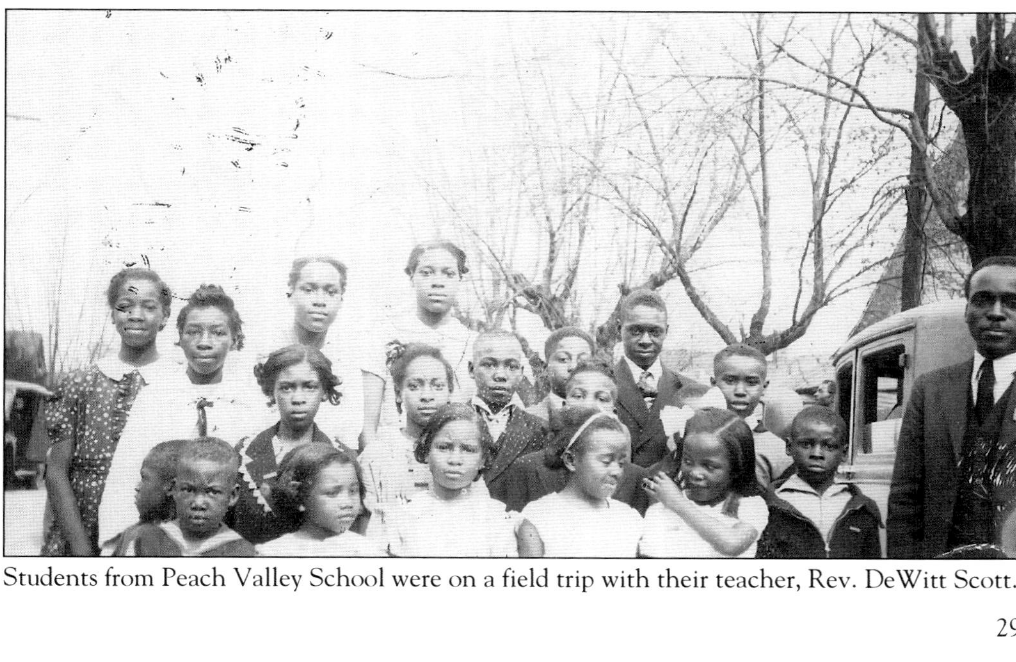

Students from Peach Valley School were on a field trip with their teacher, Rev. DeWitt Scott.

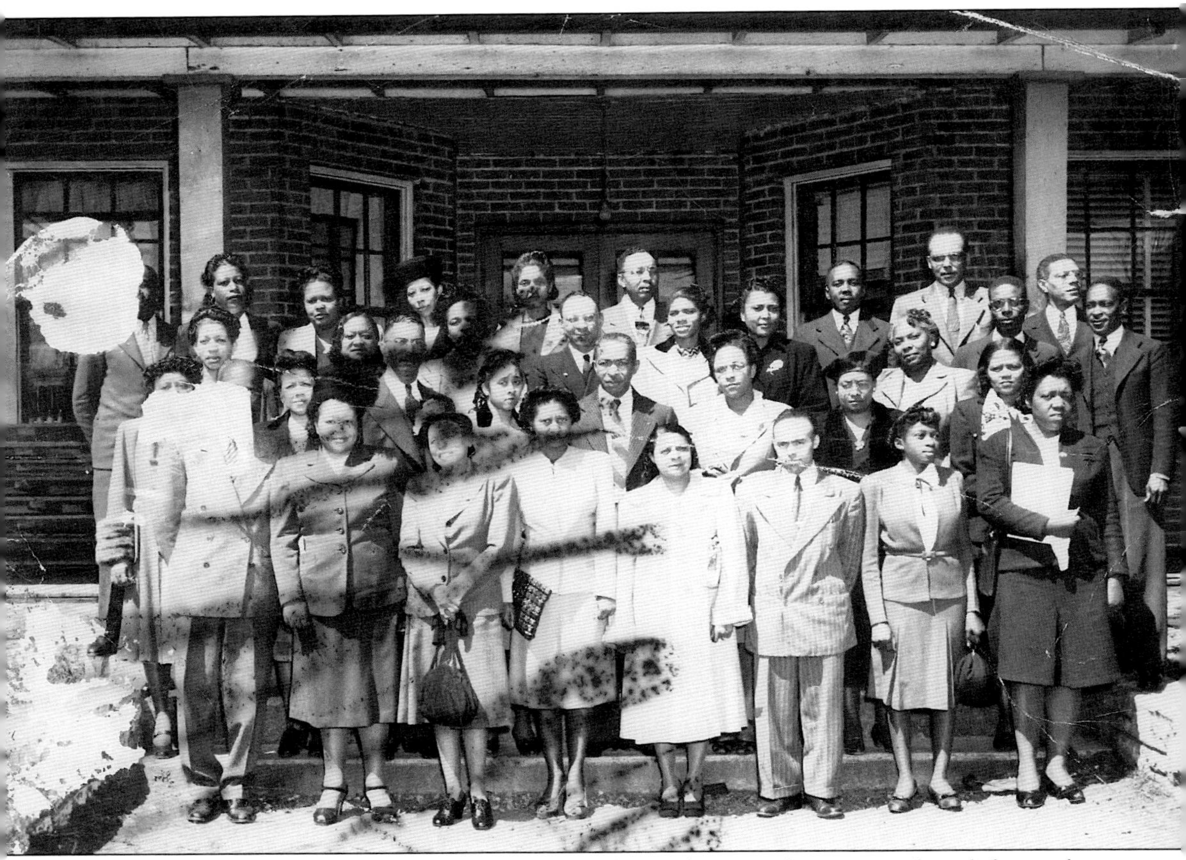

Members of the Sumner County Colored Teachers Education Association from left to right, are as follows: (first row) DeWitt Scott (Village Green), Elios Daniel (librarian at A and I State College), Sallie Jenkins (Odom Bend), Ocenia Bennett (Avondale), Queen Ola Staten (Hart's Hill), Gideon Dye (Scattersville), Florida Odom (Peach Valley), and Effie Coakley (Mt. Olive); (second row) Edna Scott (Union Elementary), Mary Stewart (Union High), R.A. Stewart (Union High), Ella Lee Dobbins (Union High), Julius Hayden (Durham's Chapel), Elois Daniels (Odom Bend), Elizabeth Wilks (Hall's Chapel), and Cora Elliott (Scattersville); (third row) Cynthia Martin (Union High), Bettie West (Stark's Knob), Lauretta Young (Hickory Grove), John Randle (Mt. Olive), Anna Ligon (Home Bound), Alice Smith (Union Elementary), Callie McKissack (Union Elementary), Odell Barr (assistant vocational agricultural teacher), and Sam Herod (Union High); (fourth row) Hutch Brinkley (Cairo), Ella Rutledge (Kansas), Catherine Herod (Hickory Grove), Mary O. Malone (Parker's Chapel), Beatrice Howse (Pilot Knob), Harold Smith (assistant vocational agriculture teacher), E.A. Gray (Union High), John Malone (Macedonia), and B.J. Hall (Union Elementary). Other Sumner County Schools included Bledsoe Chapel, Oak Grove, Rockland, St. John, and Steward's Chapel.

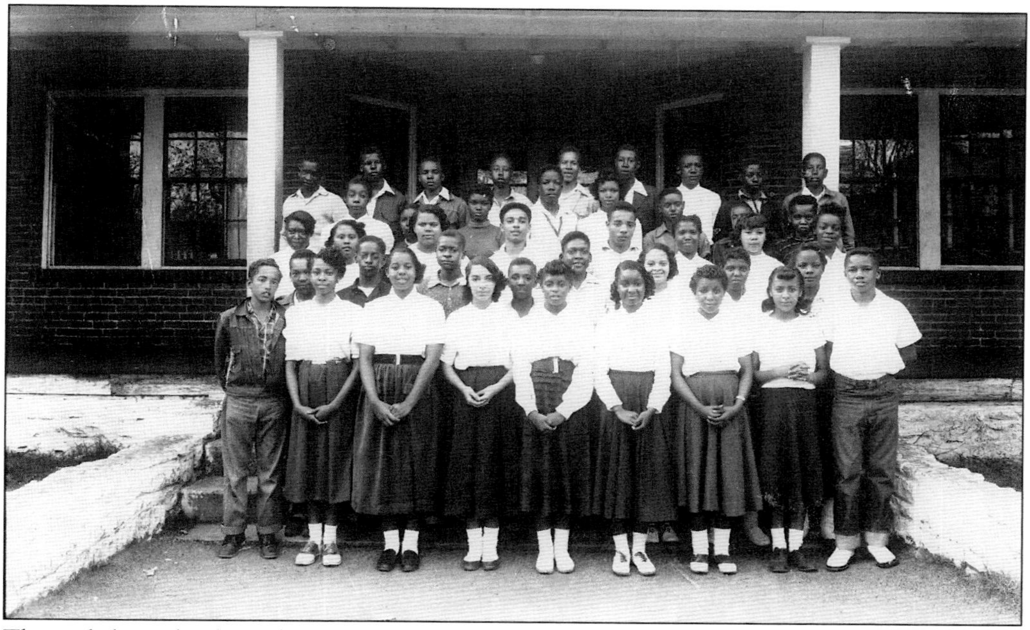

The eighth grade class of 1955 stands on the steps of Union Elementary School at 260 East Winchester Street. At the time of graduation in 1959, class officers are as follows: Robert Alexander, president; Onie Jean Flippen, vice president; Laura Green, secretary; Betty Robinson, assistant secretary; Katherine Coakley, treasurer; Irma Baker, assistant treasurer; and Jimmy Gooch, parliamentarian.

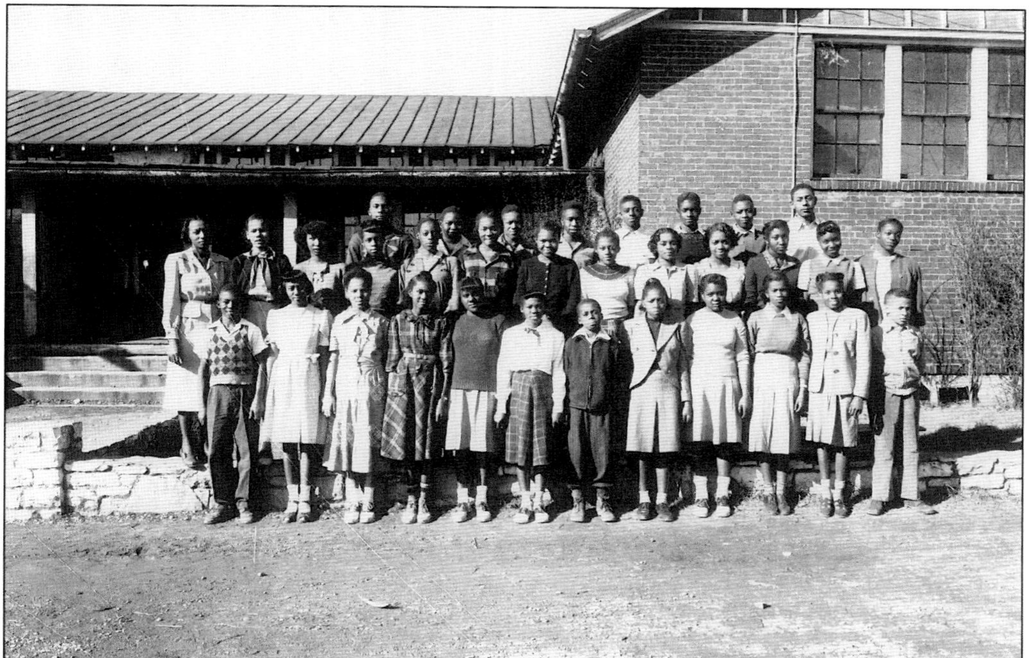

This photograph shows an early class taught by Johnnie Gray at Union Elementary School on Winchester Street.

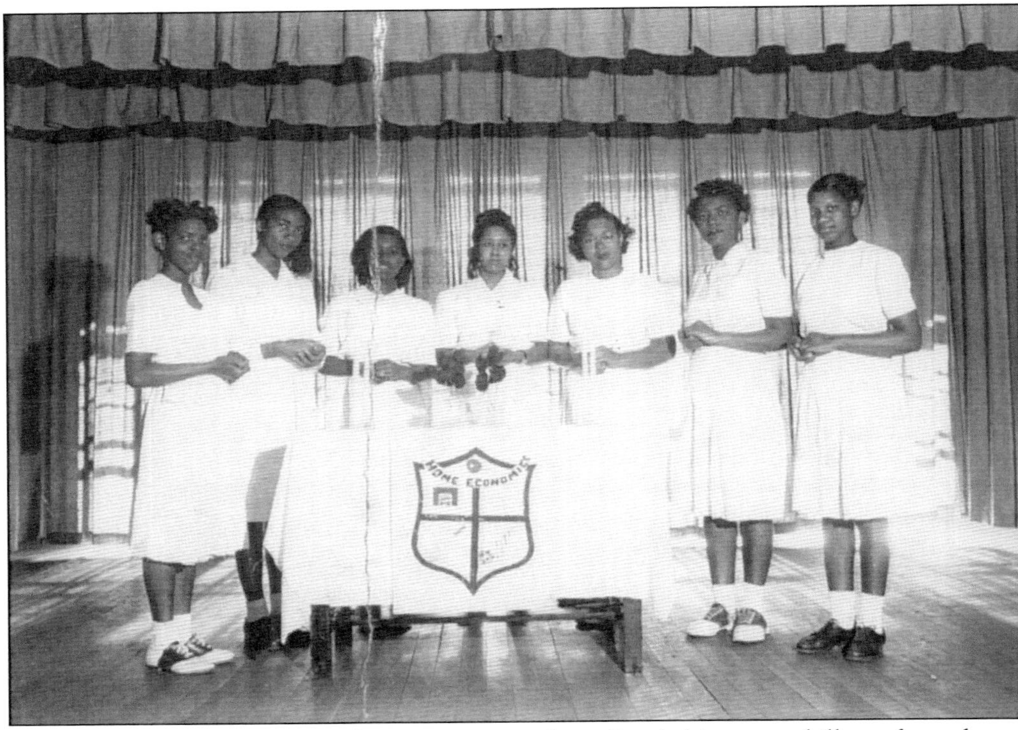

Cooking, cleaning, sewing, washing, ironing, and tending babies were skills performed on a daily basis by black girls, often as young as ten years old. Yet, when the quest for education was at hand, state and local boards portrayed home economic skills as a new venture for African Americans. Their home economic clubs were named New Homemakers of America instead of Future Homemakers of America. The 1947–1948 club officers, from left to right, are as follows: Fannie Branham, Beatrice Wilkins, Georgia Douglass, Ella Lee Dobbins (teacher), Roberta Barr, Hazel Malone, and Mattie Smith.

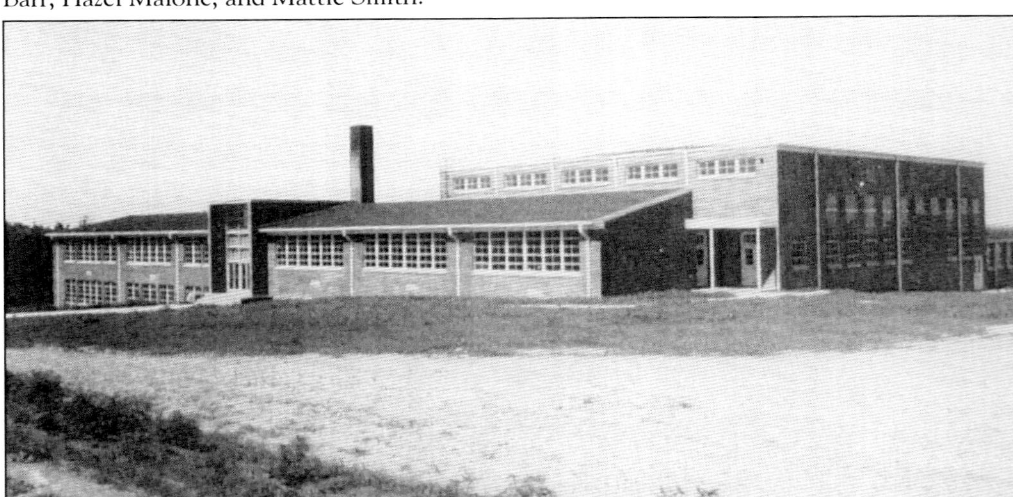

In 1950, this Union High School building was erected at 600 Small Street at a cost of $232,140. Prior to this time, high school students attended school at 260 East Winchester Street.

Two

EDIFICATION

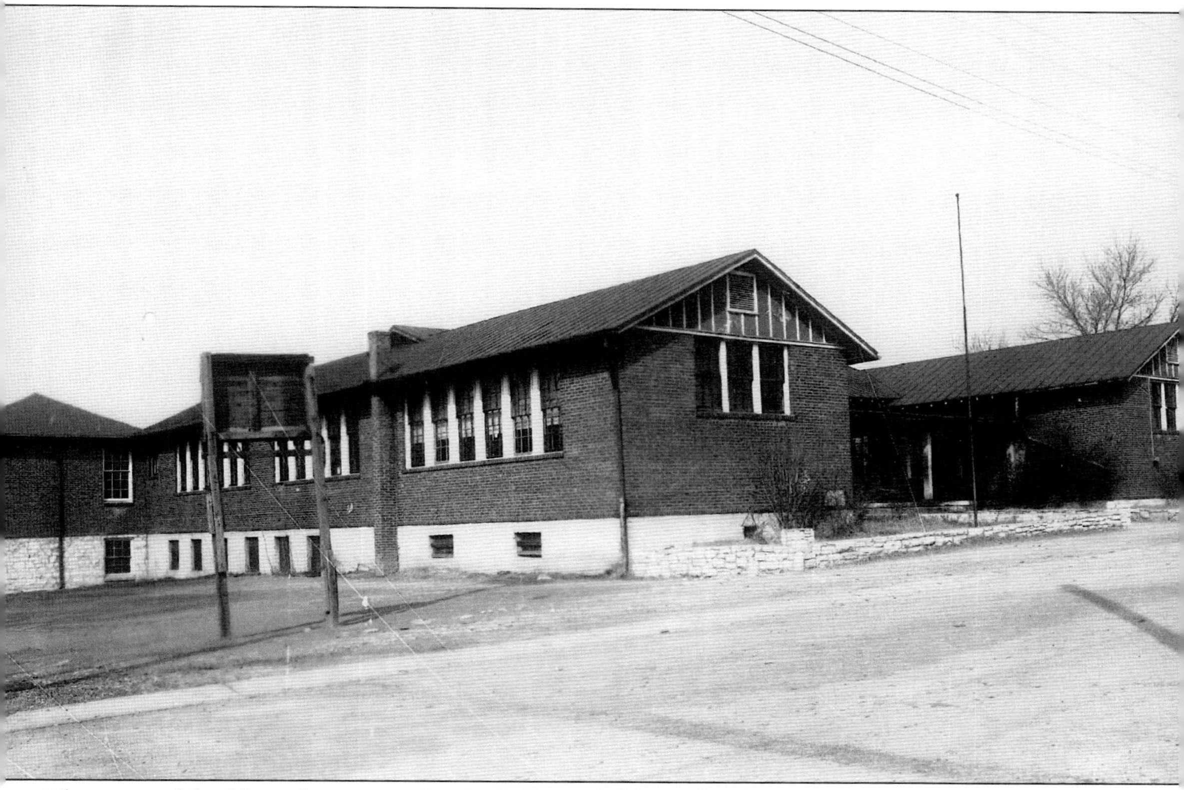

The original building, known as South Gallatin Public School, was first used by the white citizens of Gallatin as the Boys' Academy (*c.* 1888). The original building was razed and the Rosenwald school was erected in 1922. The new Union High School (Sumner County Training School) was built at a total cost of $17,875 and employed ten teachers. The African-American citizens were required to raise $5,825, the Rosenwald Fund contributed $2,100, and public funds covered the remaining $9,950.

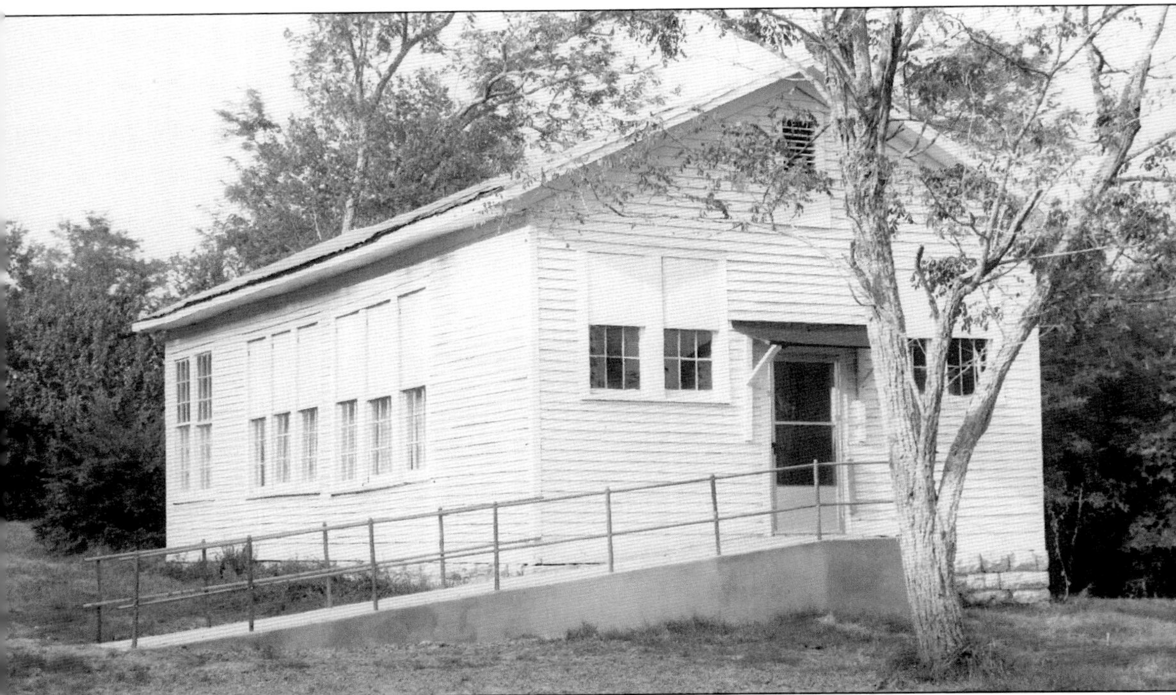

Cairo Rosenwald School was built in 1922 at a cost of $1,900. The African Americans in the community raised $700, the Rosenwald Fund supplied $500, and public funds covered the remaining $700. Local boards always required additional inducements to provide decent (albeit unequal) educational facilities for its tax-paying black citizens. The Rosenwald Fund's rural school building program provided the incentive needed in Sumner County to help secure seven schools.

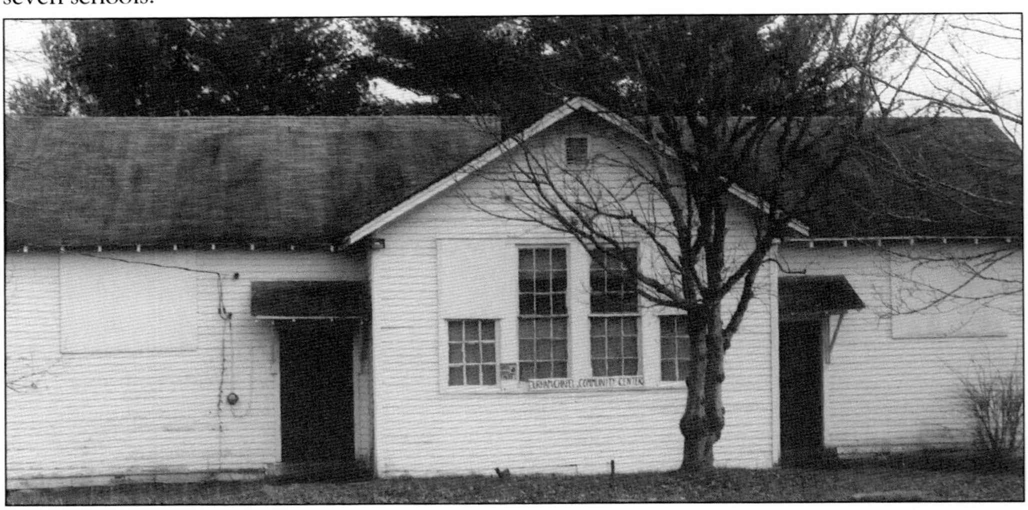

Durham's Chapel, a Rosenwald school employing two teachers, was built at a cost of $3,750. To receive this school, the black community was mandated to raise the first $1,525. The Rosenwald Fund provided a $700 grant, with the balance being paid from public funds. African Americans bore a heavy burden in their pursuit of education. John Malone and Queen Ola Staten were the last assigned teachers.

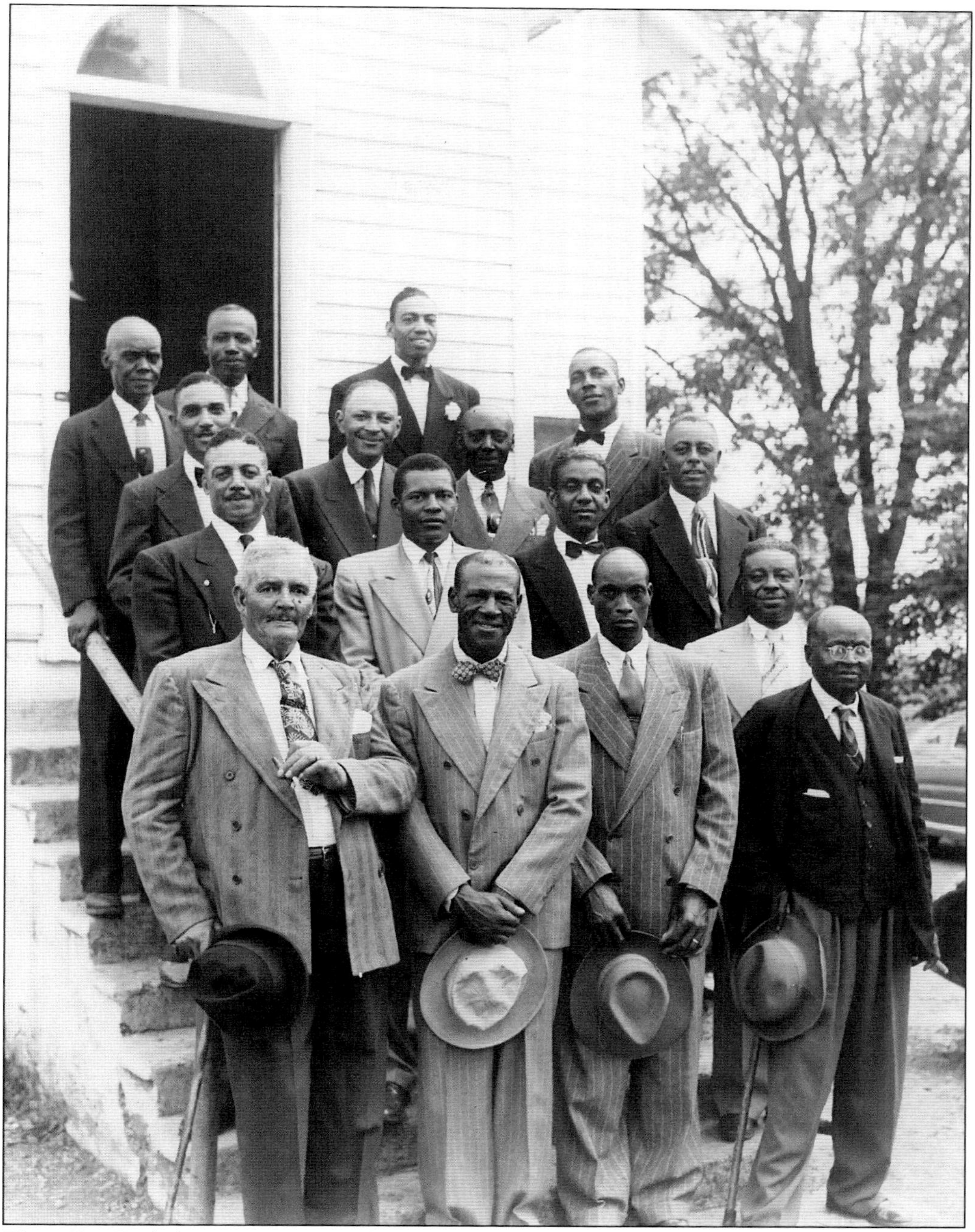

These East Fork deacons convened their service at Rockland Baptist Church in Hendersonville. They are, from left to right, as follows: (first row) unidentified, Woodson Taylor, Walter Holman, and Walter Beard; (second row) Jolet West, Tom Shaw, Rufus Grizzard, and Gene Johnson; (third row) James Lauderdale, John Randle, unidentified, and Walter Cole; (fourth row) Frank Walton, unidentified, Roy Frye, and unidentified.

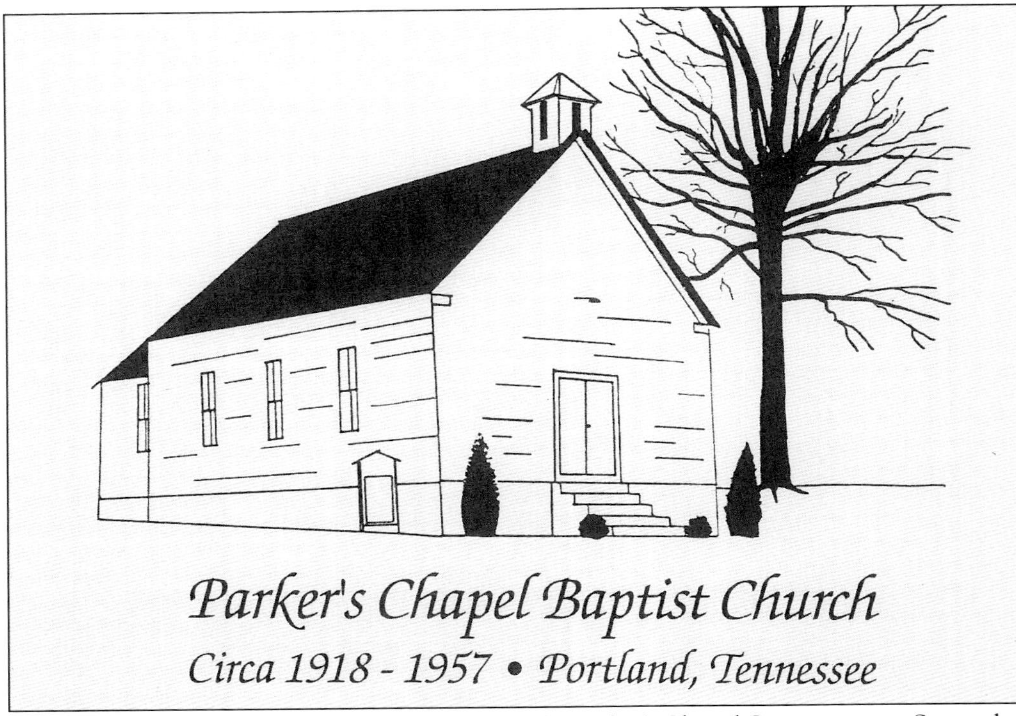

A dedication and unveiling ceremony was held in the Parker's Chapel Community on September 27, 1997. The Tennessee Historical Commission erected a marker to serve as a tribute to area settlers and their descendants for contributions made. The marker is located on the northwest side of the intersection of State Highway 52 and Airport Road in Portland. The above image appeared on invitations the Parker's Chapel Historical Marker Committee designed and used for this even.

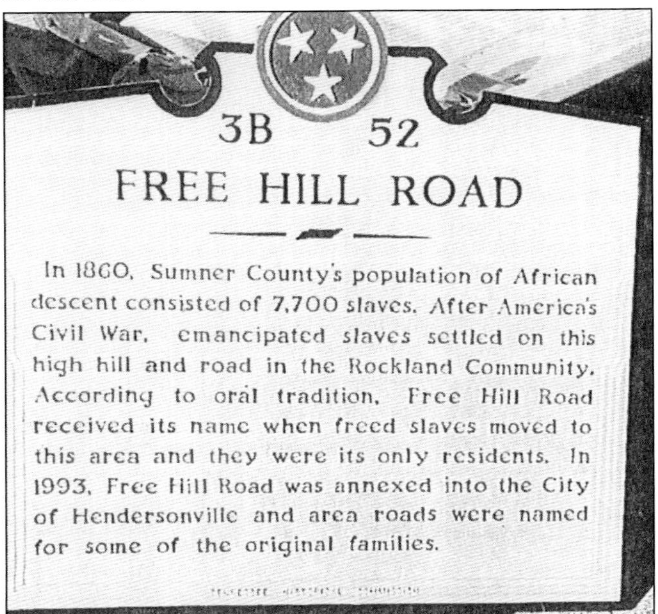

After emancipation, many former slaves bought land and moved to the Rockland area of Hendersonville, forming a unique black community. In 1996, the year of the Tennessee Bicentennial Celebration, the Tennessee Historical Commission erected a marker to serve as a tribute to the areas settlers and their descendants for contributions made. The Bicentennial Planning Committee members included Rev. Cordell Haynie, James Johnson, Edward Boone, Rev. Dennis Page, Rev. Daniel Bender, Maxine Collier, Gus Simpson, Elizabeth Wallace, and Dr. Robert Boone (chair).

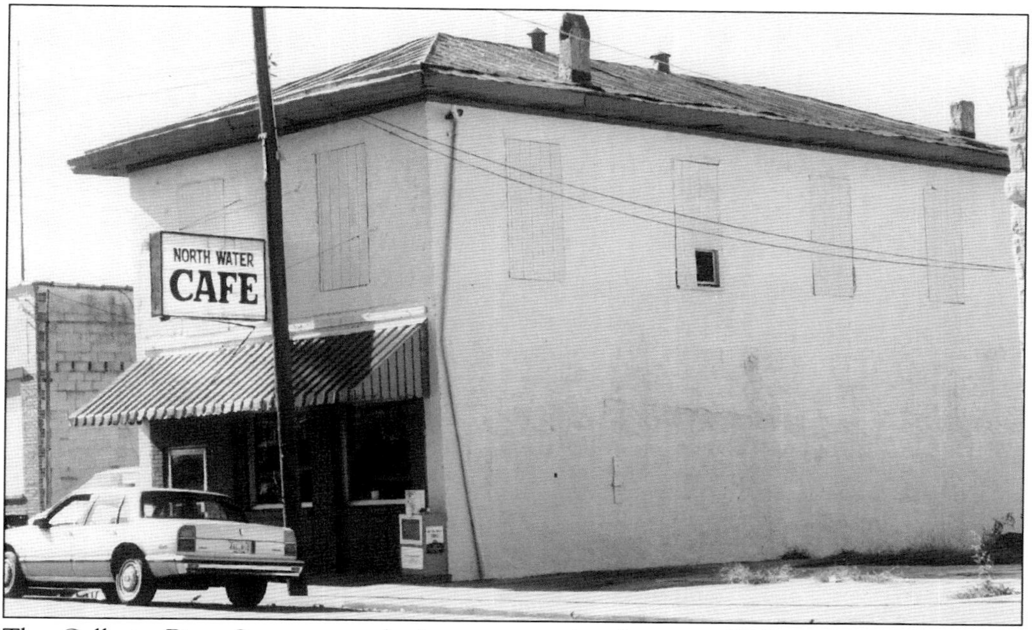

The Gallatin Drug Store was a business partnership between William Kenneth Wilson, pharmacist, and Dr. I.C. Ramsey. Many different uses were made of the second-floor space through the years. Joseph Frank Laird, M.D., (1904–1962) and W.E. McKissack, D.D.S., operated respective general practices from the area. Charlie Crowder, business associate, and employee Clarence Malone operated Crowder's Funeral Parlor from one section prior to relocating to Nashville.

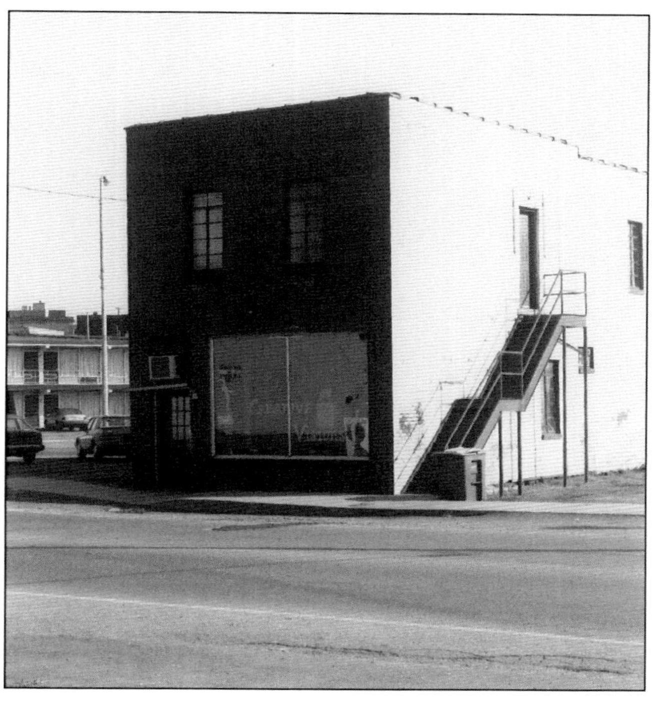

Owned by the IOC until 1996, the second floor of the Immaculate Hall was reserved for meetings. The first floor housed a medical practice for Dr. Frank Laird and later, for Dr. Gardner Dixon. The local societies were the Bethel Lodge No. 75 (men), Queen Esther Court No. 7 (women), and the Children's Fraternity. A parade preceded the Easter Ceremony each year. Members included E.A. Gray, Glen Rutledge, Marion Gwynn, Melvin Vaughn, Sadie DeMoss, Florence Green, Hazel Corbin, Flora Miles, Lucy Black, and Secenara Adams.

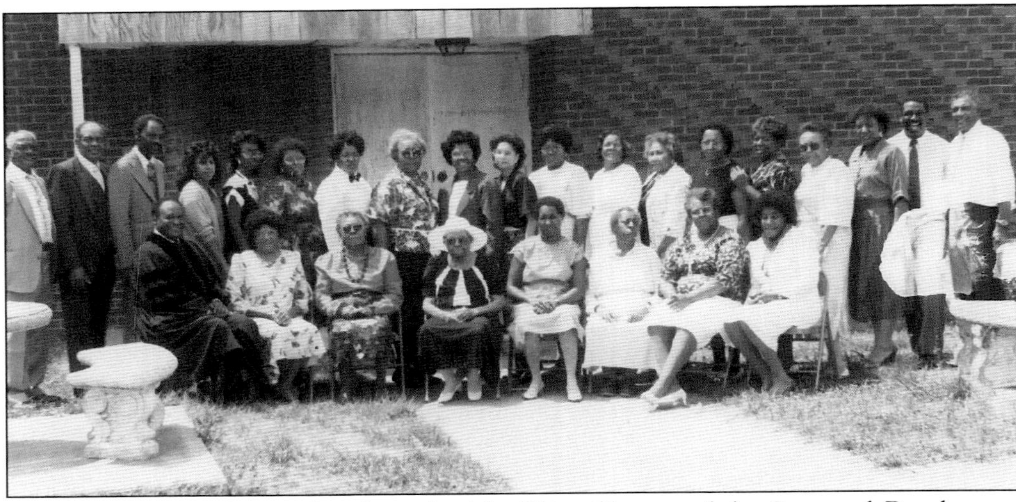

Ninety-four years after its founding, the Mt. Olive Chapter of the Sons and Daughters of Charity Lodge is still active. Members of the organization, from left to right, are as follows: (seated) Dr. Odell McGlothian, Fannie Latimer, Louise Watkins, Florida Holder, Sally Sawyer, Lucille Holder, Christine Shaw, and Louise Holder; (standing) Henry Shaw, George Shaw, Rev. Thomas Clark, Shirley Black, Beverly Staten, Mable Shaw, Mary Brinkley, Louise Rutherford, Gloria McGlothian, Parniece Johnson, Eunice Shaw, Eva Wright, Mattie Shaw, Faye Wright, Betty Branham, Frances Watkins, Annie Douglas, Thomas Staten, and Tom Shaw.

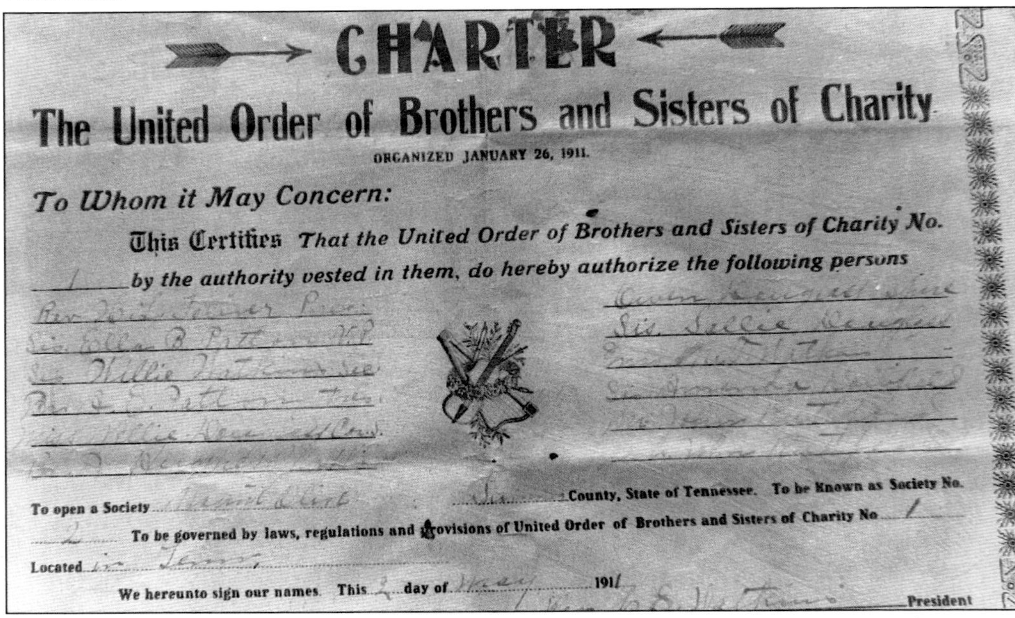

CHARTER

The United Order of Brothers and Sisters of Charity

ORGANIZED JANUARY 26, 1911.

To Whom it May Concern:

This Certifies *That the United Order of Brothers and Sisters of Charity No.* 1 *by the authority vested in them, do hereby authorize the following persons*

To open a Society .... County, State of Tennessee. To be Known as Society No. 2 To be governed by laws, regulations and provisions of United Order of Brothers and Sisters of Charity No 1

Located in Tenn.

We hereunto sign our names. This 2 day of May 1911

President

The Mt. Olive Chapter of the Sons and Daughters of Charity Lodge was started in 1904. The official charter was signed on May 2, 1911, by Rev. Charlie Watkins, who served as president. Present officers are as follows: Rev. Floyd Shaw (president), Ida Durham (vice president), Christine Shaw (secretary), Mattie Shaw (treasurer), Pearline Manning (chaplain), Dewey Brinkley (spy), Louise Rutherford (teller), Lula Brinkley (marshall), and Eunice Shaw (good of order).

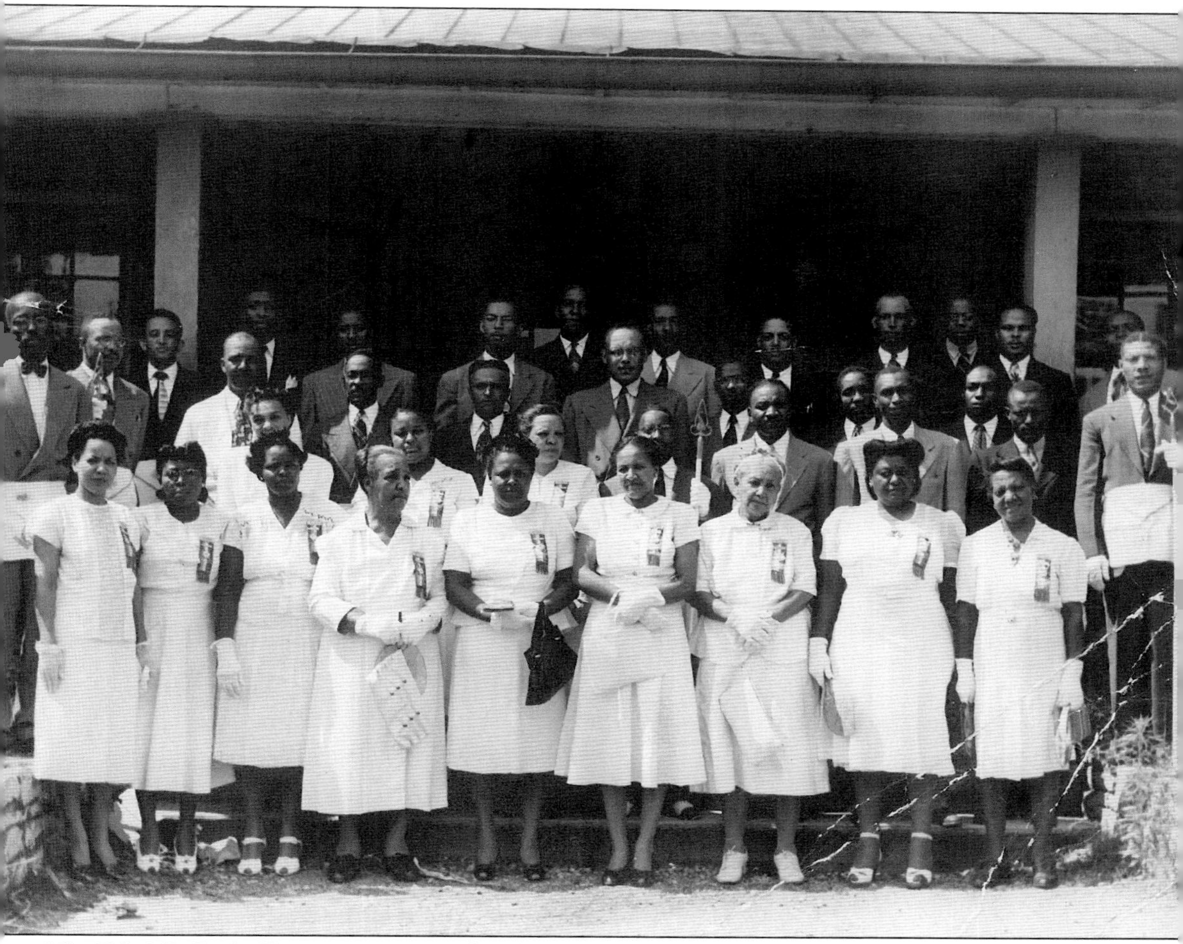

The Ethel B. Beck Chapter No. 22, Order of the Eastern Star, was photographed with members of the Freemont Lodge No. 274 during the late forties. Members, from left to right, are as follows: (first row) Mary Stewart, Edna Scott, Alice Malone, Diora Vertrees, Catherine Herod, Margaret Alexander, Jennie Jamison, Betty West, and Ellen Corbin; (second row) DeWitt Scott, Mary Dobbins, Estella Herod, Clara Vertrees, Horace Herod, Thomas Odom, Robert Smith, unidentified, and B.J. Hall; (third row) Harold Smith, unidentified, Russell Vertrees, Sam Herod, Thomas Alexander, John Malone, unidentified, John Dobbins, Robert Fitts, and unidentified; (fourth row) Bill Bettis, unidentified, Rev. R.A. Stewart, Dee Patterson, Thomas Malone, Jolet West, Herbert Duncan, James Debow, and Edward Anthony.

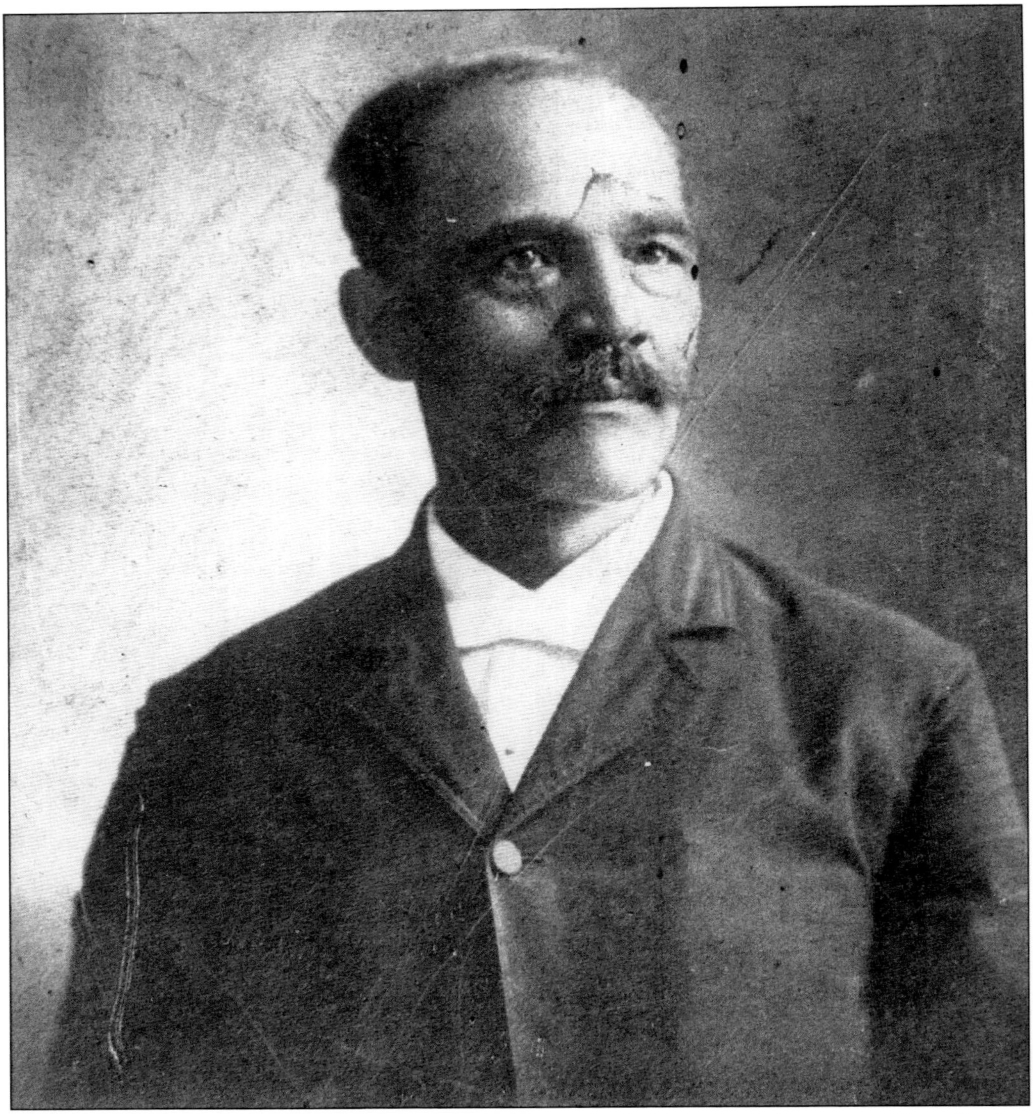

Peter Vertrees (1840–1926), the mulatto son of Mary "Polly" Elizabeth Skaggs and Rev. Booker Harding, was born in Edmonson County, Kentucky. At age five, he was awarded to the court and was apprenticed to his paternal grandparents, Jacob Vertrees and Catherine Davis. For four years, Vertrees served in the Confederacy under his father's half brother, Dr. John Luther Vertrees, a surgeon to the 6th Kentucky Infantry. He was mustered out at Dalton, Georgia, in 1865 and left for Gallatin, where he lived with another uncle, Judge James Cunningham Vertrees. He attended Roger Williams University and went on to accomplish many outstanding achievements. Rev. Vertrees was the founder of Durham's Chapel Baptist Church, Williams' Chapel, Franklin's Chapel, the Sons and Daughters of Charity Lodge, East Fork Missionary Baptist Association, and he assisted in the founding of Sylvan Street Baptist Church. He served over 30 years as principal of South Gallatin School and 52 years as pastor of the First Baptist Church. Under his leadership, two of four edifices of the First Baptist Church were erected. The following page contains an excerpt from a message given by Rev. Peter Vertrees to the East Fork Association on August 14, 1925, during annual session.

MODERATOR'S ANNUAL ADDRESS
August 14, 1925

Who is on the Lord's side? Who is willing to bear criticism and stand up for Jesus at all times and under all circumstances? We need no cowards in our band, but soldiers true. The great questions of today, which confront us are things which only God's wisdom can solve, and God's children must stand for. Ministers and all Christian leaders must be led and controlled by the Almighty God in order, to carry out God's command: "Go and teach all nations."

This is a day when prayer is needed in the home and everywhere.

The minister should pray for God's indwelling spirit, then prepare his mind to teach God's word, and then preach to convince men and help save the world. The minister or any Christian leader who prays and resigns himself to God will be a model leader, one worthy of emulation. A minister's life will have more effect on the people than all the sermons he could ever preach.

Our Theological Seminary, the only one in the world for Negroes, is a great asset to our denomination. We should be encouraged to pursue our work, and patronize the seminary. Every preacher in our district should sacrifice some time and money and attend this seminary. We cannot be too intelligent; the thing to fear is that we will not learn enough, and the result is we fall short of God's glory. We should be concerned about Jesus, and learn his will, and how to be fishers of men. God's cause is perishing each day for lack of strong men who are bearers of burdens, not grumblers, who never see one thing that is carried out correctly. We need in our pulpits and pews those who have really been with Jesus, and are living a life which testifies to the world that they are kingdom builders.

I wish my people could be aroused from the slumbers of negligence and vice, and do their whole duty for missions and education. The request made by Rev. Harris concerns each member giving three cents per month, or thirty-six cents a year is easy to comply with. Any member can pay that amount and not feel it. Let us be up and doing. Faith without works is dead.

We should be more determined to do our Christian duty than ever before. Roger Williams is still appealing to us for aid. Roger Williams is to us as a child to its parent. A parent is unkind and unfit to be called a parent if he fails to support his child. Roger Williams is sending out through this country men and women religiously trained, who are lifting our people to higher plains of living, and we should appreciate the work to the extent that we will do what we can to support our school.

We, as leaders of our people, should follow the commandment of our God. Let it be our object to do the right, and follow our leaders as Christ directed, and he will be with us until the end.

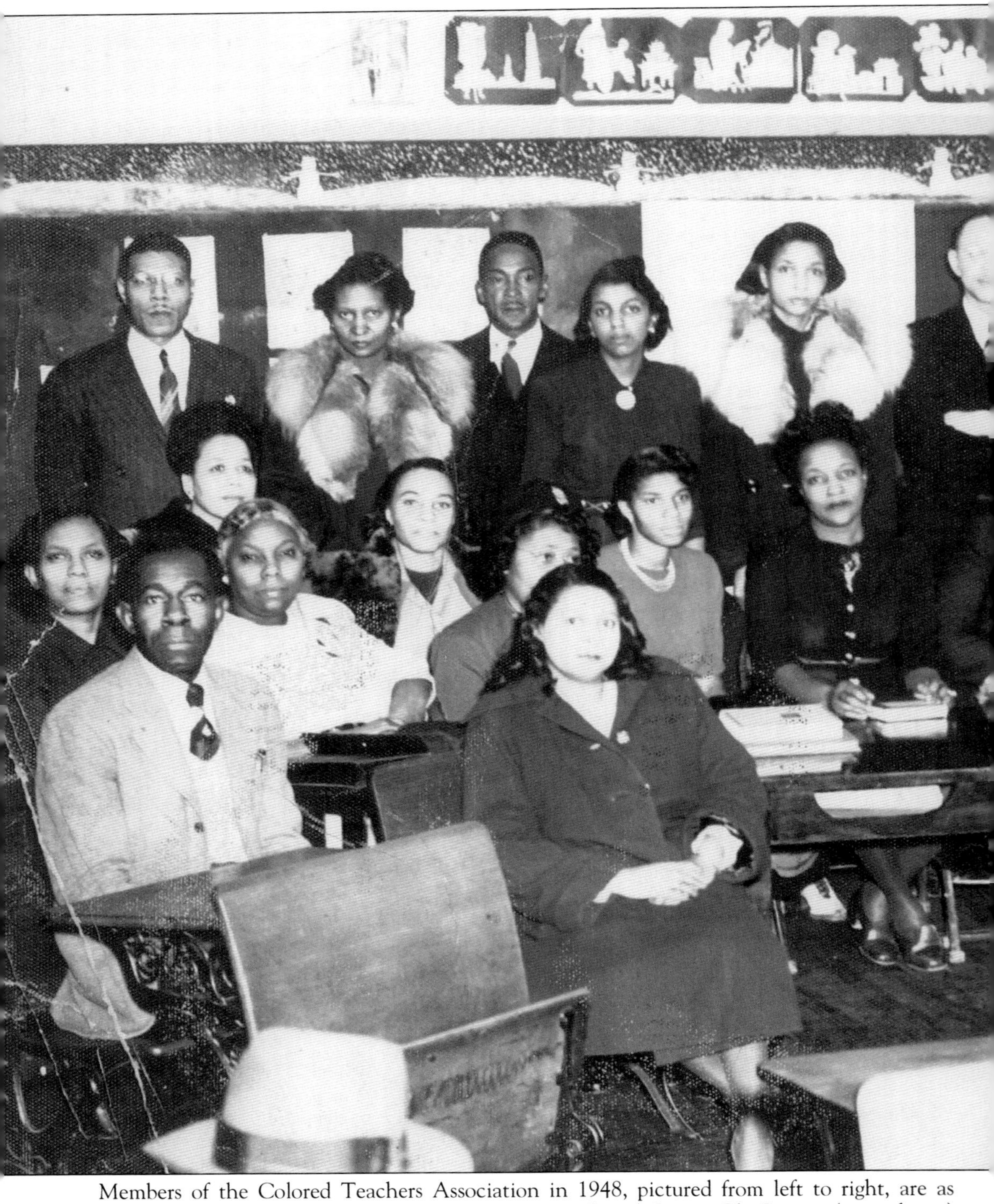

Members of the Colored Teachers Association in 1948, pictured from left to right, are as follows: (first row) John Hutch Brinkley (1908–1995) and Queen Ola Staten; (second row) Ola Bate Robinson, Mary Stewart, Callie Apple McKissack (1896–1982), Mary Alexander Dobbins (1918–1984), Edna Mai Scott, Anna Bransford Ligon, Lauretta Young (1907–1990),

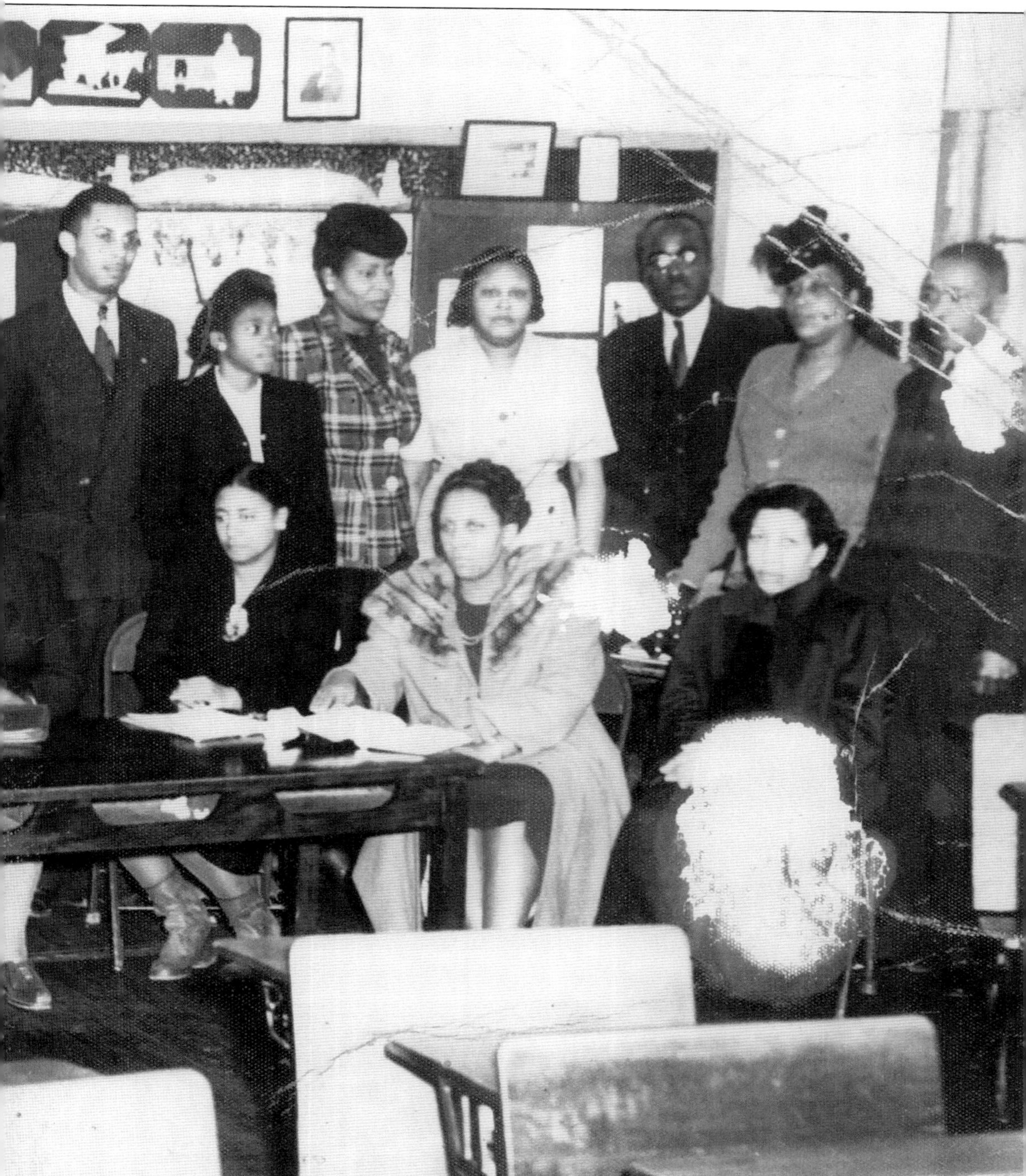

Bettie West, Elizabeth Wilks, Elois Daniels, and Cynthia Martin; (third row) Billy Hall, Ocenia Bennett, Samuel Herod, Dorothy McKissack Jordon, Beatrice Howse, John Randle, Roy Stewart, Florida Odom, Evelyn Parker Hall, Catherine Herod, DeWitt Scott, Ella Lee Rutledge, and Julius Hayden.

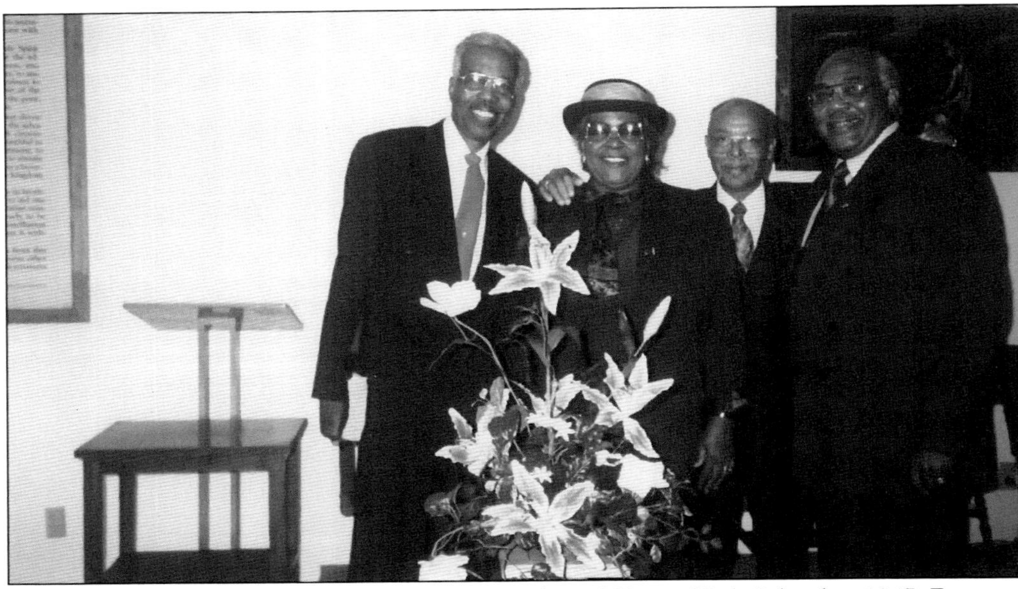

Rev. Talmadge Dewitt Scott Jr. (1929–1996) graduated Union High School in 1947. For more than 30 years, he worked in the retail grocery industry as a butcher. Reverend Scott served as associate and interim pastor of First Baptist Church and as pastor of Durham's Chapel Church. He was a graphic artist who expressed his talent through sign-making. Family members are, from left to right, as follows: Rev. Talmadge Scott, Alva Scott Ray, Rev. H.L. Ray, and Rev. Joseph Frank Scott.

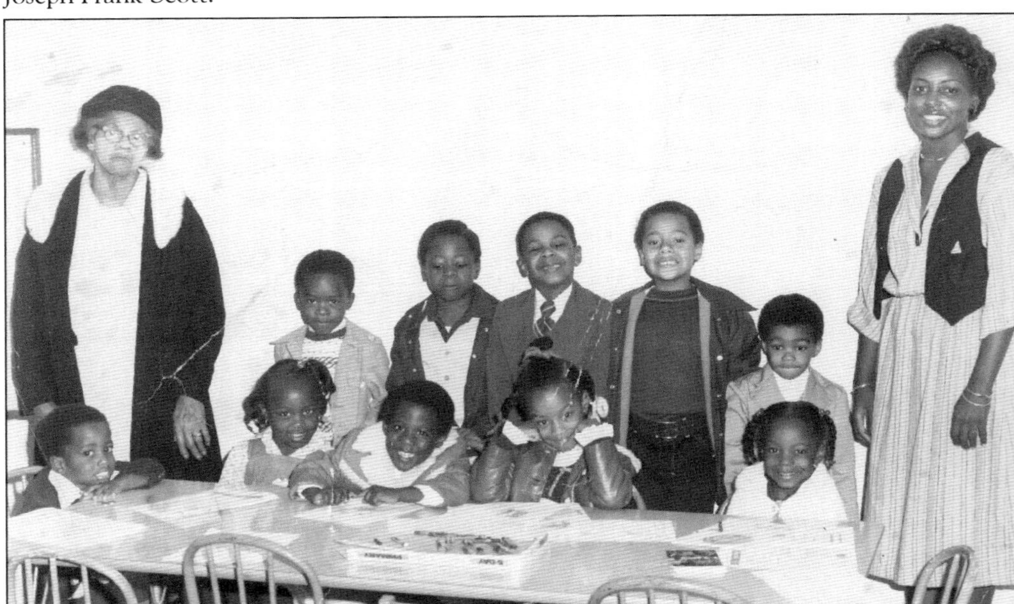

This kindergarten class at First Baptist Church (*c.* 1978) was taught by Callie Stanford (1900–1995) and assisted by Alice Malone. The members, from left to right, are as follows: (seated) Joseph Smith Jr., Crystal Malone, Jacoby Malone, Tasha McQuarters, and Lisa Malone; (standing) Callie Stanford, Charles Brinkley Jr., Mark Rickman, Anthony Carter, Christopher Brinkley, Antonio Duncan, and Alice Malone.

Michael L. Douglas, son of Georgia Sadler and Arthur Douglas, is a 1986 graduate of Gallatin High School. His mother recalled that he began drawing exact replicas of pictures at age seven or eight. Doris Bills, his high school art teacher, taught him to measure and shade from light.

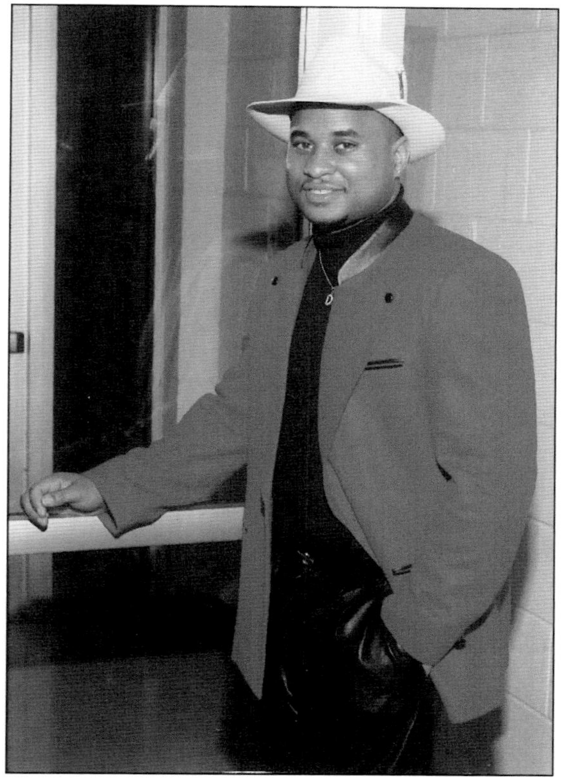

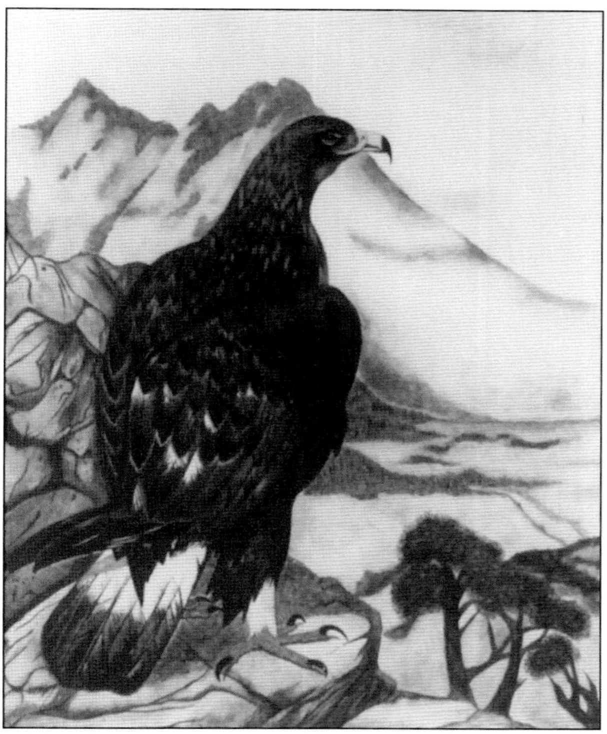

As a second-year art student, Mike painted this watercolor entitled "the Overseer." It was entered in the Senior Mid-State Art Show and was awarded second place.

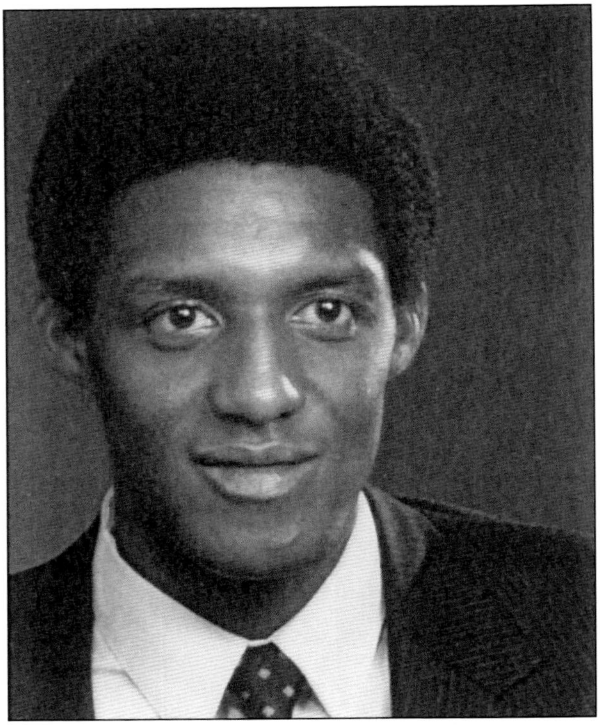

James Tyree Ligon graduated from Gallatin High School in 1973 and attended Volunteer State Community College (VSCC). He received a B.A. degree in fine arts from Austin Peay State University and attended Southern Illinois University at Carbondale. Tyree served as an art instructor at VSCC.

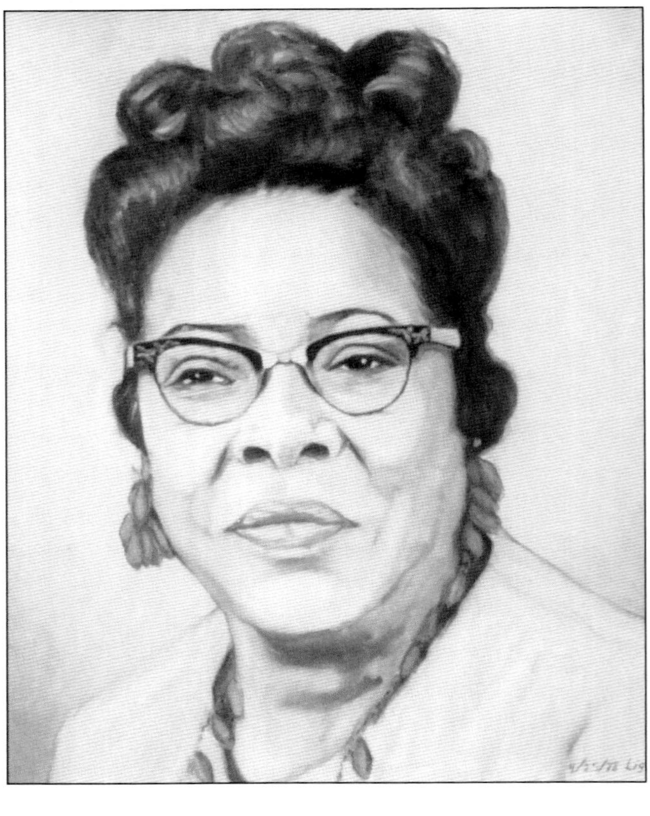

This oil portrait of Evelyn P. Hall, a Sumner County home economics teacher, part-time librarian, and Jeanes supervisor for 46 years, is one of Tyree Ligon's treasured works.

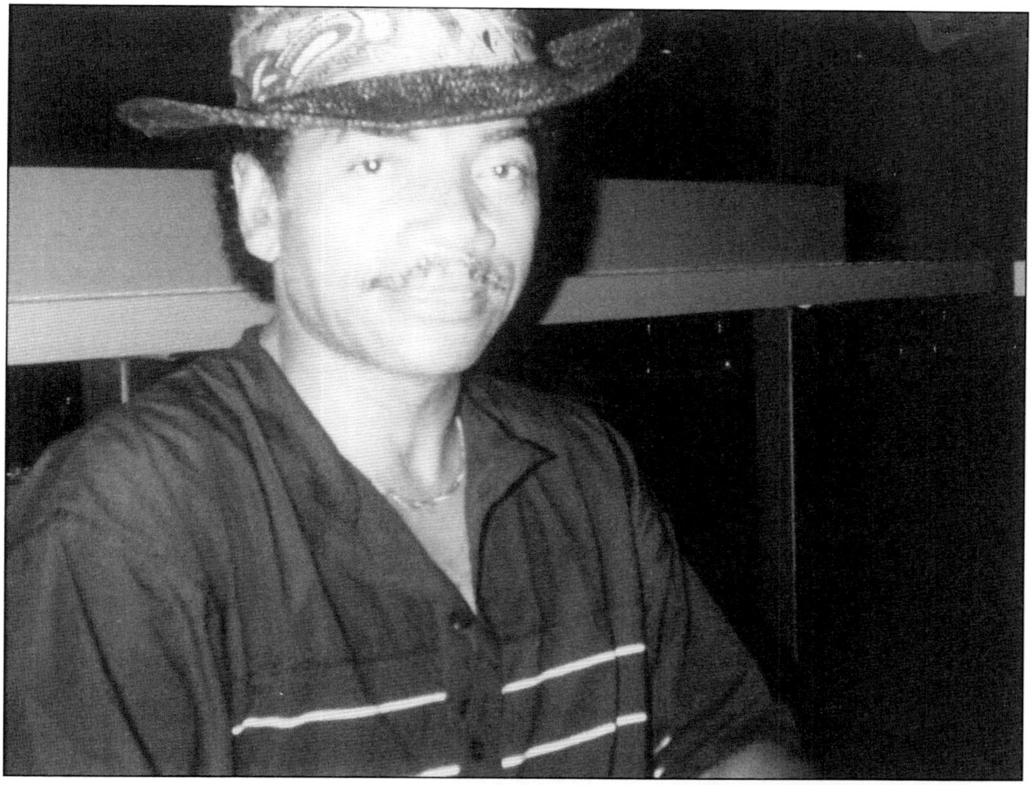

John Hanna Jr. was honorably discharged from the U.S. Army in 1957. Upon returning home, he soon finished high school and entered Tennessee State University (TSU) on a basketball scholarship. One year later, he transferred to Mississippi Valley State University (MVSU) on a basketball scholarship and earned a B.S. degree in art education. A former teacher, John is a commercial artist and works for the State of Tennessee as a detention facilities specialist.

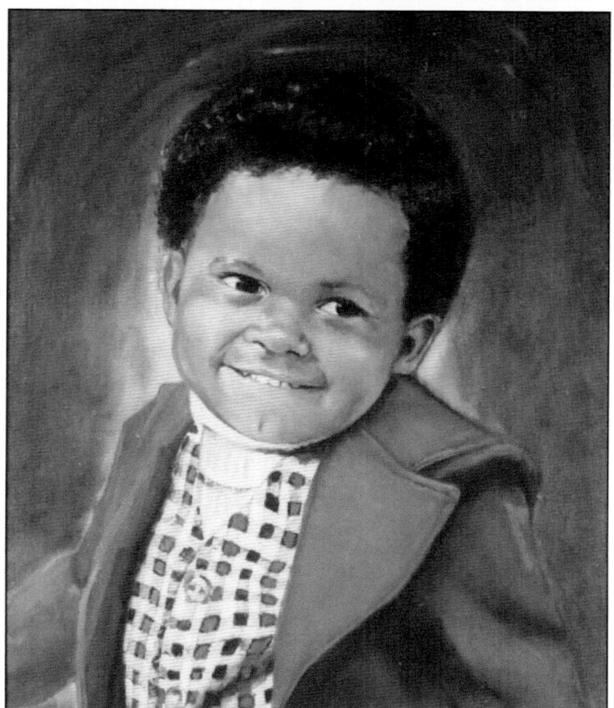

This oil painting on canvas is one of many commissioned portraits done by John Hanna Jr.

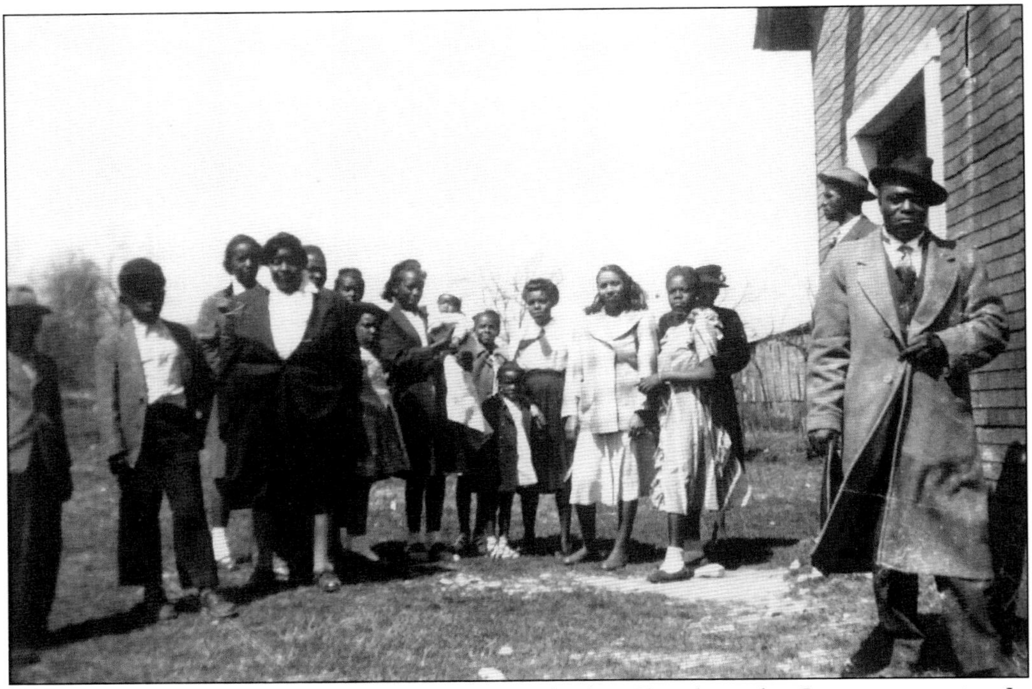

These worshippers are leaving St. Matthews Methodist Church in the Cairo community. In addition to St. Matthews, Williams' Chapel Baptist Church is also located in Cairo. There is much unity and cooperation between the congregations, as they generally worship together by spending two Sundays at each church on a monthly basis.

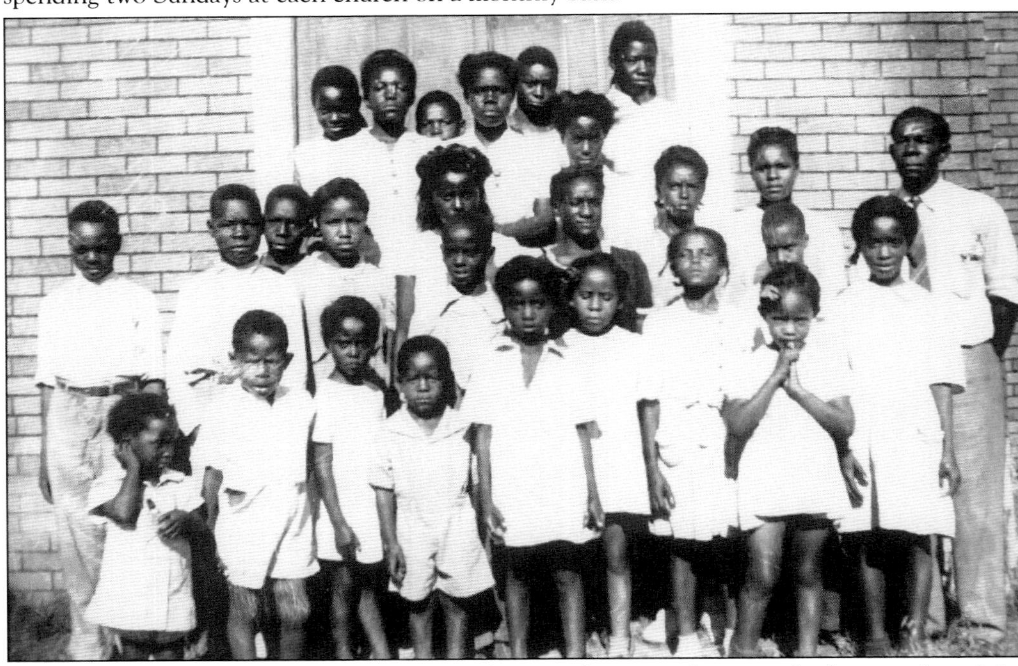

It is vacation Bible school time in Cairo. These students are shown with their teacher, John Hutch Brinkley, in front of St. Matthews Methodist Church (*c.* 1945).

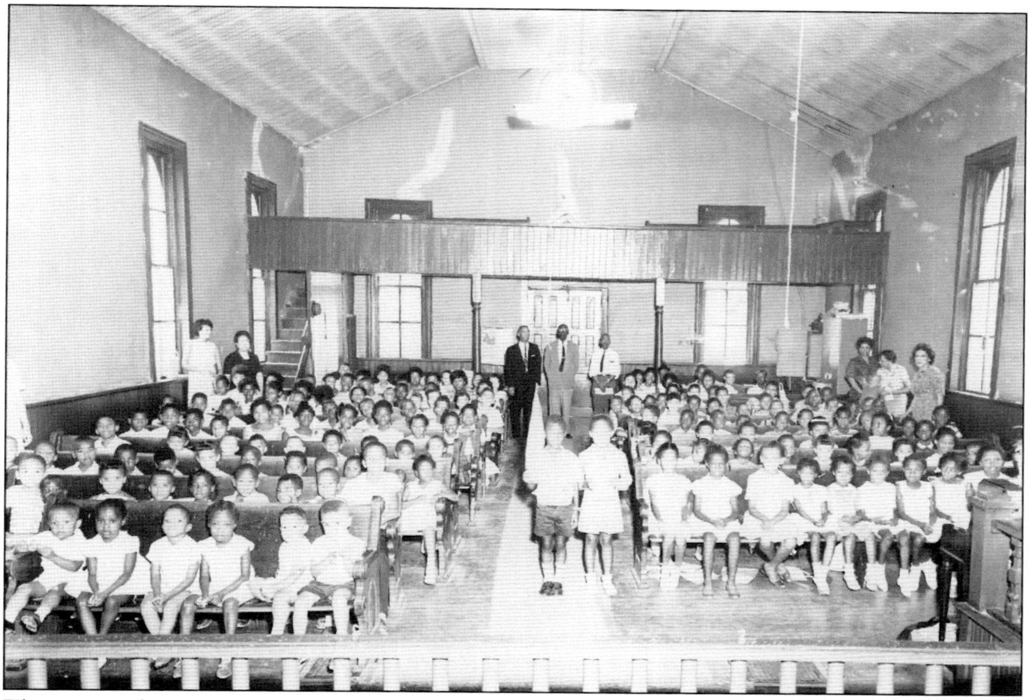

This group of community children is attending vacation Bible school at Key Memorial Methodist Church, which is now the Key Stewart United Methodist Church.

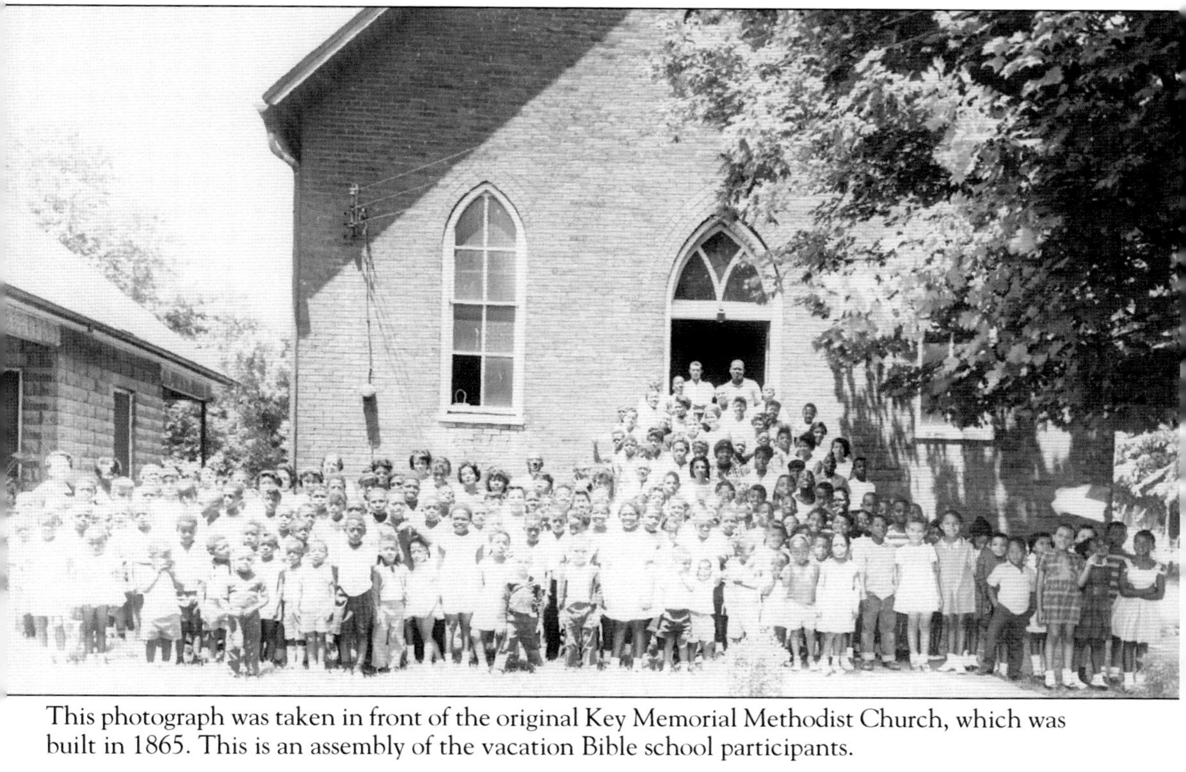

This photograph was taken in front of the original Key Memorial Methodist Church, which was built in 1865. This is an assembly of the vacation Bible school participants.

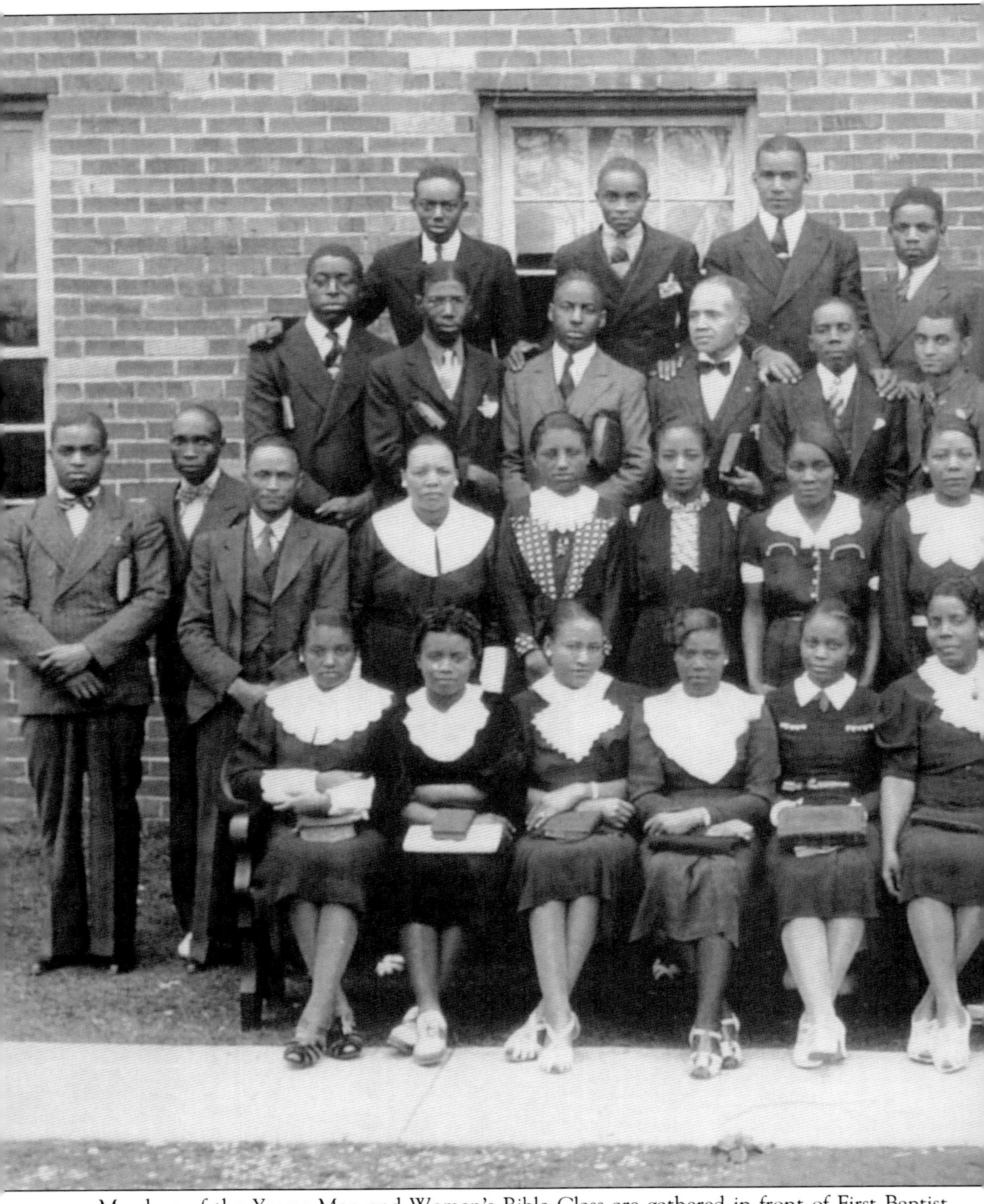

Members of the Young Men and Women's Bible Class are gathered in front of First Baptist Church (*c.* 1951). Some members identified are as follows: Horace Herod, Johnnie Gray, Evelyn Hall, Martha Patterson, Peter Rucker, Clara Vertrees, Irene Coakley, B.J. Hall, Mamie

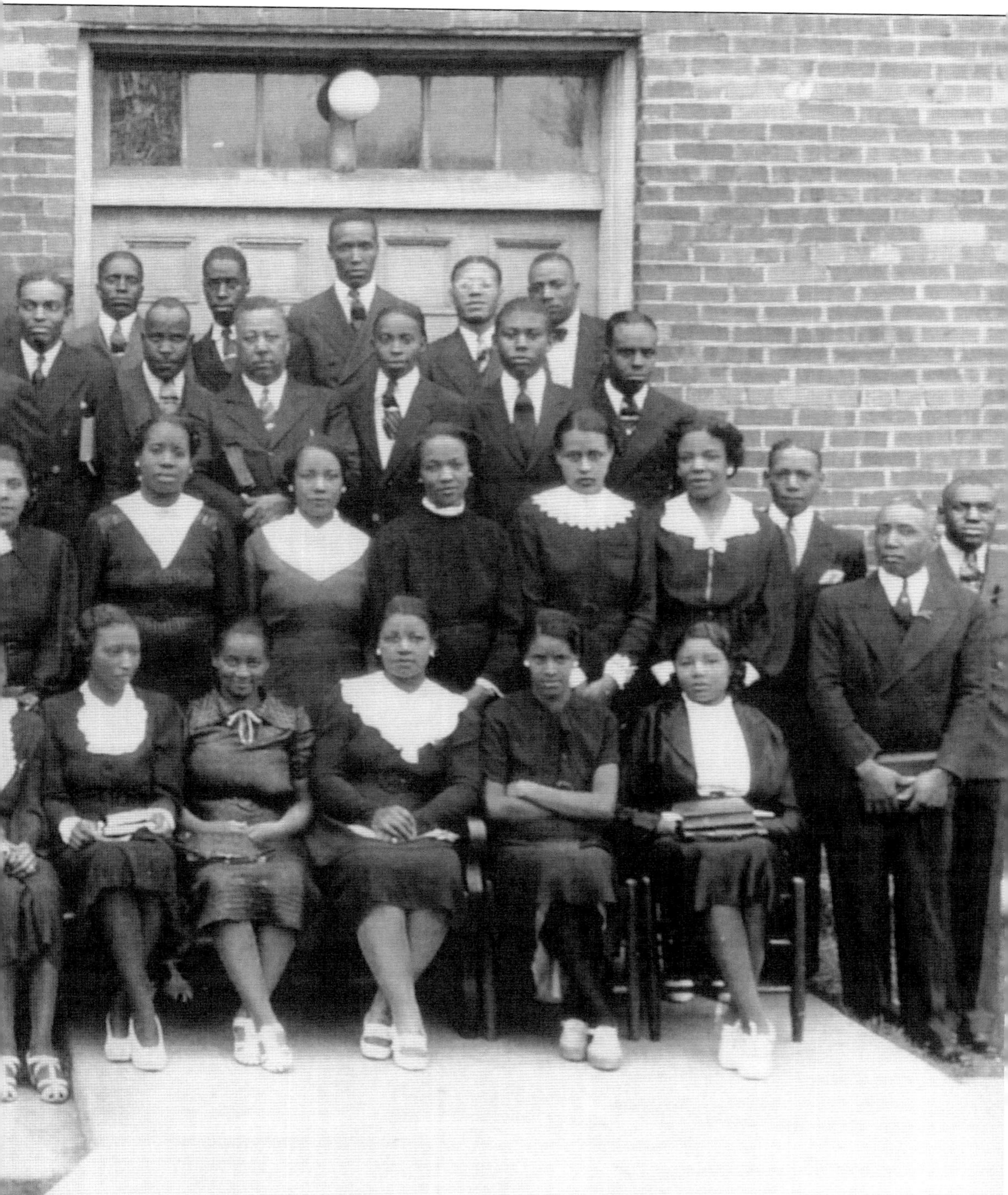

Malone, Verna Lee Anderson, Johnny Bowers, Russell Vertrees, James Hunter, E.A. Gray, Loretta Young, John Frank Horton, and Willie Barksdale.

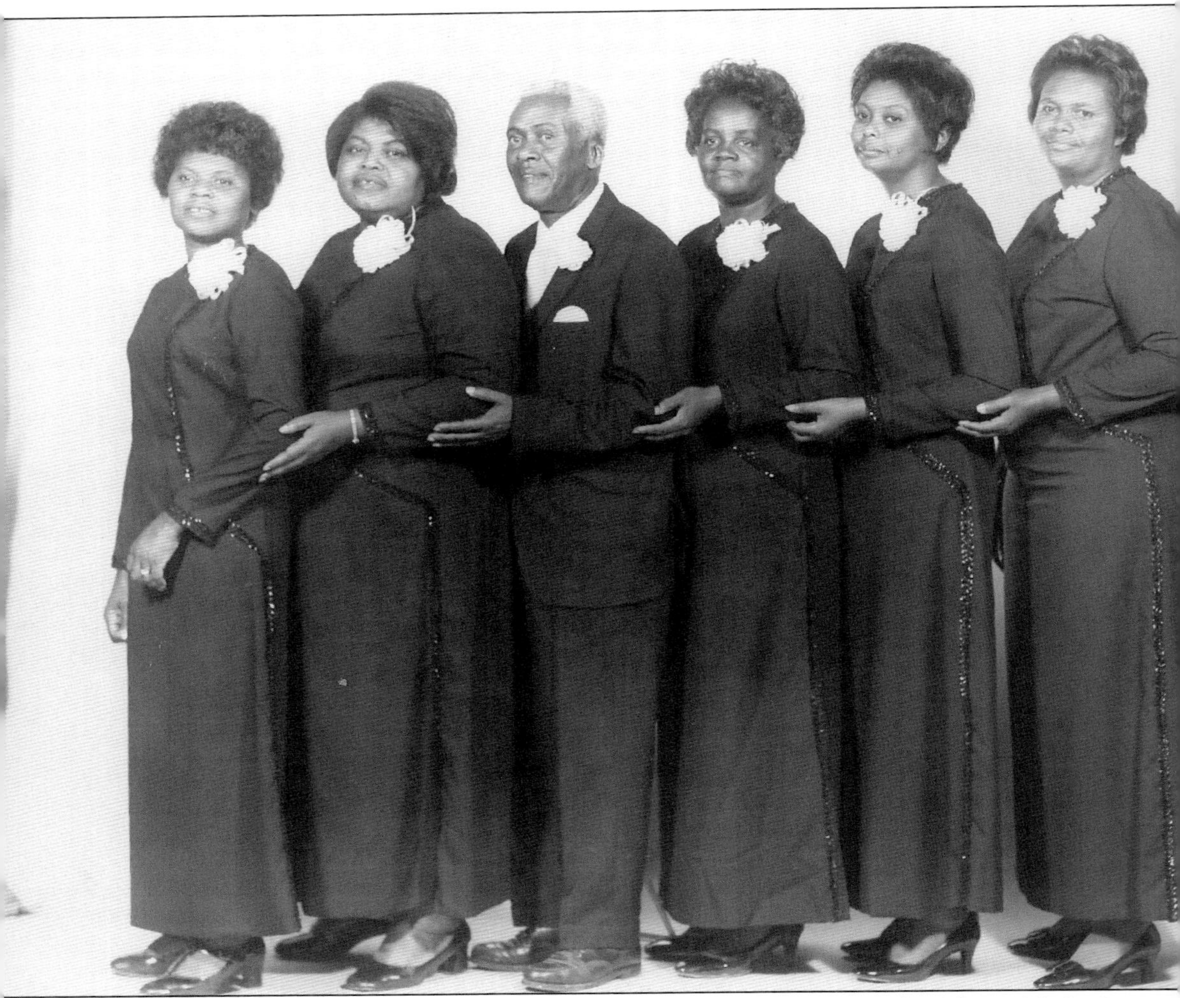

This singing group was organized in 1959 under Rev. M.M. Cole of St. Luke African Methodist Episcopal Church at 355 North Blythe Avenue. At that time, the group was called "the Colettes"; however, in 1963, Rev. L.W. Johnson became pastor and the name was changed to "Johnson Spirituals." The group members, from left to right, are as follows: Allie Robb Bell, Catherine Carey Hassell (1925–1984), Will Henry League (1922–1997), Nevada Watkins, Flora Carey Sweat, and Rachel Turner Cowan. Mildred Bell (not pictured) was a member of the original group and remained until 1969.

Johnnie Ransom Gray retired in 1974 after a successful 34-year teaching career. She holds both a B.S. and M.S. degree from TSU. Next to her love for teaching is a great love for music. She has been director of the music department at First Baptist Church for several decades and church pianist for 61 years. She also directs the male chorus, the senior choir, and is a member of the Happy Trio Club.

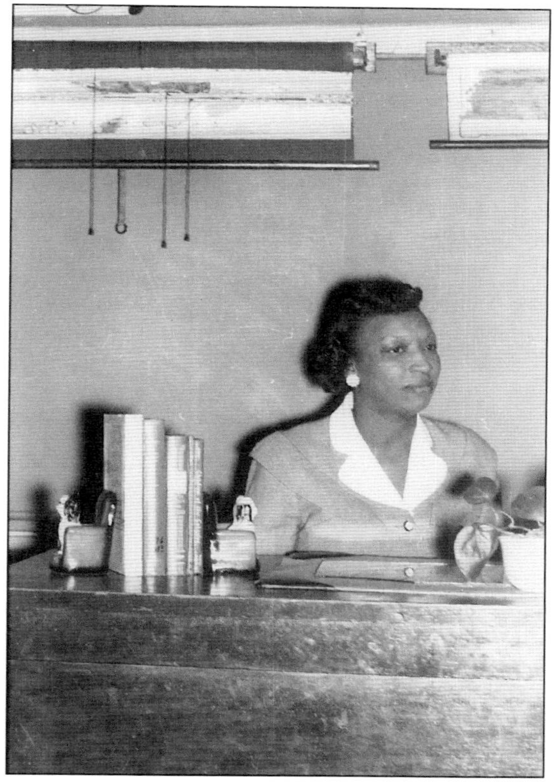

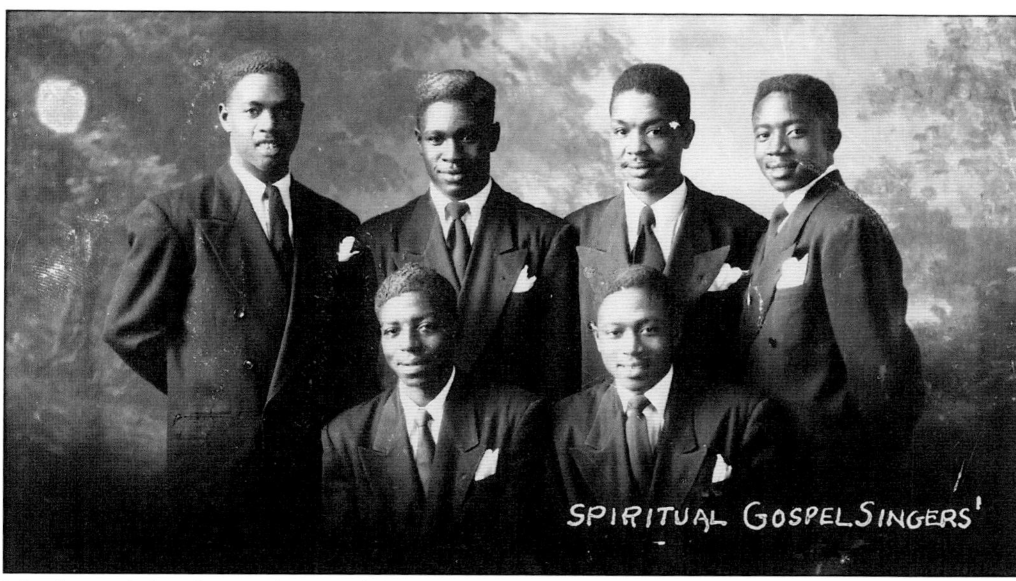

Members of the Spiritual Gospel Singers (*c.* 1948), from left to right, are as follows: (front row) Billy Ray and Jimmy Goodrich; (back row) Miller Bender, Miller Woodson Taylor, Earley Stanton, and George Goodrich.

The Pastor, Deacons, Trustees and Members of
The First Baptist Church, Gallatin, Tennessee
request your presence at
The Opening Of Their Parsonage on Winchester Street
Sunday Afternoon, October 4th, 1953
Hours from three to seven o'clock
Will you please register with \$1.00; funds will be used to eradicate the indebtedness of the parsonage
Thanks,
Rev. W. L. Shaw, Pastor

Chmn. of Deacon Board, Idyll Roberson — *Chmn. of Trustee Board, E. A. Gray*
Church Clerk, B. J. Hall — *Church Treasurer, J. V. Malone*
Building Fund Treasurer, John Cowan

In 1946, Rev. Walter L. Shaw Sr. (1898–1991) became the fourth pastor of First Baptist Church. In 1953, the parsonage at 288 East Winchester Street was erected. This is an invitation to the opening of the parsonage in 1953.

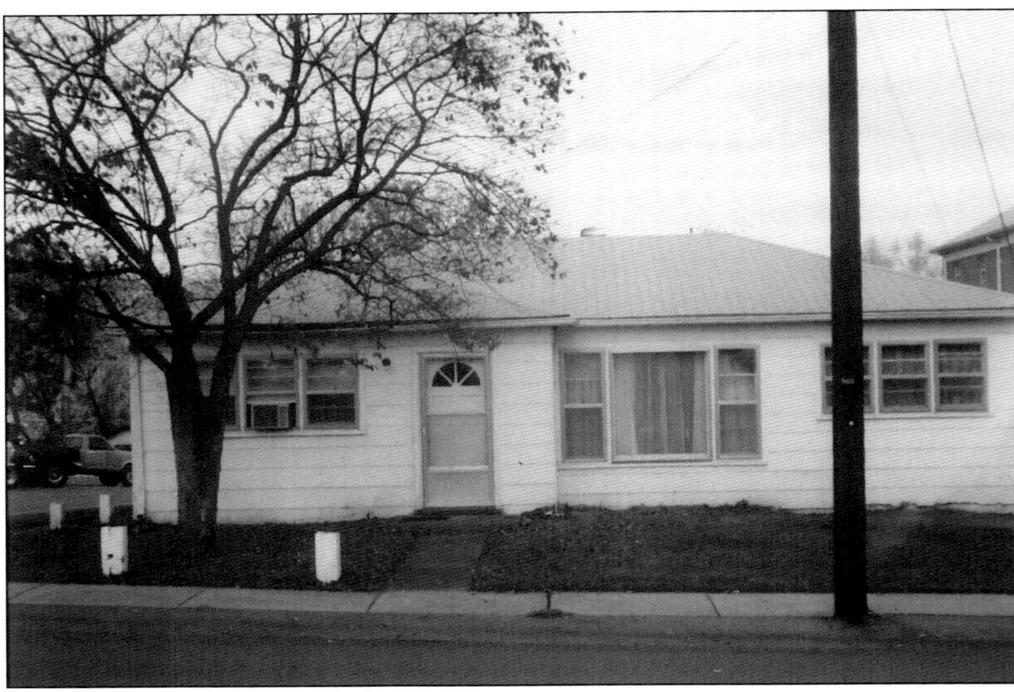

The First Baptist Church Parsonage was built at a cost of \$17,500. It was the home of the Shaw family from 1953 to 1975. It presently houses the Wallace Sewing Center and is used for other church functions.

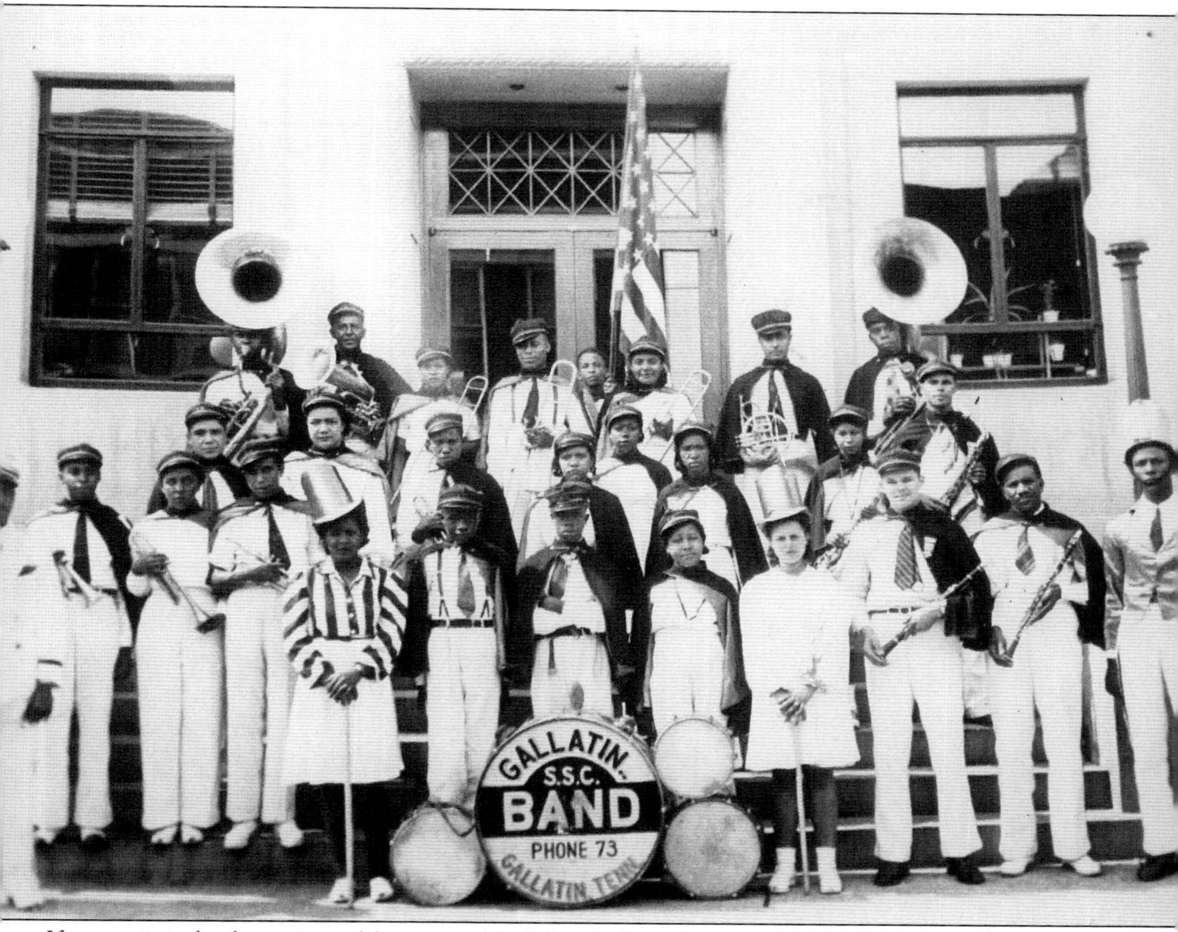

If music is indeed a universal language, black bands from Sumner County have shared in the interpretation of that language. Members of the Sunday School Congress Band, from left to right, are as follows: (first row) Tom Gwynn, unidentified, Eloise Webster, Louis Offitt, unidentified, John "Stack" Chumbley, unidentified, Marie Brown, Katherine Osborne, Foster Anthony, Joseph Thomas Odom, and Clarence Allen Day; (second row) Randolph Offitt, Lillie Harding Vertrees, James Willis Green, Carietta Offitt, Katie Mai Alexander, and three unidentified; (third row) Peter Wylie Vertrees, Hart Winston, unidentified, Walter Horsley, Talmadge Harris, Alice Taylor, James Harold Bryant, and unidentified.

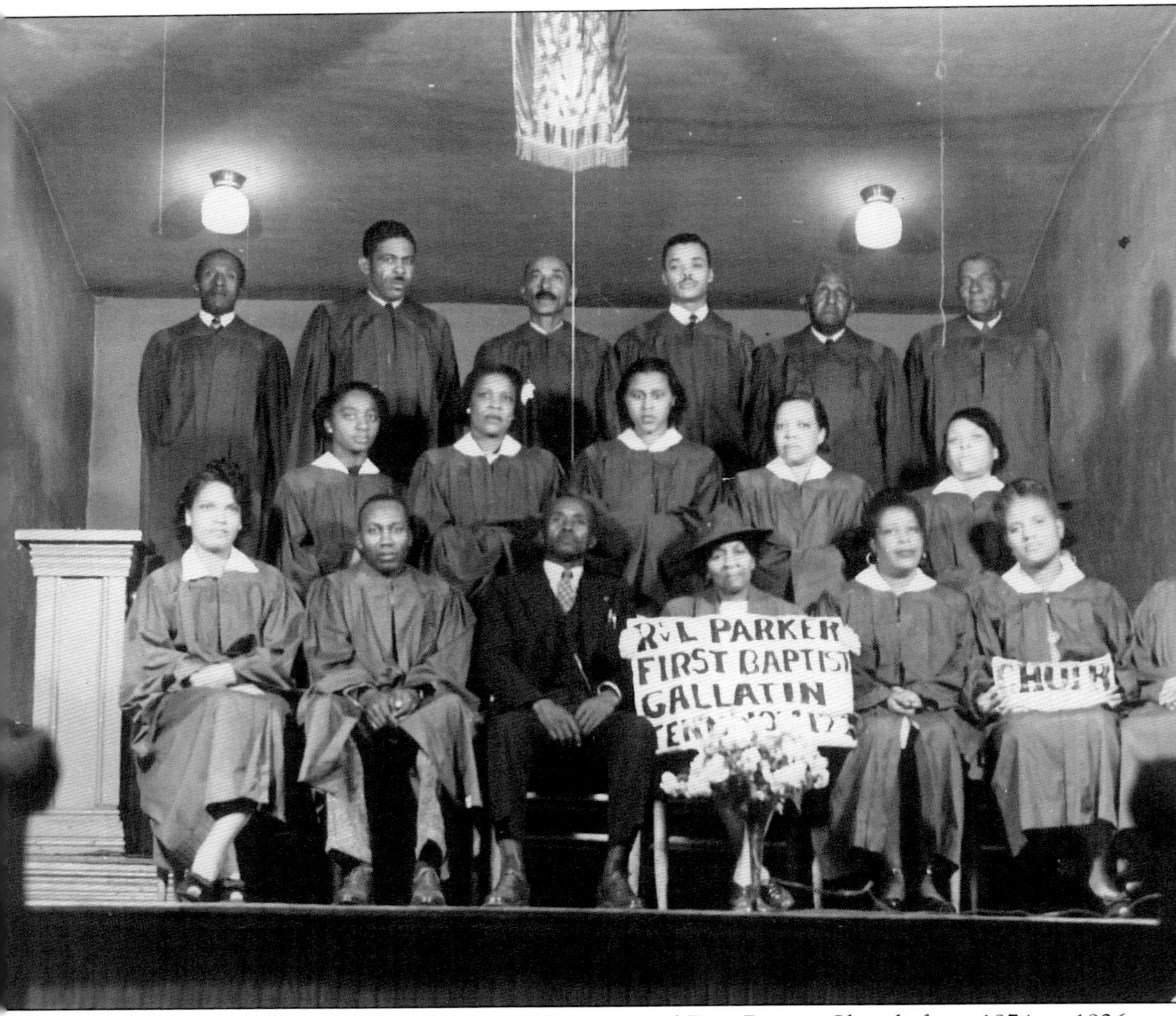

Rev. Peter Vertrees (1846–1926) was the pastor of First Baptist Church from 1874 to 1926. During this time, the senior choir was organized with Mariah Locke as the first organist. The early members, from left to right, are as follows: (front row) Everlina Rucker, Richard Hogg, Rev. Lawson Parker (interim pastor 1945–1946), Ada Parker, Ella Lee Rutledge, Glendolyn Flippin, and Jennie Hogg; (second row) Margaret Fitts, Martha Patterson, Irene Coakley, Clara Vertrees, and Pearl Douglas; (third row) Guy Vaughn, John Dee Flippin Sr., Howard Douglas, Glen Rutledge, W.E. Hamilton, and W.H. Tollinger.

Callie Bell Apple McKissack (1896–1982) was a vocalist, musician, founder/director of a privately owned kindergarten, and a teacher for 40 years. Her daughter, Dorothy Rebecca McKissack Jordon, graduated from Fisk with a B.A. degree, TSU with the M.S. degree, and taught school for 39 years. She has been the minister of music at Key Stewart United Methodist Church since 1982. Her son, William Edward McKissack, graduated from TSU and from Meharry Medical College with a D.D.S. degree. He, too, is musically inclined but followed in his father's footsteps and became a practicing dentist.

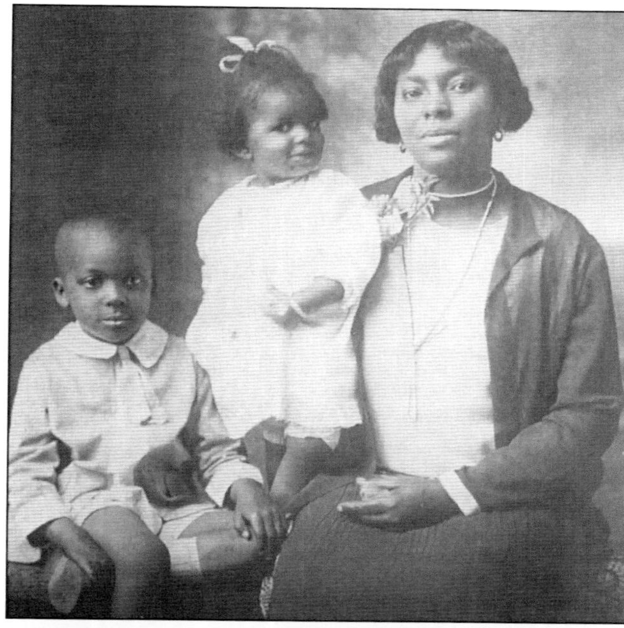

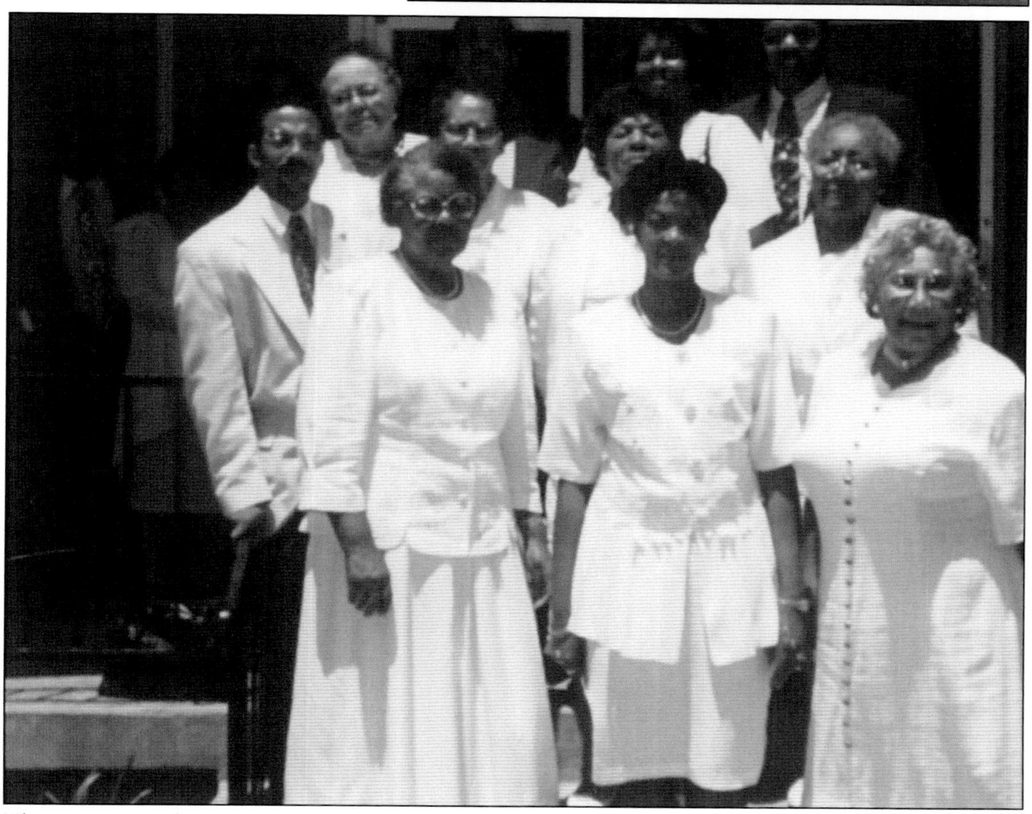

The sanctuary choir at Mt. Olive Baptist Church is part of a body that gave name and meaning to a community over 100 years ago. The church serves an immediate community of about 40 families, plus an extended community of former residents and descendants.

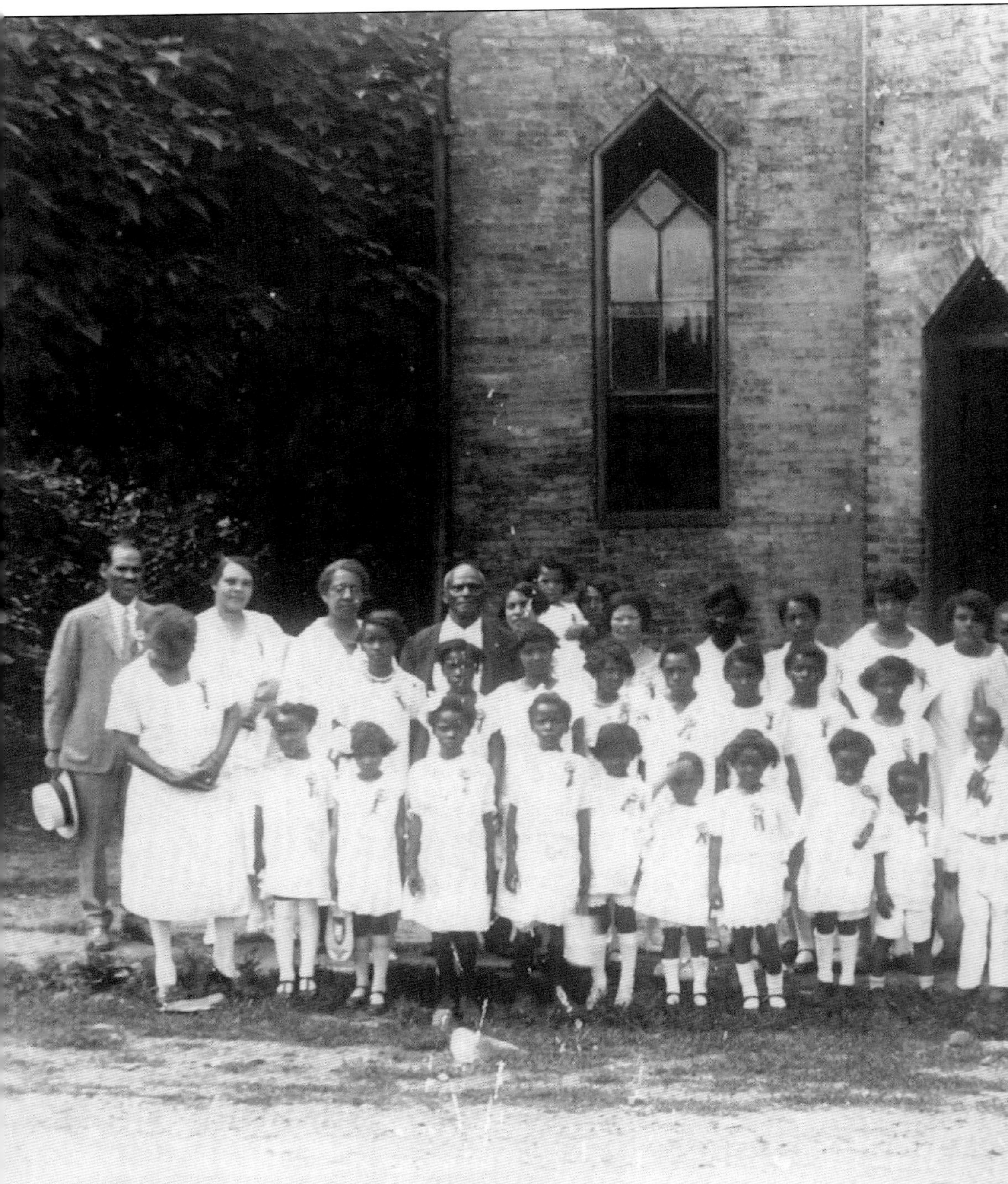

After emancipation, African Americans quickly learned the advantages arising from combined effort and welcomed every organization that promised to secure religious, political, social, or material benefit. The rich, lasting legacy of secret societies in Sumner County proves that members were devoted to them and spent much time and money maintaining them. Some

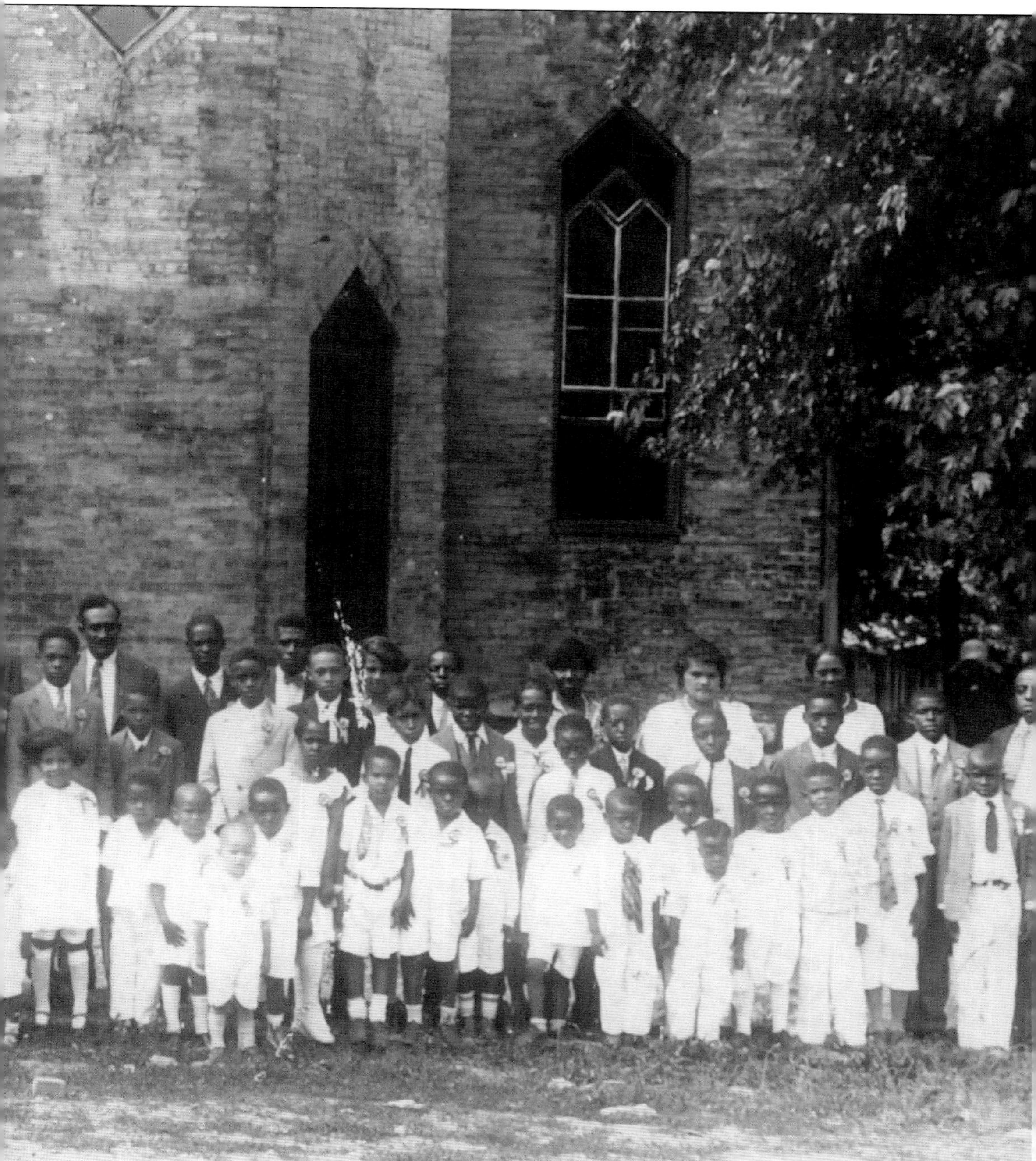

known members of the Knights of Pythias (men) and Calanthe Court (women) included Edward Anthony, Dr. W.E. McKissack, Diora Vertrees, Jimmy Young, Tom Odom, George Harris, Annie Malone, and Richard Hogg.

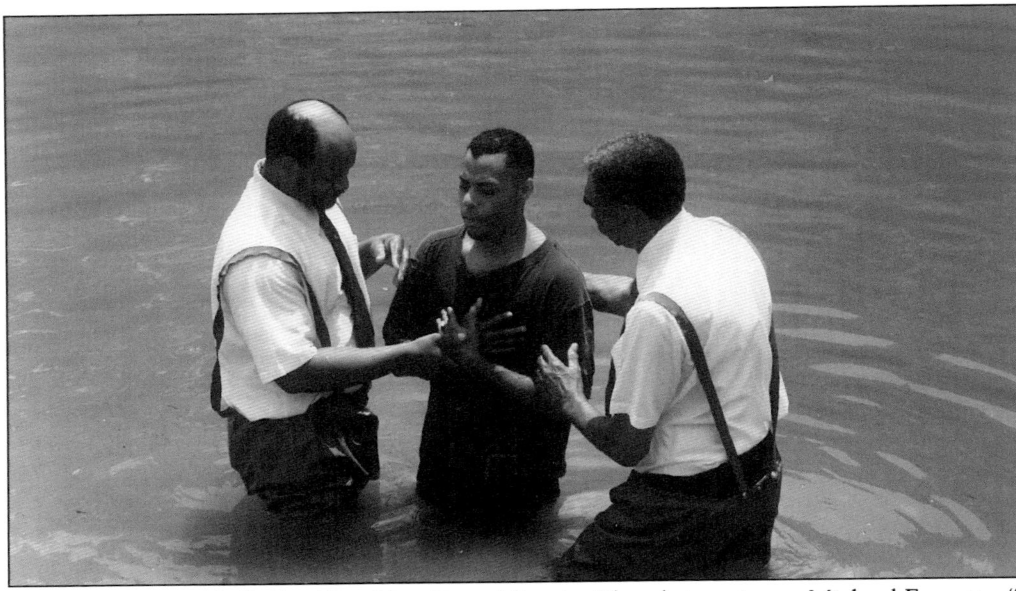

Rev. Anthony Robb (left) of Franklin Chapel Baptist Church is saying to Michael Everette, "I baptize thee in the name of the Father, and of the Son, and of the Holy Ghost." Assisting with the baptism by immersion is Willie James Bush, a church deacon. This baptism was conducted in 1996 in the waters of Old Hickory Lake.

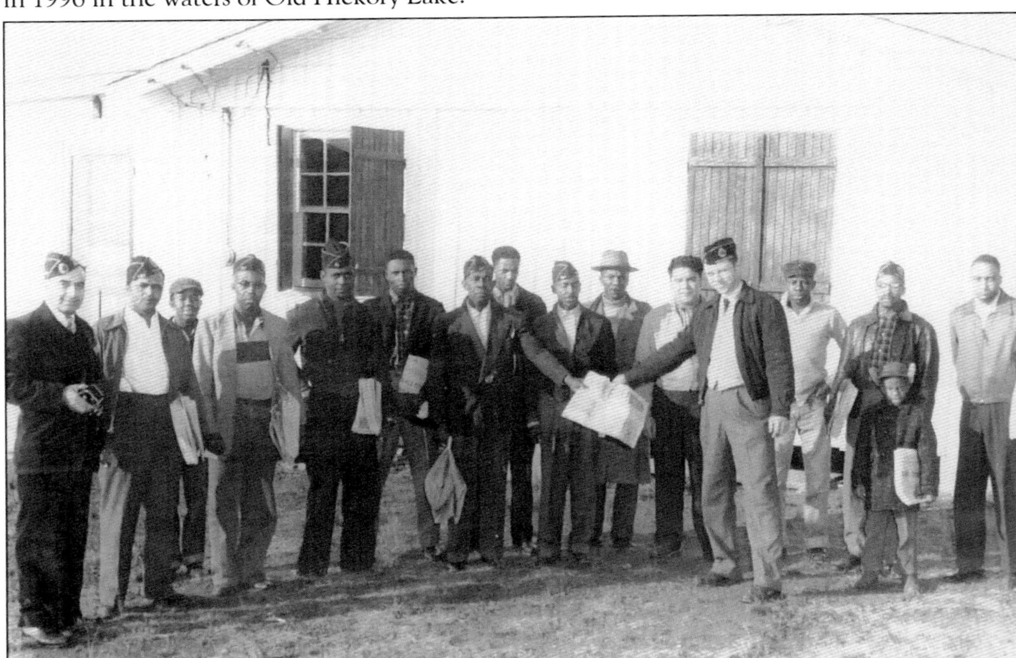

Clearview Center on Chambers Street was the established distribution center for the Big Brothers Paper Sale (c. 1952). Participants included Joe St. Charles, Thomas Alexander, Charles Brinkley, Arthur Lee Hall, Roy Gardner, Billy Black, J.H. Brinkley, James Herman Carter, Samuel Herod, William Rogan, Randolph Offitt, Frank Brinkley, Horace Herod, and Harold Herod.

Three

Artifacts and Remembrances

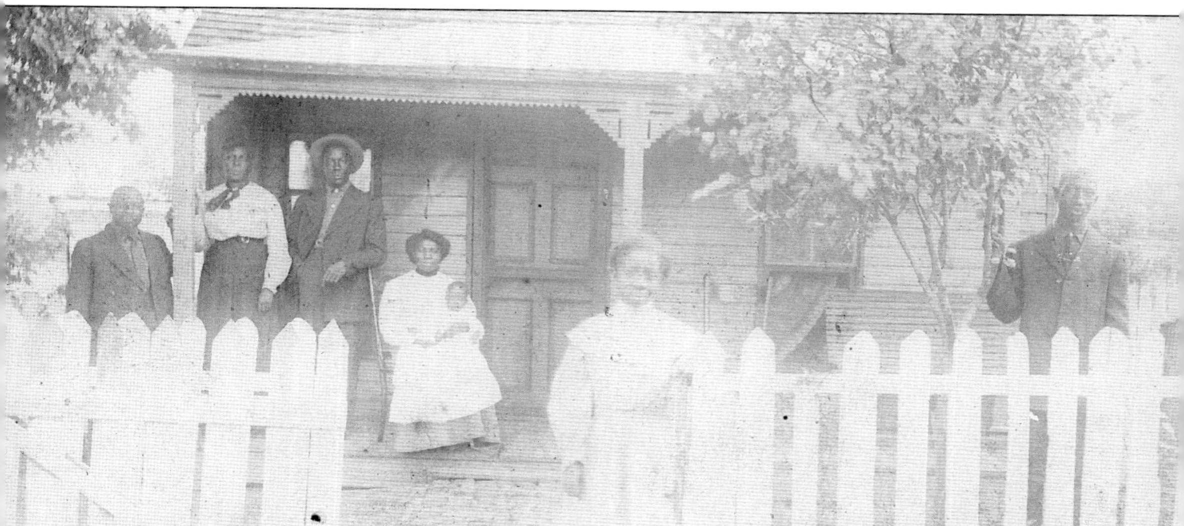

The Dobbins family has a long-standing reputation for being industrious, creative, and good managers of both time and resources. Not long after emancipation, the Dobbins family owned their own home. The family owned this quality home on Enlow Street, which runs from the present Gallatin Police Department toward Town Creek. The family had this picture made in 1907. From left to right, they are as follows: James Dobbins, Pattie Dobbins, Johnny Dobbins, Pattie Martin (with baby), Katie Dobbins, and James M. Dobbins Jr.

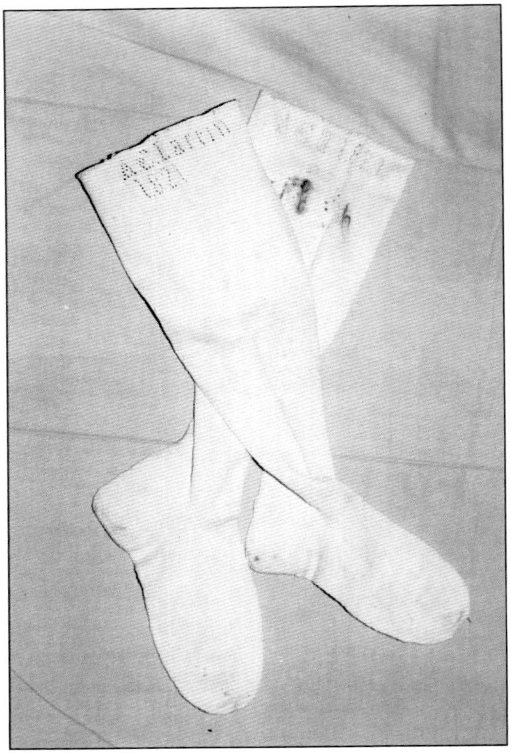

Sock makers, Anee C. Martin (1784–1830) and a slave named Lucy Richerson (1798–?) made and marketed socks locally. Anee C. Martin and family members immigrated from Hanover County, Virginia, to Sumner County in 1806. Lucy Richerson was owned by John B. Hoy, whose family was among the earliest settlers of Kentucky. Note the name A.C. Martin and the year 1821 knitted into the socks pictured to the left.

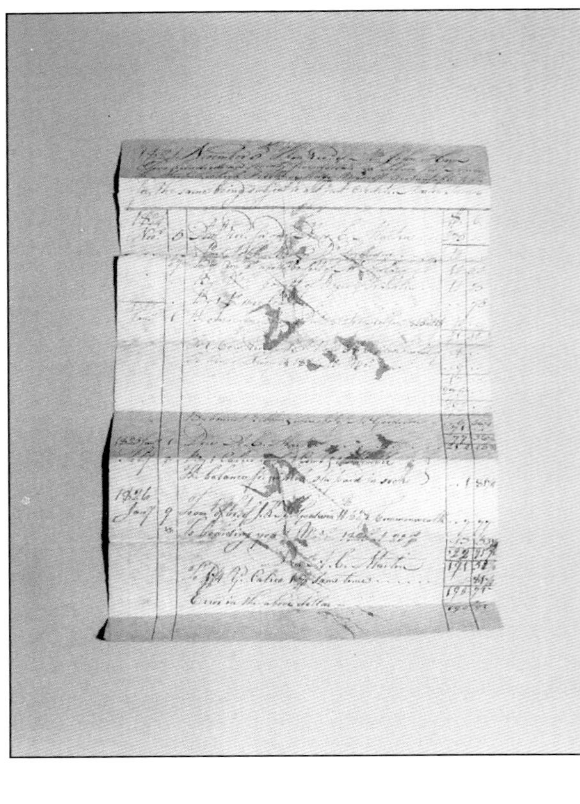

This ledger page, dated 1824, documents that Lucy Richerson was leased to Anee C. Martin by John B. Hoy of Simpson County, Kentucky. Various supplies, purchased from Gallatin merchants for the purpose of making socks, are also listed.

This cast-iron double betty lamp is from a slave cabin (c. 1830). Tallow was burned with a wick, which resulted in a dim light. The lower section provided a reservoir, which caught grease drippings from the wick. This was an improvement over the simpler design of the betty lamp, which had no lower reservoir.

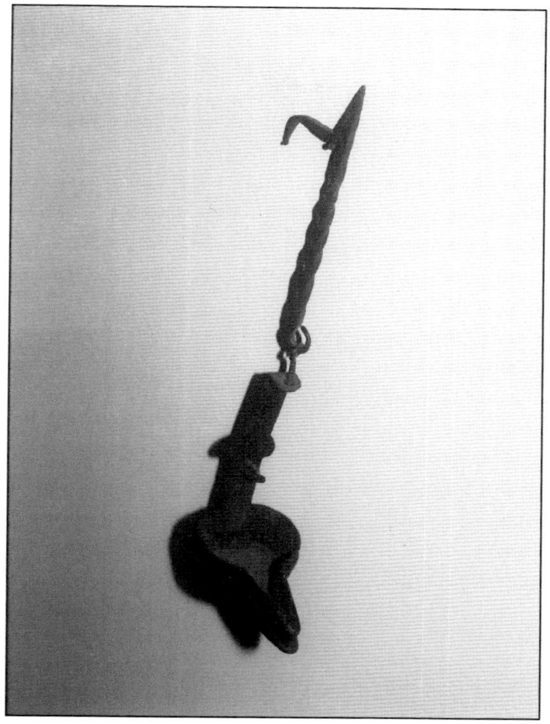

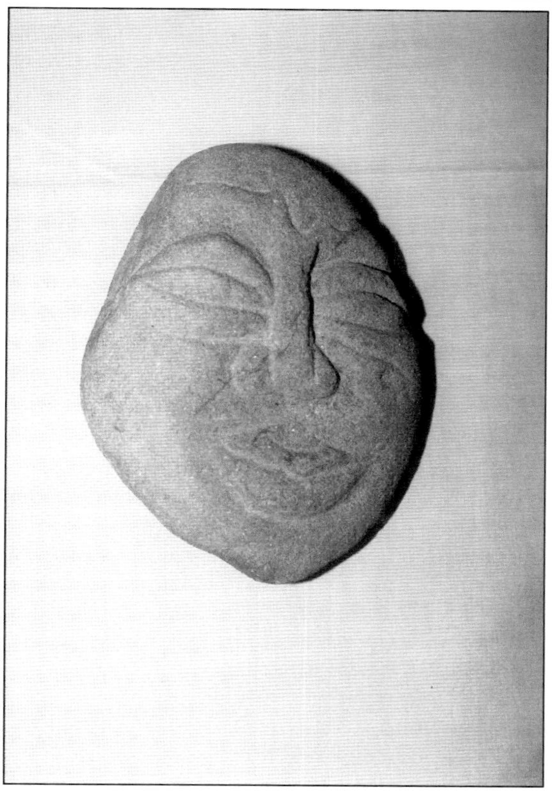

This type of stone carving, depicting a human likeness, is rare. Known examples are strikingly similar to wooden tribal masks of Zaire. This similarity has resulted in the conclusion that their creation was directly influenced by traditions from Africa. At least two such sculptures have been discovered in Sumner County. The sandstone piece shown is from Logan County, Kentucky.

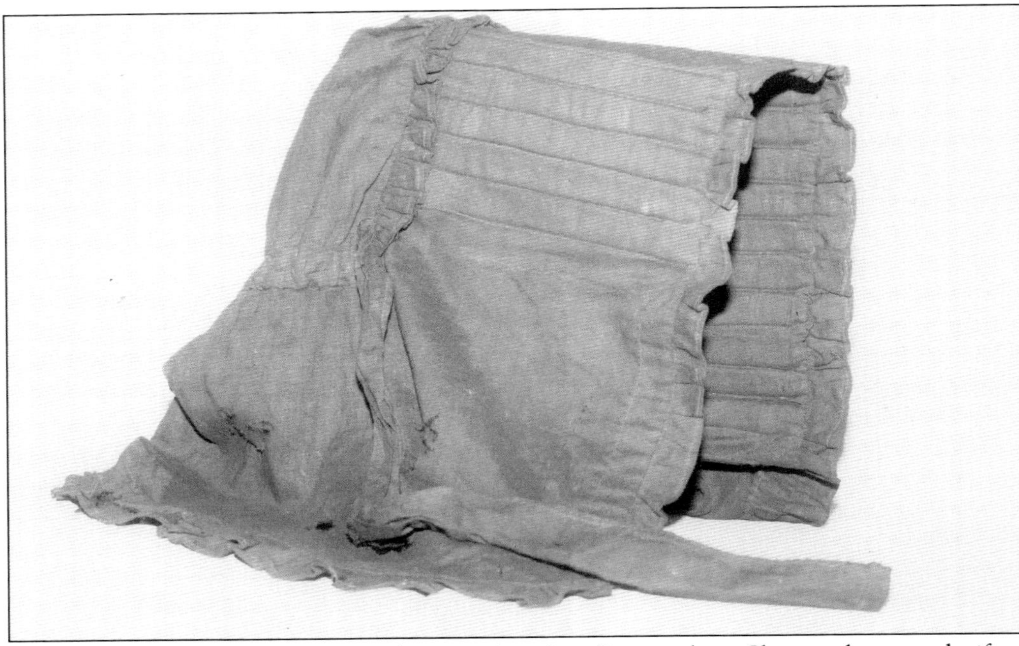

This bonnet belonged to Maria Head Bate, a Castalian Springs slave. She was the second wife of Mark (Marcus) Bate, and together, they had seven children: James, Ben, Lucy, Emma, Nanna, Annison, and Charles Brimage Bate. They raised their children on the William Brimage Bate farm in Castalian Springs.

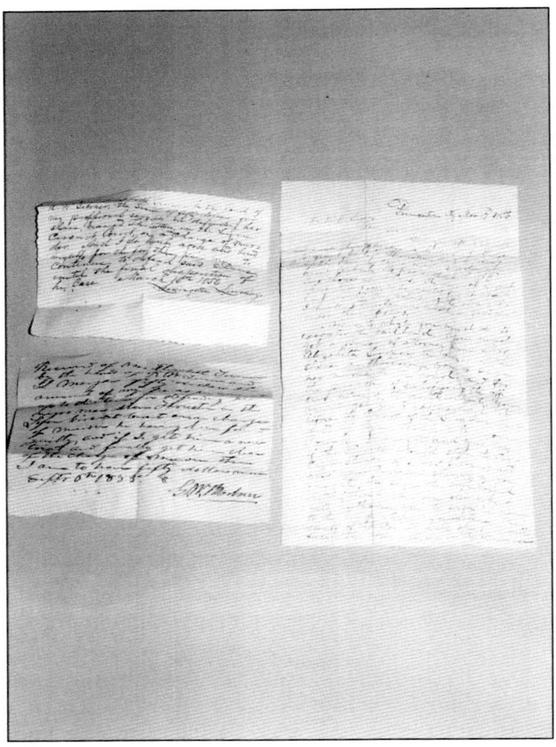

While he was leased to William Kelly, an iron works magnate in Lyon County, Kentucky, a slave named Thurston Turner was charged with the murder of a Chinese man. Thurston was indicted on November 30, 1854, and convicted in 1855. Much attention was drawn to this case because Thurston's owner, Elizabeth Turner, hired prominent defense lawyers to appeal his conviction. The two trials that followed resulted in Thurston's acquittal on October 23, 1856. The three papers pictured are trial-related documents written to Robert W. Turner (Elizabeth's son) of Mitchellville.

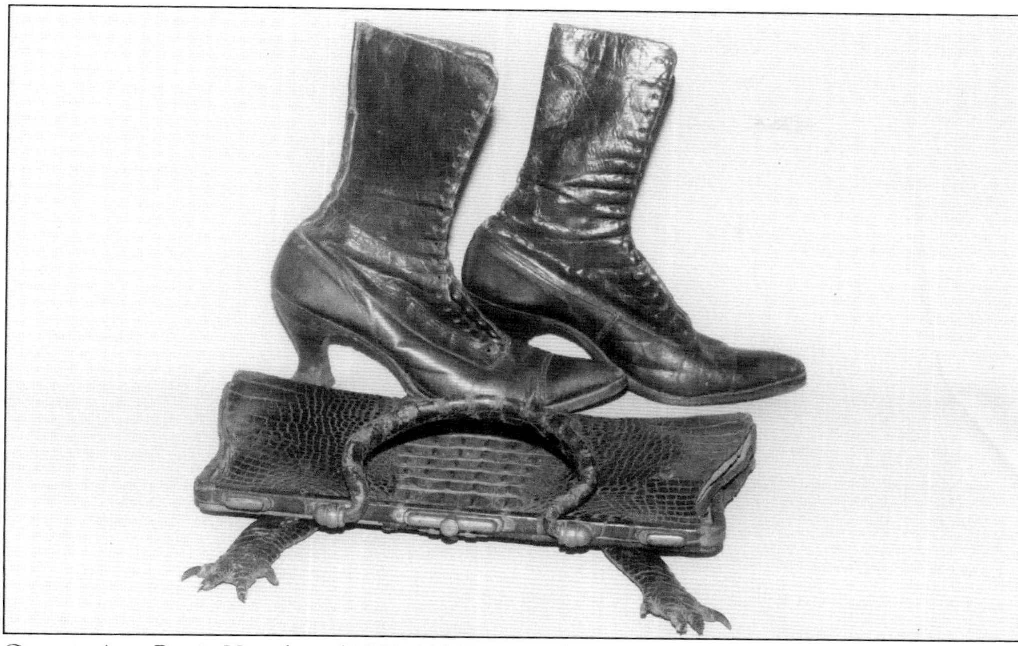

Georgia Ann Bettis Hamilton (1876–1939), a member of the Cairo Community, owned these brown leather boots with stacked wooden heels. She also owned the alligator skin purse which sports the gator's front feet. Both the bag and the shoes are in good condition. Georgia worked for the Will Gray family in Rock Town for many years.

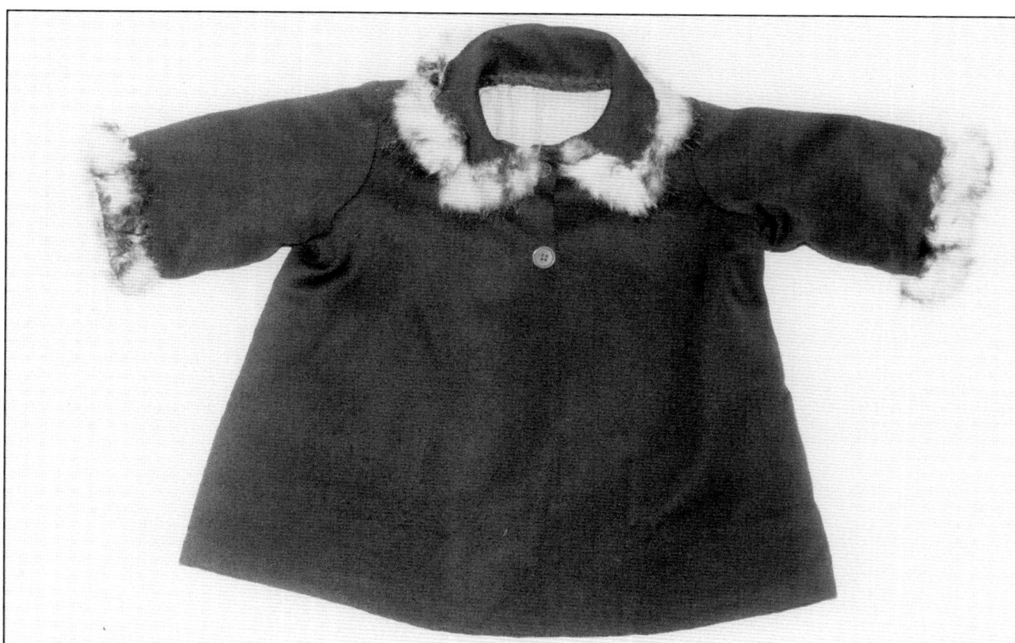

This fully lined wool coat was made by Sallie Dobbins in 1930. The black wool, fox-fur trimmed coat was made for her youngest daughter, Julia Dobbins Carter.

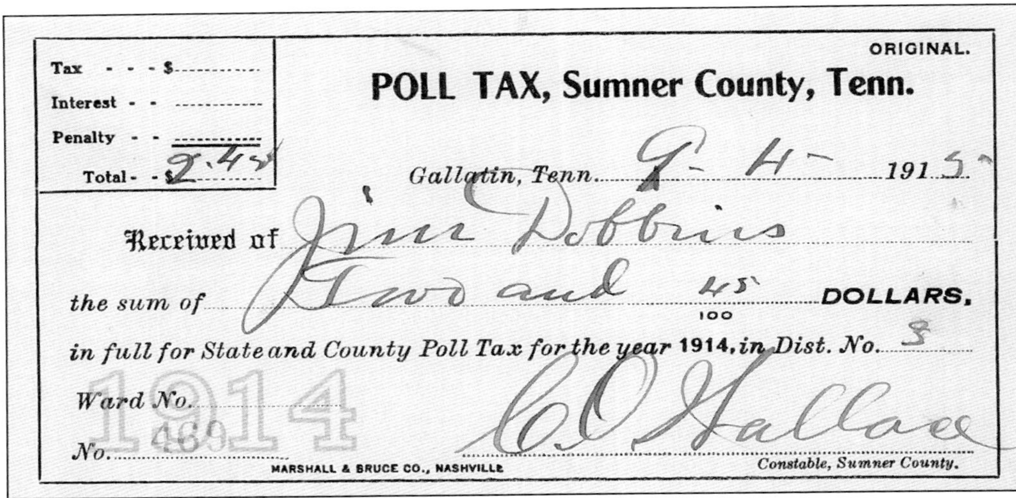

ORIGINAL.

POLL TAX, Sumner County, Tenn.

Tax - - - $
Interest - -
Penalty - -
Total - - $2.45

Gallatin, Tenn. 9-4- 1915

Received of Jim Dobbins

the sum of Two and 45/100 DOLLARS,

in full for State and County Poll Tax for the year 1914, in Dist. No. 3

Ward No.

No. 469

1914

C O Wallace
Constable, Sumner County.

MARSHALL & BRUCE CO., NASHVILLE

The Voting Rights Act of 1965 showcased national consensus in favor of eliminating suffrage barriers. Since the First Reconstruction, the structure of disenfranchisement of African Americans was built upon literacy tests, poll taxes, and intimidation.

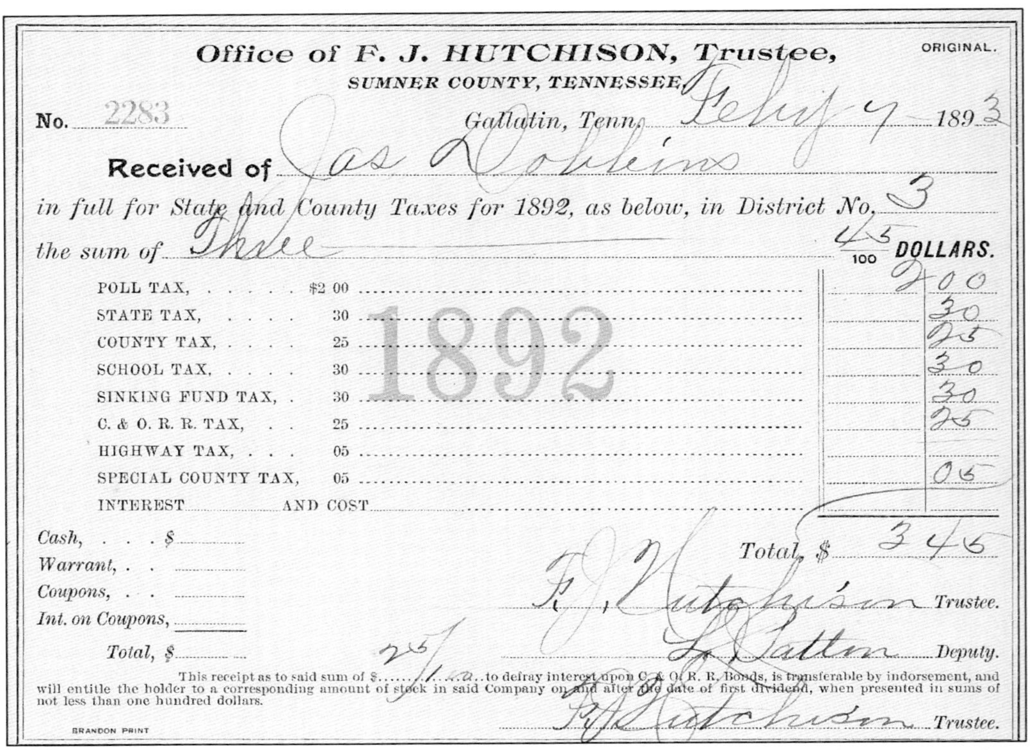

ORIGINAL.

Office of F. J. HUTCHISON, Trustee,
SUMNER COUNTY, TENNESSEE.

No. 2283 Gallatin, Tenn. Feby 7 1893

Received of Jas Dobbins

in full for State and County Taxes for 1892, as below, in District No. 3

the sum of Three 45/100 DOLLARS.

POLL TAX,	$2 00	2 00
STATE TAX,	30	30
COUNTY TAX,	25	25
SCHOOL TAX,	30	30
SINKING FUND TAX,	30	30
C. & O. R. R. TAX,	25	25
HIGHWAY TAX,	05	
SPECIAL COUNTY TAX,	05	05
INTEREST ... AND COST		

1892

Cash, . . . $
Warrant, . .
Coupons, . .
Int. on Coupons,
Total, $

Total, $ 3 45

F. J. Hutchison Trustee.
L. Patton Deputy.

This receipt as to said sum of $ 25/100 to defray interest upon C. & O. R. R. Bonds, is transferable by indorsement, and will entitle the holder to a corresponding amount of stock in said Company on and after the date of first dividend, when presented in sums of not less than one hundred dollars.

F. J. Hutchison Trustee.

BRANDON PRINT

This is a receipt for 1892 state and county taxes paid by James Dobbins on February 7, 1893.

This Christening gown (right) was first worn by Vines Lucas Collier Jr. (1822–1900). He was the son of Sarah Keithley Collier and Vines Lucas Collier Sr. It is said that while the Collier family was living in West Feliciana Parish, Louisiana, a slave made this Christening gown. It is completely hand-stitched with gathers, cutwork, and intricate embroidery. Even the minuscule buttons in the back have sewn coverings. The gown clearly displays a high level of artistry. The Collier family moved to Sumner County, Tennessee, in 1833. Six additional generations of Collier descendants have used the gown.

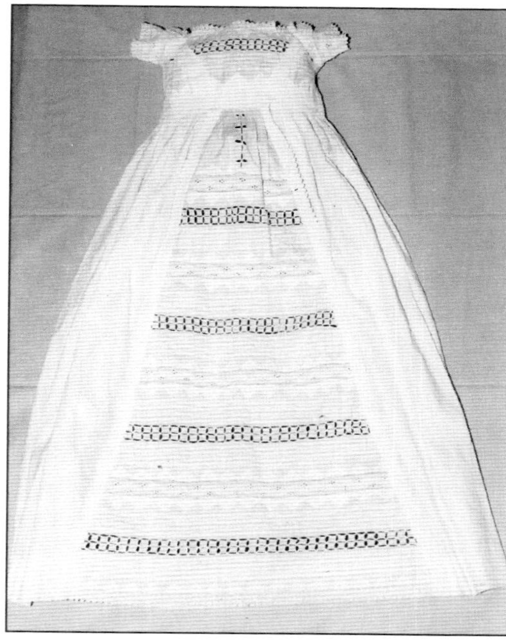

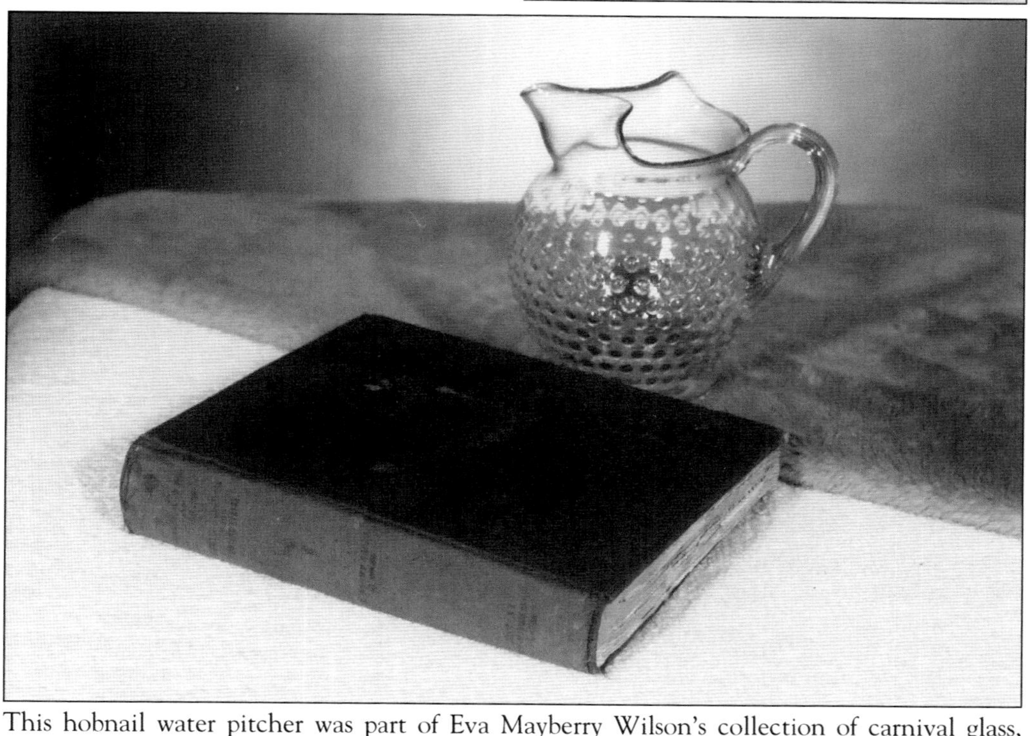

This hobnail water pitcher was part of Eva Mayberry Wilson's collection of carnival glass, ceramics, china, and other collectibles. In addition to working as a registered nurse, Eva taught school for 30 years, many of which were spent at Rockland School. As she began her teaching career in 1925, E.B. Wilson became superintendent of Sumner County Schools (1925–1930). One of his books, *Fishery Industries of the United States* (1884), was converted into a scrapbook many years ago.

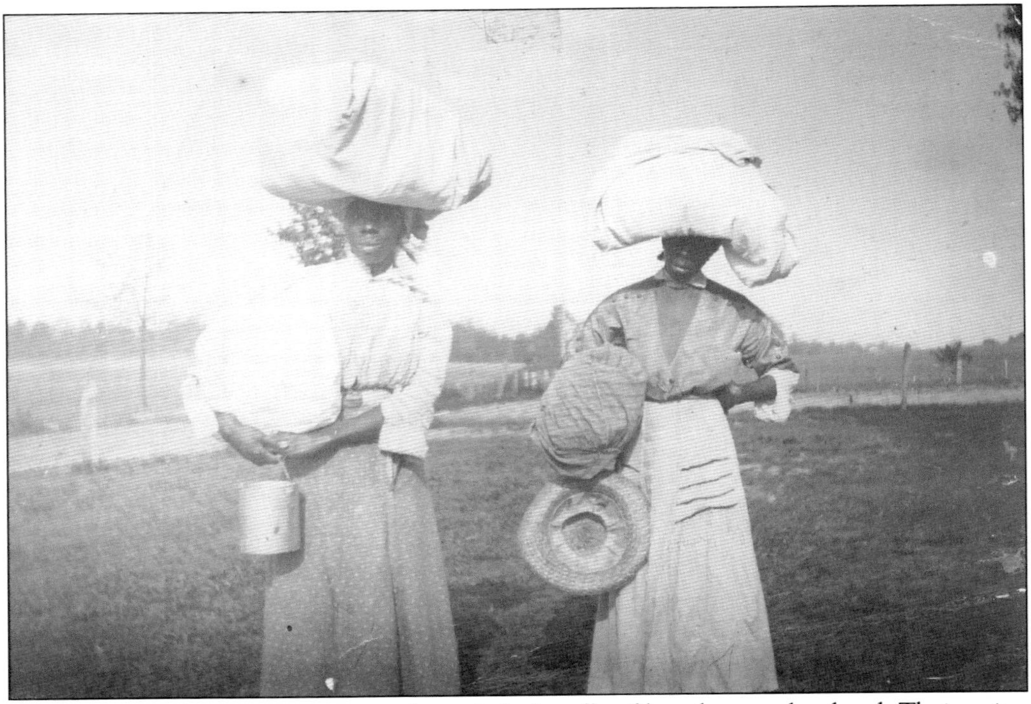

These African-American women each carried a bundle of laundry atop her head. Their poise, balance, grace, and posture speak of their "Mother Land." At this time in history, many black women supplemented the family income by doing laundry and/or ironing for white families.

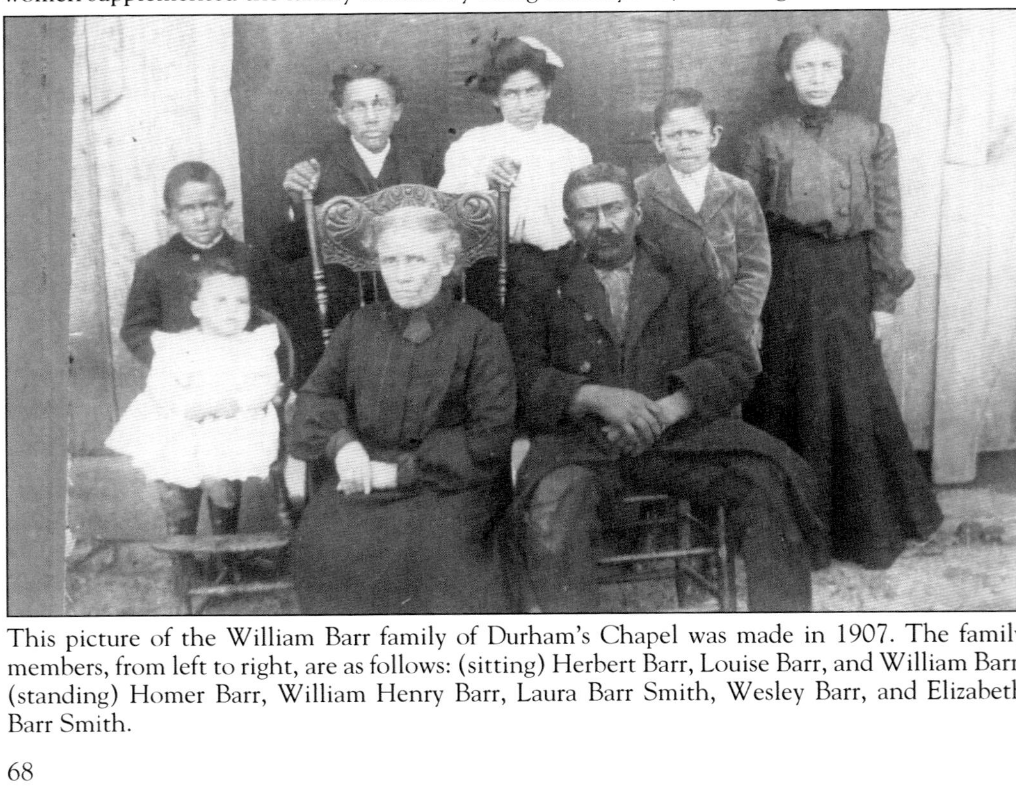

This picture of the William Barr family of Durham's Chapel was made in 1907. The family members, from left to right, are as follows: (sitting) Herbert Barr, Louise Barr, and William Barr; (standing) Homer Barr, William Henry Barr, Laura Barr Smith, Wesley Barr, and Elizabeth Barr Smith.

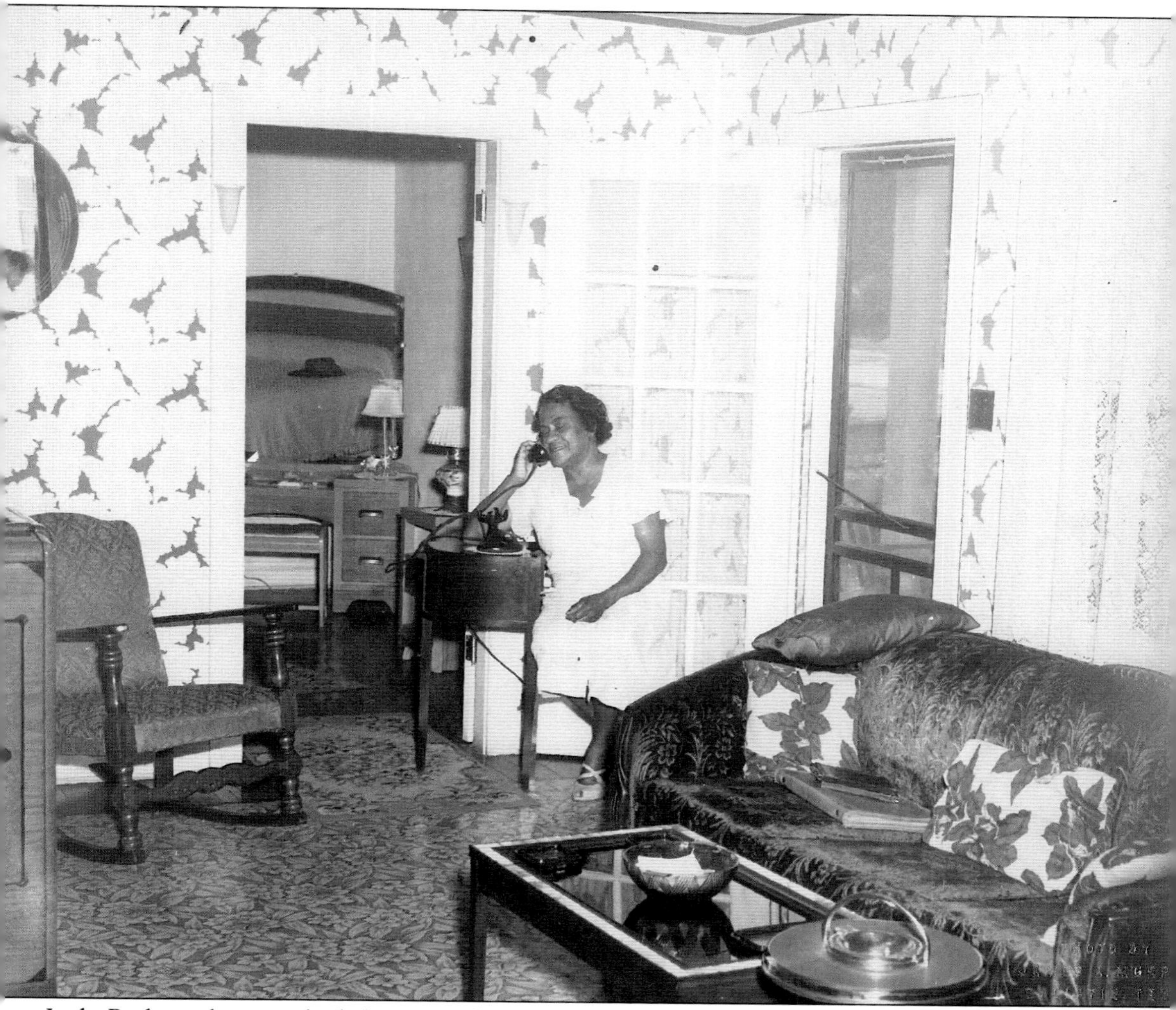

Lady Bush is photographed showing off a well-appointed 1945 living room. The phone was characteristically placed near the front door to accommodate neighbors and friends who were without the benefit of phone service. Some telephone numbers in use at that time were as follows: Della Armstrong, 1060-M; Odell Barr, 414-M; Felix Baker, 865-W; Frank Vaughn, 1042-J; and Alfred Herod, 676-J. Lady Bush built this modern home at 633 North Blythe Street in 1945.

Educators Speak At Colored High School

Dr. Sheperdson, S. L. Smith and O. H. Bernard, representatives of the Rosenwald Fund, J. L. Harnard, state superintendent, J. W. Brister, high school superintendent of the state, J.B. Brown, elementary superintendent and C. H. Horn of the city schools of Franklin were speakers on the all day program at the Gallatin colored high school Tuesday, which received an endowment from the Rosenwald fund. Luncheon was served by the school at noon.

Following the afternoon program, the guest and local workers who have given the colored school aid, including city and county superintendents, board of education, high school faculty, Mrs. Ewing, executive secretary of the local Red Cross chapter, Miss Whaley and Mrs. Morris Wile were entertained with a tea by Miss Virginia Pearl Moore at her home on the Scottsville Pike.

Other colored schools in this county which have received aid from the Rosenwald fund are the Kansas and Durhams Chapel schools. An endowment from the fund has also been given for the new school to be erected at Cairo.

Marriage in Colored Circles.

A notable wedding took place in the upper circles of colored society last Wednesday morning, the groom being Mr. Sam Williamson, the obliging porter at Knight's drug store, and the bride Miss Jennie Howser, a popular and fascinating rustic belle. The affair was due on Tuesday night, but for some unexplained cause the groom did not materailize at the appointed hour. The marriage took place at the residence of Henry Williamson, and was attended by quite a number of white citizens.

Aunt Bettie Baker Dies, Age 110 Years

The death of Aunt Bettie Baker, colored, the oldest person in Sumner county occurred Saturday at her home at Peach Valley. Aunt Bettie was 110 years old. Just ninety eight years ago, together with her parents and a number of brothers and sisters, she was purchased by Isaac Franklin of this county from John Washington, adopted son of General George Washington in Virginia, and brought here. Several years later she married and reared a family of nine children. Aunt Bettie was industrious and thrifty and at all times enjoyed the confidence and good will of the white folks. Her declining years were spent in comfort at her home at Peach Valley. The burial occurred Tuesday afternoon.

Top Left: This article appeared in the *Sumner County News* on Thursday, April 19, 1923.
Top Right: News of this wedding appeared in the *Sumner County News* on Saturday, May 4, 1889.
Bottom: This death notice appeared in the *Sumner County News* for Betsy Baker, who is pictured on page 84.

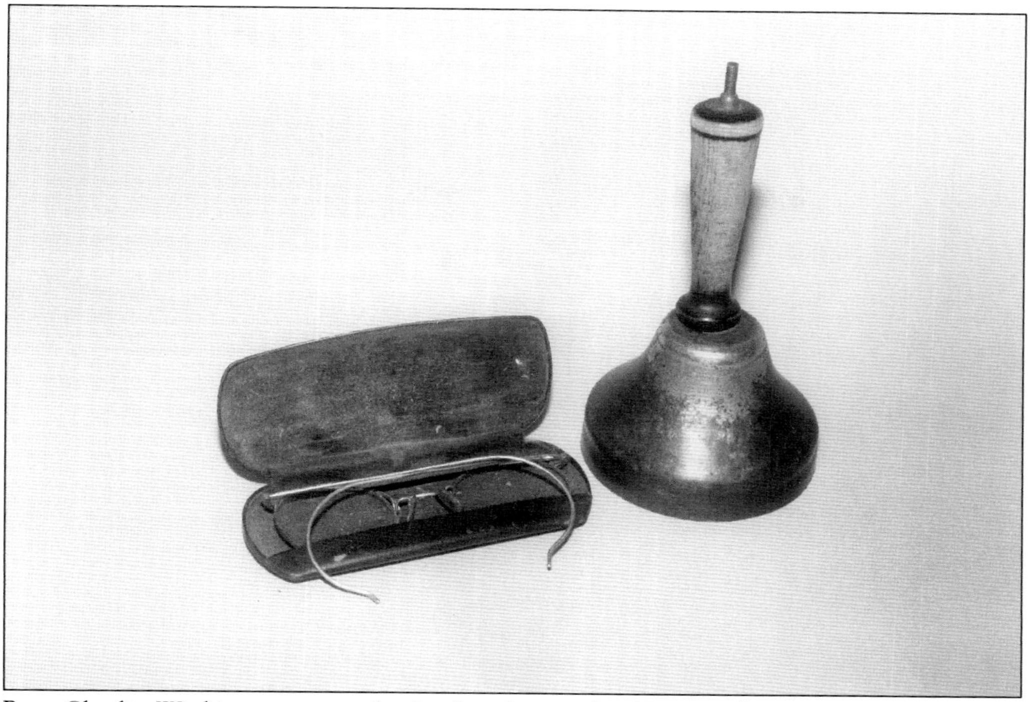

Rev. Charlie Watkins, pastor and schoolteacher in the Hart's Hill community, wore these eyeglasses. In 1925, he was elected treasurer of the East Fork Association. He was elected pastor of Peach Valley Church in 1920 and served until his death. The school bell belonged to his nephew, John Hutch Brinkley, who used it during his 16-year tenure at Cairo School.

This white-with-red-trim enamel water dipper was used by students at Cairo School during the late 1940s. In the 1950s, this modern aluminum dipper retired the older version.

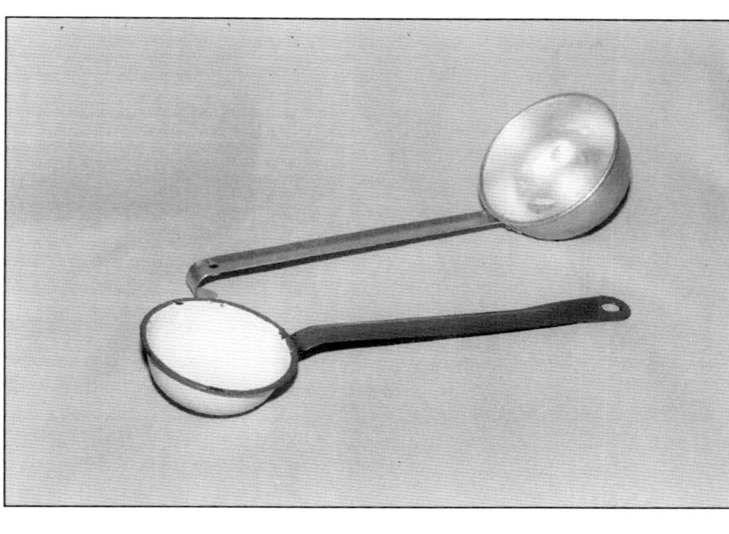

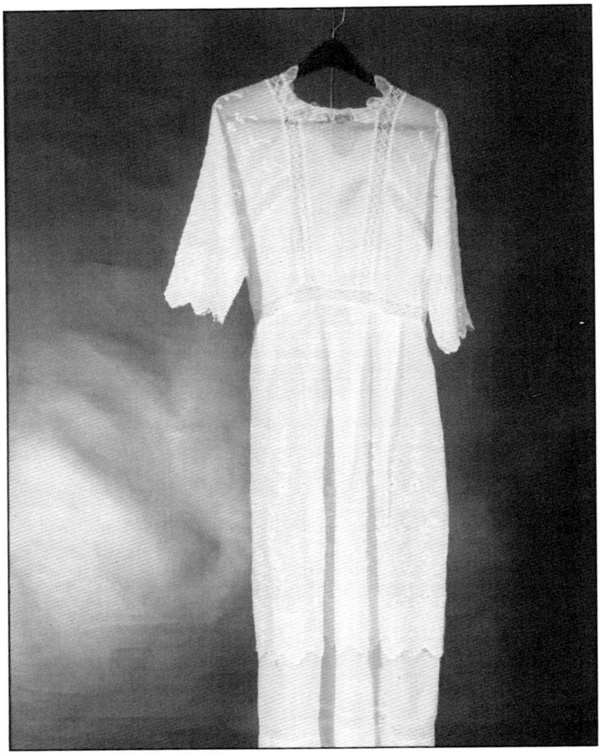

Sallie Watkins purchased this white batiste, embroidery, and lace dress from Sears, Roebuck, and Co. in 1914 for her wedding. She married James Dobbins on July 14, 1914. Her youngest daughter, Julia Dobbins Carter, maintains her mother's wedding-day attire, which includes the white, silk stockings she wore.

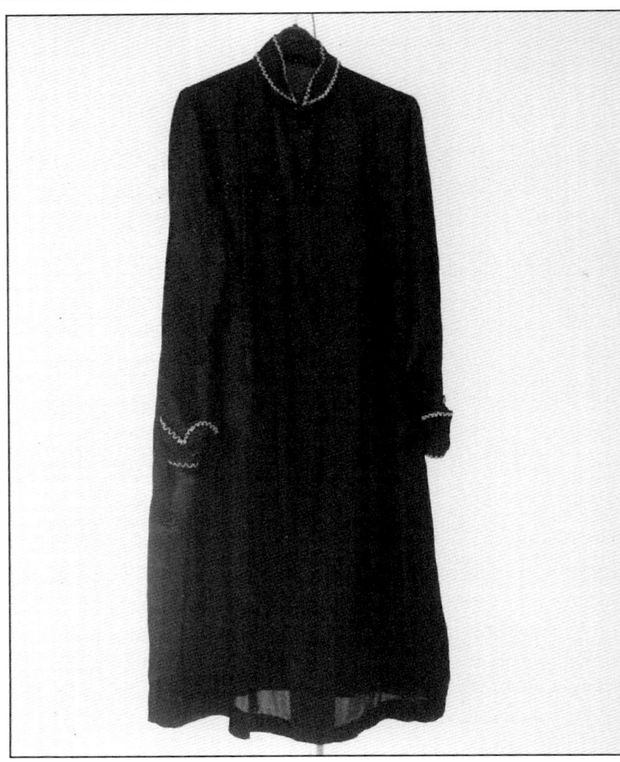

This black silk and satin dress with ecru cord-trimmed cuffs and collar was purchased in 1920. It has a self-tie belt and center front crepe inset with covered buttons. The dress was owned by Eliza Watkins.

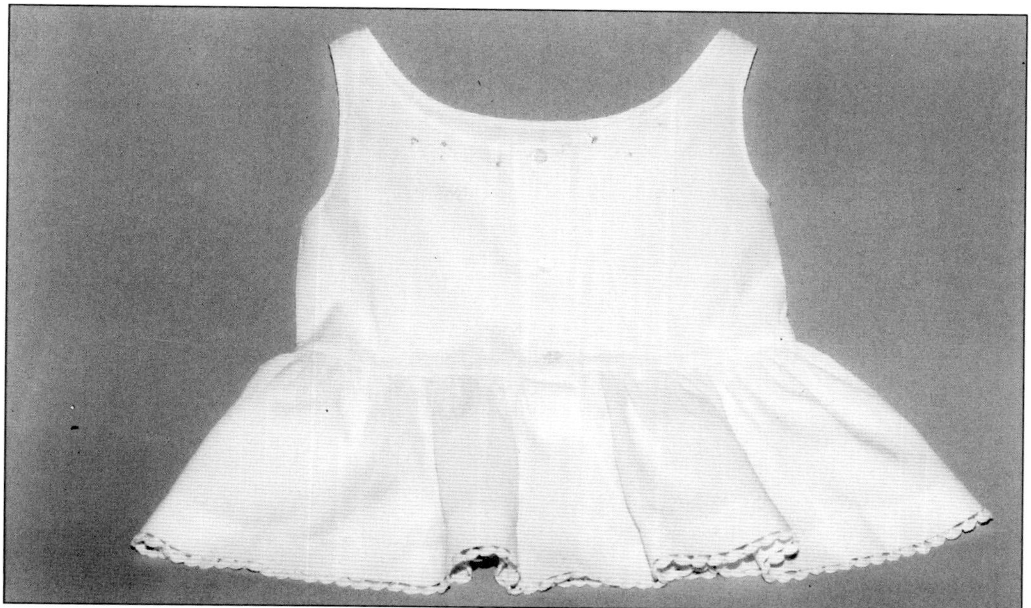

The child's white domestic undershirt has hand-made shell lace trim and a buttoned back. It was made for John Dobbins in 1918 by his mother Sallie Dobbins.

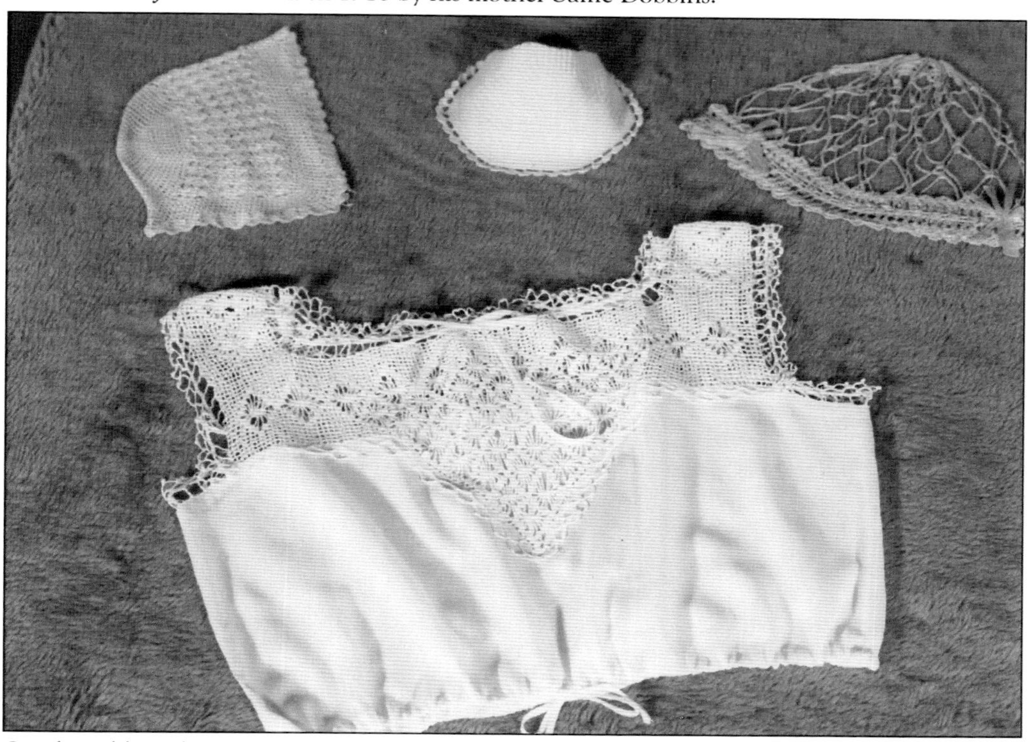

Crocheted by Julia Ishup in 1929, the clothing items from left to right are as follows: a baby's bonnet, a bib, and a lady's nightcap. Rib crochet, shells, and chains were largely used in making these designs, with the nightcap requiring a ribbon drawstring. The white, batiste crocheted camisole was made by Elsie Brackins in the early 1920s.

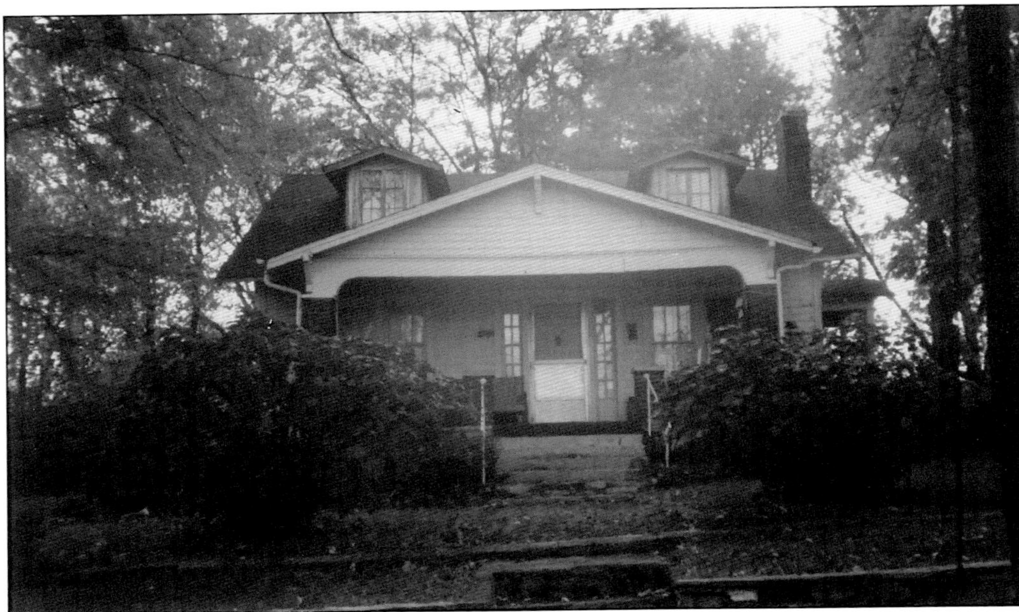

This is the home of Robert Benjamin and Clara Seay Baker, built in 1925, after fire destroyed the original family home at the same East Winchester Street location. Clara and her daughter, Hattie Offitt Herod, were known as great hostesses. It was difficult to find a black citizen who had not dined at either this or the original family home.

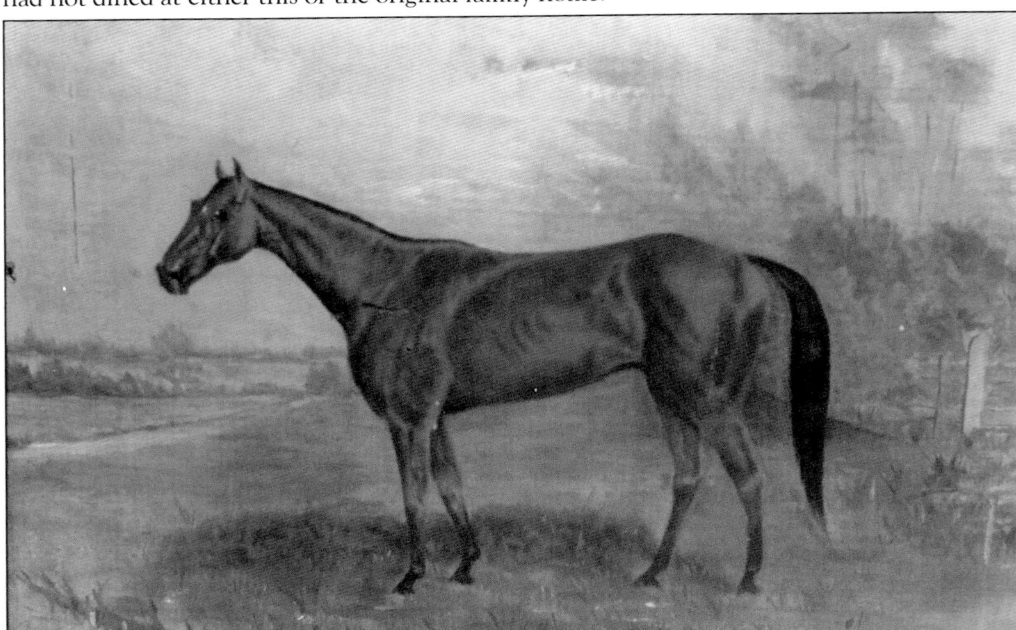

Robert Benjamin "Chuck" Baker Jr. is the creator of this work. This painting was entered into the Tennessee State Fair art competition in 1914. It was judged to be the best and was awarded a first-place ribbon. Reportedly, Chuck had neither drawing instruction nor a single painting lesson throughout his entire life.

Four

People

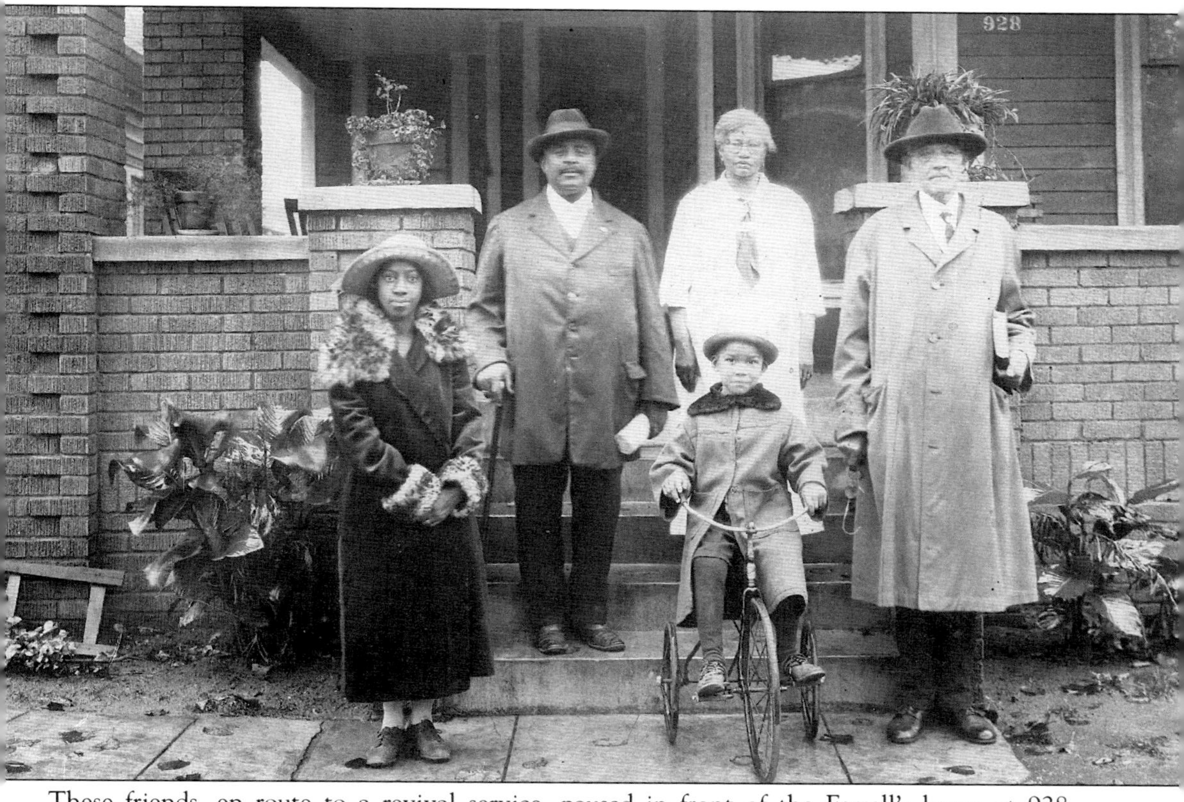

These friends, en route to a revival service, paused in front of the Ferrell's home at 928 Missouri Street in Indianapolis, Indiana (*c.* 1922). Rev. Benjamin Ferrell founded Mt. Paran in 1906 and continued his pastorate until his death in 1927. From left to right are as follows: (front row) Thelma Ferrell, Peter Wylie Vertrees, and Rev. Peter Vertrees; (back row) Rev. Benjamin Ferrell and his wife, Mattie Ferrell. Reverend Vertrees was in Indianapolis to conduct a fall revival.

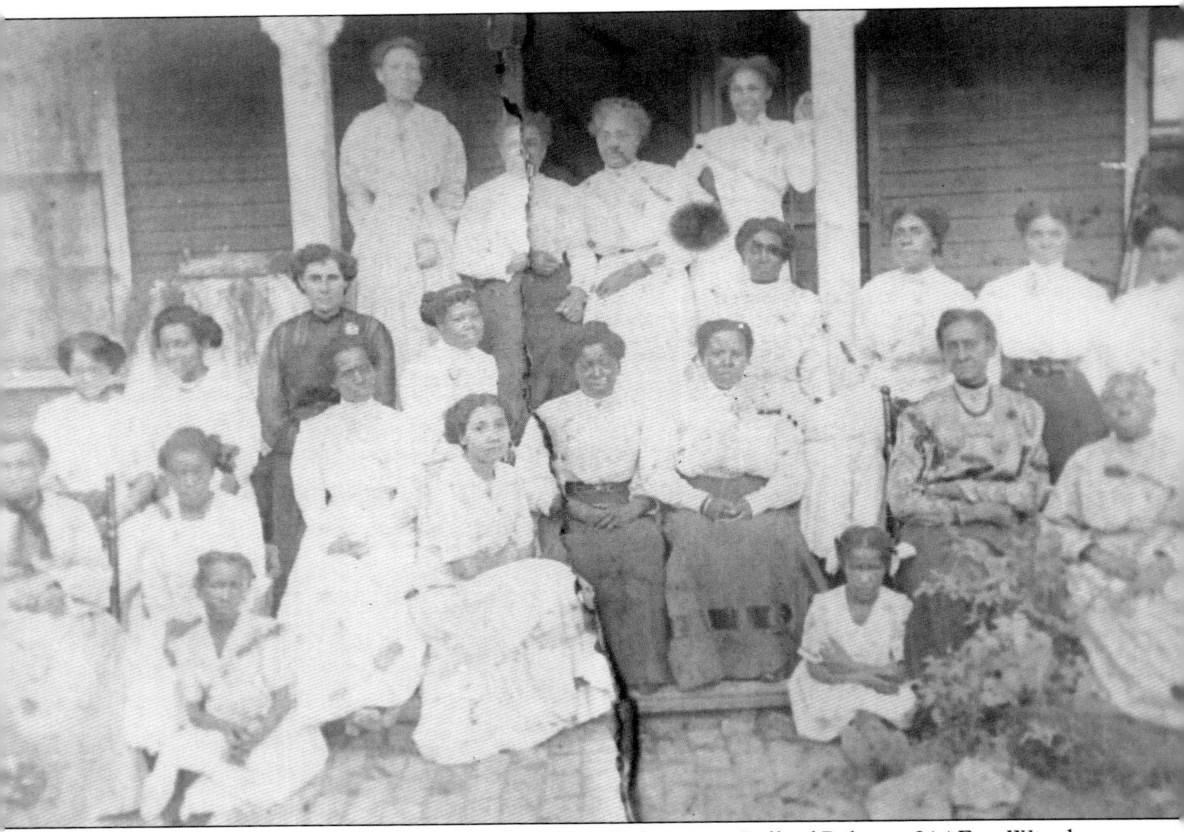

This is a social gathering of ladies at the home of Clara Seay Ballard Baker at 314 East Winchester Street. From left to right are as follows: Abigail Clara "Shea" Baker and Hattie Offitt Baker (children); (first row) Martha Baker, Callie Belle Apple, Louise Matthews, unidentified, Nolie Steel, Sallie Harris, unidentified, and Harriet Ballard; (second row) Carrie Mayberry, Nannie Light, Ophelia Franklin, Elcie Baker, Nora Payne, Ida Woods, Mary Jane Apple, and Narcissas Head; (third row) Georgia Odom, unidentified, Nancy Anderson, and Clara Ballard Baker.

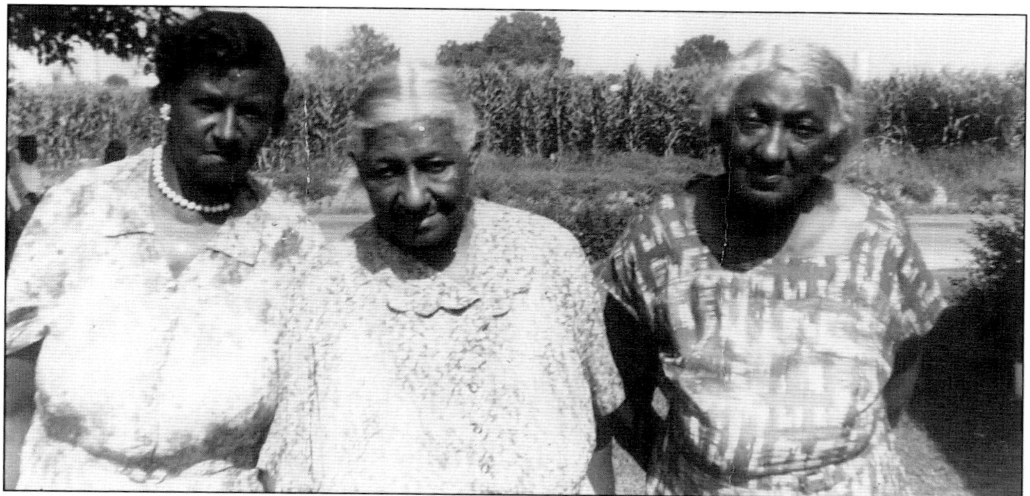

These sisters are the daughters of James and Betty Valentine of the Gravel Hill community. They are, from left to right, as follows: Nellie Valentine Walker, Cora Valentine Epperson, and Fannie Valentine Stewart. Nellie and her husband, Rev. Tom Walker, spent their lives in the Gravel Hill community. Cora married Thomas Jefferson Epperson, and together they had six children: Lena Valentine Adams, Lelia Valentine Russell, Leonard Epperson, Wesley Epperson, James Ellis Epperson, and Nellie Epperson Stokes. Fannie married Ed Stewart, and they lived in Franklin, Kentucky.

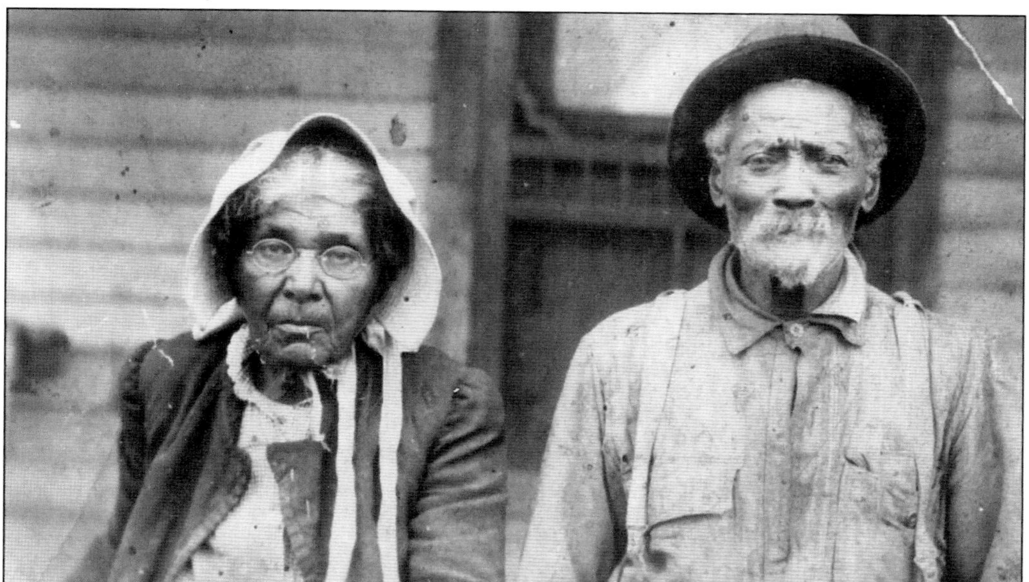

Phil and Caroline Douglas purchased land and a small home in the late nineteenth century. A white landowner, whose property adjoined theirs, wanted to annex their acreage. He arranged an even exchange of 6 acres on a gravel road (now Nashville Pike) for their land. The only building on the newly acquired land was a barn, and that is where they lived until they were able to build a home. Eventually, plans were set into motion to turn the narrow gravel road into a wide paved one. Through treachery, Phil received no compensation for his land while his neighbors were paid.

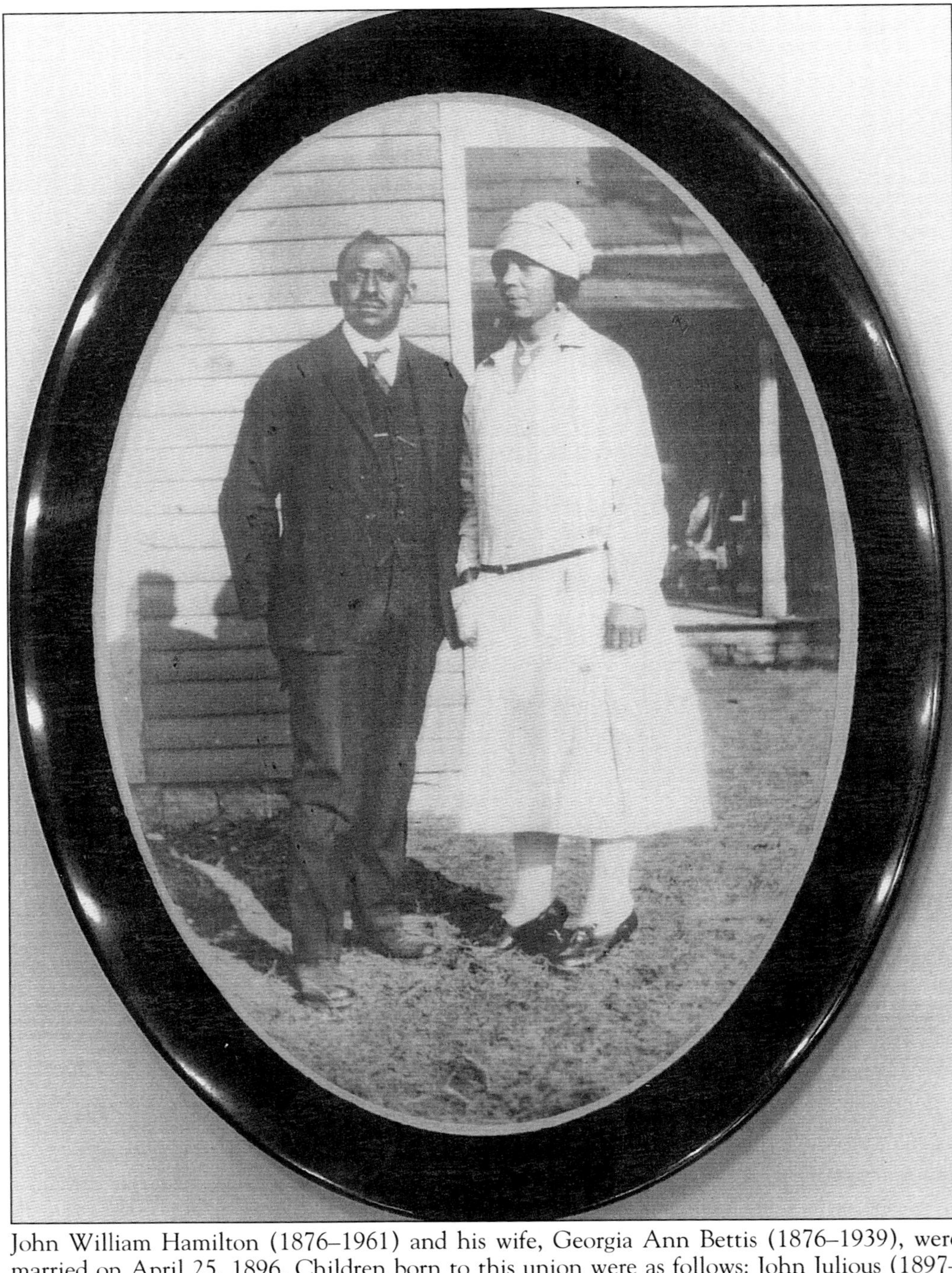

John William Hamilton (1876–1961) and his wife, Georgia Ann Bettis (1876–1939), were married on April 25, 1896. Children born to this union were as follows: John Julious (1897–1897), Leslie Harrison (1900–1986), Bessie Gray (1902–unknown), Collins Landstreet (1906–1996), and Charlie Gray (1907–1917). Will was a sharecropper and later became an employee at Du Pont in Old Hickory, Tennessee.

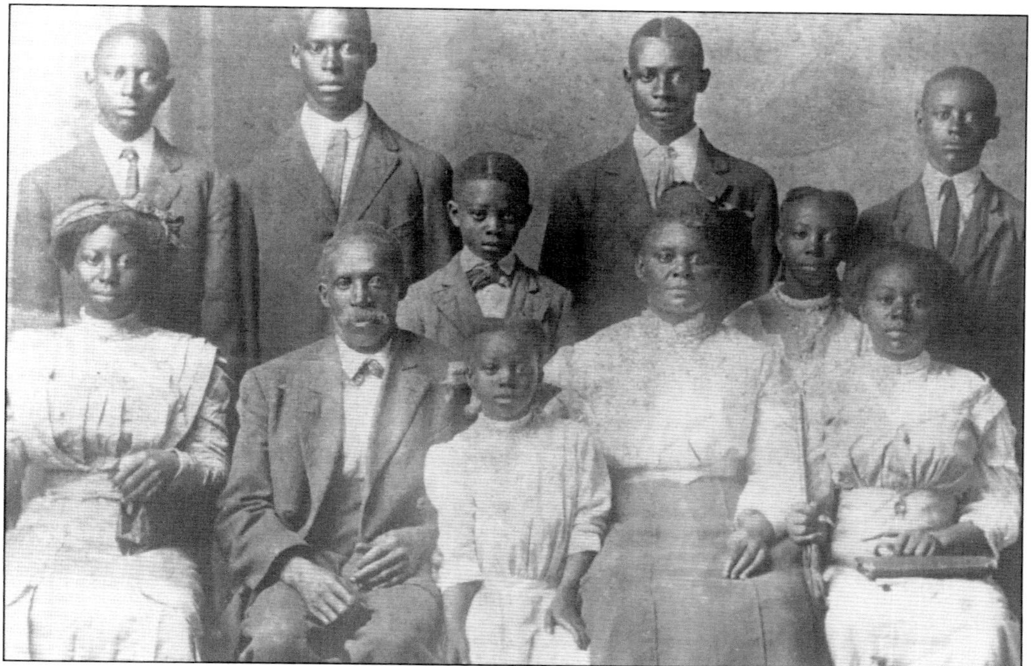

According to oral family history, the Sumner County Robb family started from three siblings: Henry Hubert, Mary, and Cornelia—all of whom were bought at auction. After emancipation, they remained in Cairo with Henry Hubert marrying Etta Williams of Macedonia on September 25, 1884. His sister, Cornelia, was married to Jack Wilks of Cairo. Henry Hubert's immediate family members, from left to right, are as follows: (first row) Mary Ann, Henry Hubert, Hattie Rachel, Etta, and Lillie; (second row) Jack, Jim, Hosa, David, Sally, and Silas.

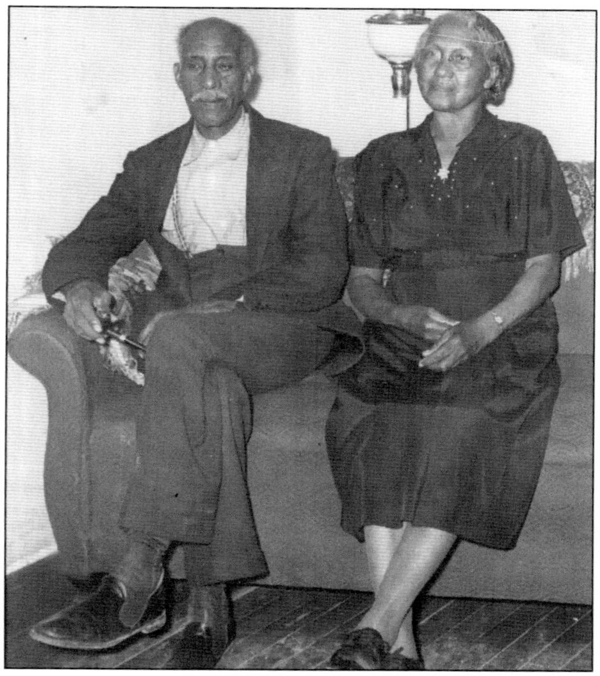

Roscoe Smith (1874–1963) and Carrie Groves Smith (1886–1967) reared a close-knit family in the Parker's Chapel community. They are remembered for their strong support of education and public schools. Two of their children, Robert and Harold, are believed to have been the first college graduates from Parker's Chapel. Their children were Berry Smith, Vester Smith Rogan, Harold Smith (1914–1976), and Robert Smith (1904–1972).

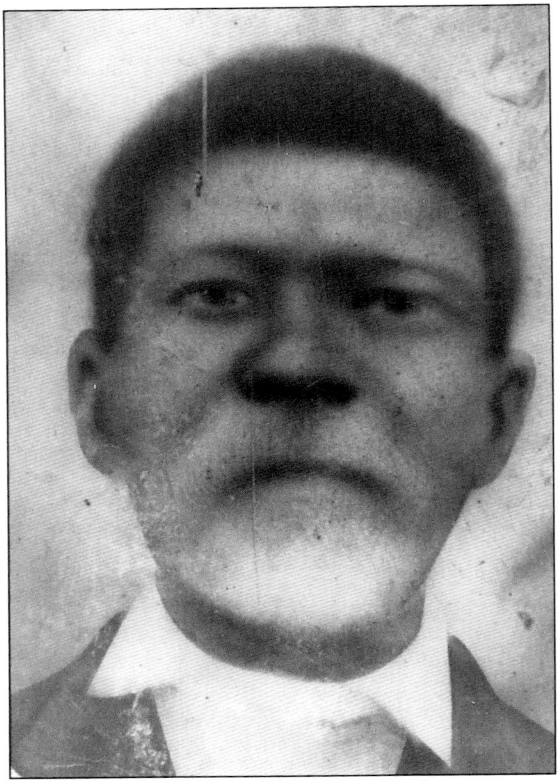

Halifax Wylie married Polina Brown Miller (1831–1905) in 1863. Mary Eliza Moore Brown (1831–1884) was the owner of Polina. In 1877, Halifax purchased an 80-acre farm on Woods Ferry Pike, only to have his banker take it through treachery. Eventually, he settled his family 6 miles west of Gallatin on the farm of Captain Alfred E. Bell (1836–1913). There he and Polina reared their children, grew gardens, and raised cattle, colts, and hogs, in addition to the regular farm work he was hired to perform. Because of his strength and imposing stature, he was often referred to as "Black Hercules."

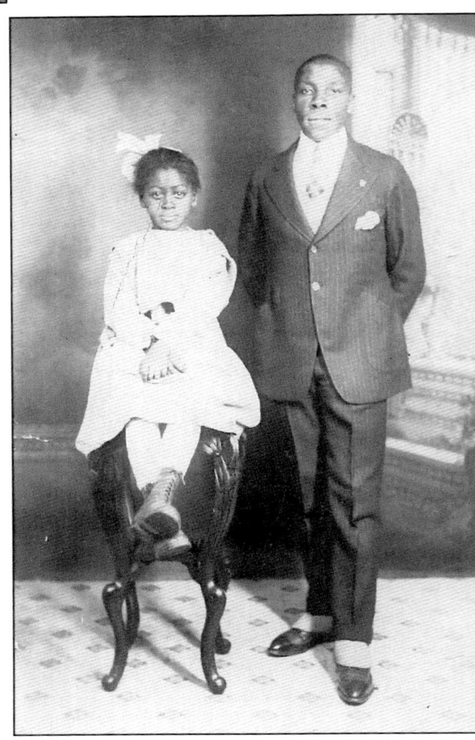

Lucy Mary Rush was born in the Hatten Track community to Dianah Barber and Samuel Brown on February 14, 1913. Unable to read or write, Dianah, the daughter of Lucy Woodfork and Walter Barber (ex-slave) was determined that her daughter would not grow up illiterate. In 1918, Lucy was sent to live with two great-aunts in St. Louis, Missouri, to attend school. She is pictured with an unidentified cousin.

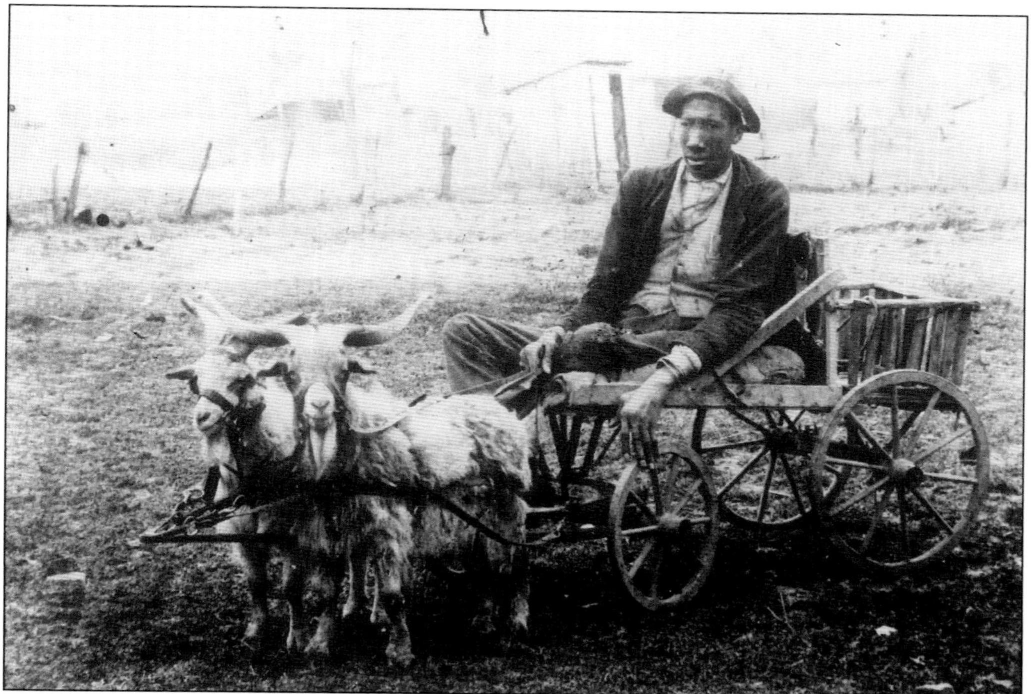

This photograph is one of the few known to exist of Gallatin native John William "Bud" Rogan (1868–1905). Gallatin photographer C.C. Horn captured Rogan, "the world's tallest man," in a setting near Blythe Street. Due to the fusion of joints in his hips and knees, Rogan was physically unable to stand. Rogan's mobility, as seen here, was provided by a goat wagon. This enabled him to travel daily from his home, a few blocks away, to the Louisville and Nashville Railroad depot. There, he sold postcards of his image to railroad passengers, which provided him with an income. Rogan's obituary stated his height to be 8 feet and 9 inches.

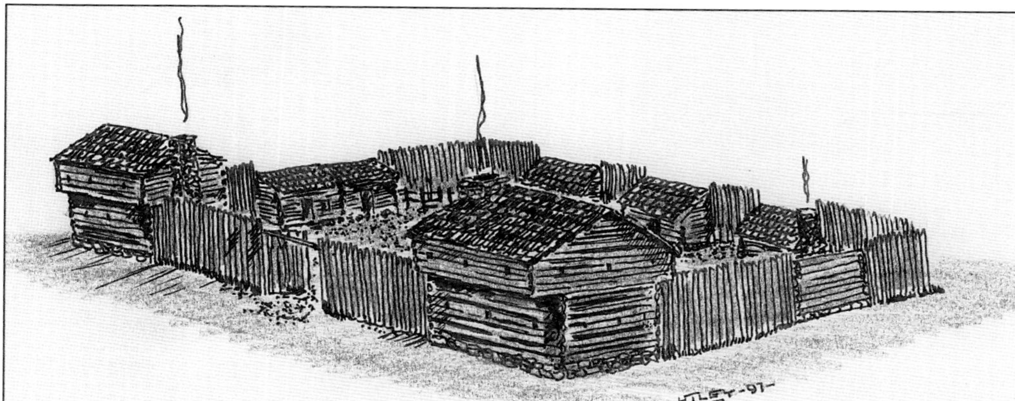

Abraham, a mulatto slave, was owned by Col. Anthony Bledsoe and was described by Gen. William Hall as "one who was very brave, intelligent, an active fellow, who was indeed a good soldier and marksman." The owner of a horse, saddle, and rifle, Abraham's heroic feats include the following: when attacked, his alertness and marksmanship protected a poorly manned Greenfield Fort; upon encountering two dangerous Native American chiefs Mad Dog and Taylor, he fatally wounded Mad Dog; and found in the wilderness a lost ten-year-old, Jo C. Guild, who became a noted jurist, statesman, and historian.

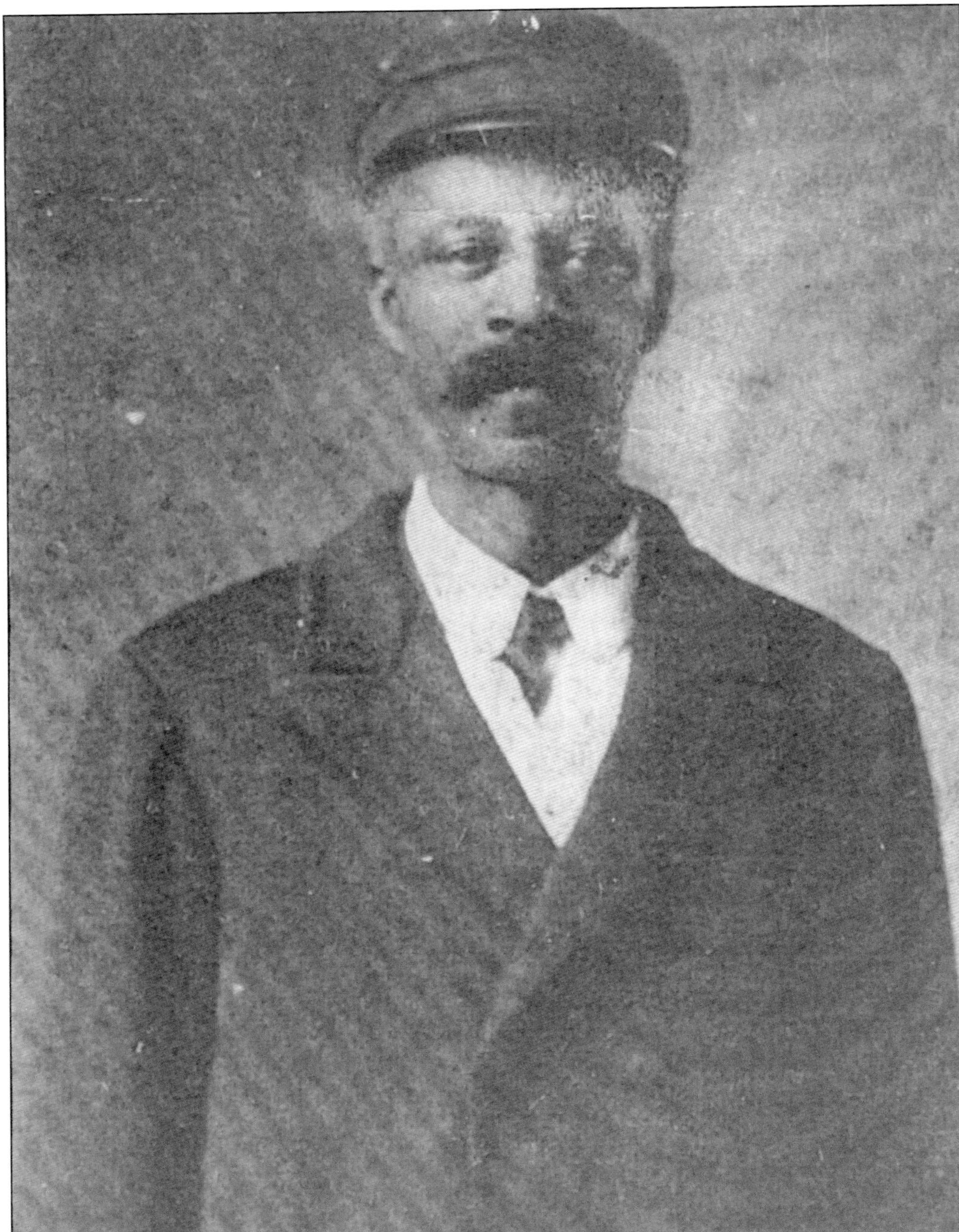

Dock Bracken, who was born into slavery, managed to purchase a small farm from his previous owner, John Bracken, sheriff of Sumner County from 1900 to 1904. The desire for his grandson to get an education forced Dock to exchange his small rural farm for a little house in Gallatin. There his grandson, James Herbert White (1903–1974), entered South Gallatin Public School. White became an assistant principal, college president, and eventually the founder and president of Mississippi Valley State University.

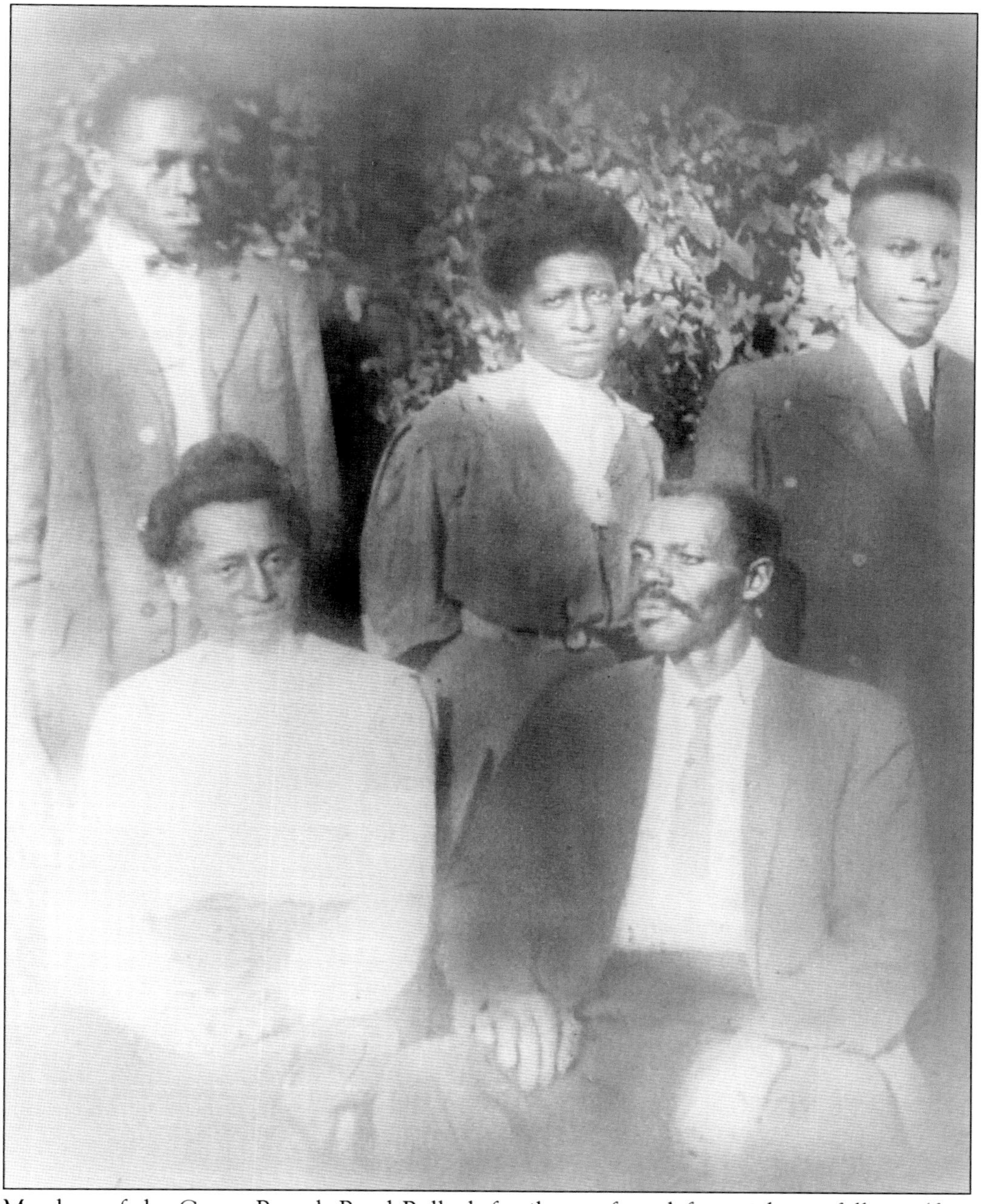

Members of the Canoe Branch Road Bullock family are, from left to right, as follows: (first row) Emma Bate Bullock and Jack Bullock; (second row) Van, Mazie, and Jimmy Bullock. After Jack's death in 1908, the family moved to Texas to accommodate Van's educational pursuits. Van died in 1912 after drinking water from a contaminated well. The family returned to Sumner County in 1913. Jimmy died from pneumonia in 1914, leaving his sweetheart, Eva Baker distraught. Meanwhile, Mazie became engaged to Winston Payne, but she died from typhoid fever in 1915. Winston Payne then married Eva Baker, much to Emma's delight, and she forever considered them her family.

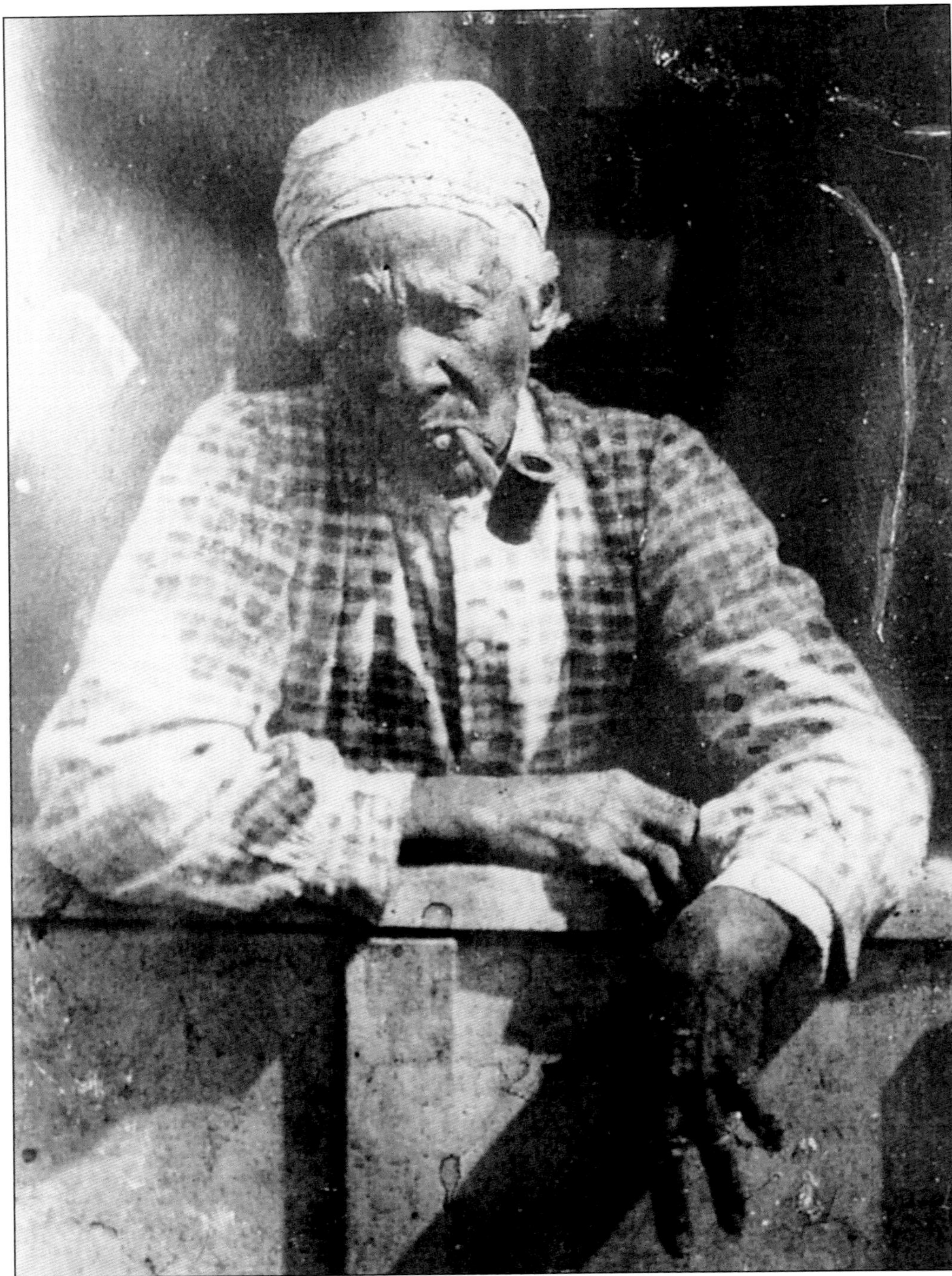

Betsy Baker, a slave of Gen. John Washington of Mt. Vernon, was sold to a slave trader named Issac Franklin, of Gallatin, in 1825. Betsy lived at Fairvue and in the Peach Valley community until her death. She had nine or ten children, one of whom was Mark Baker. He was born at Fairvue.

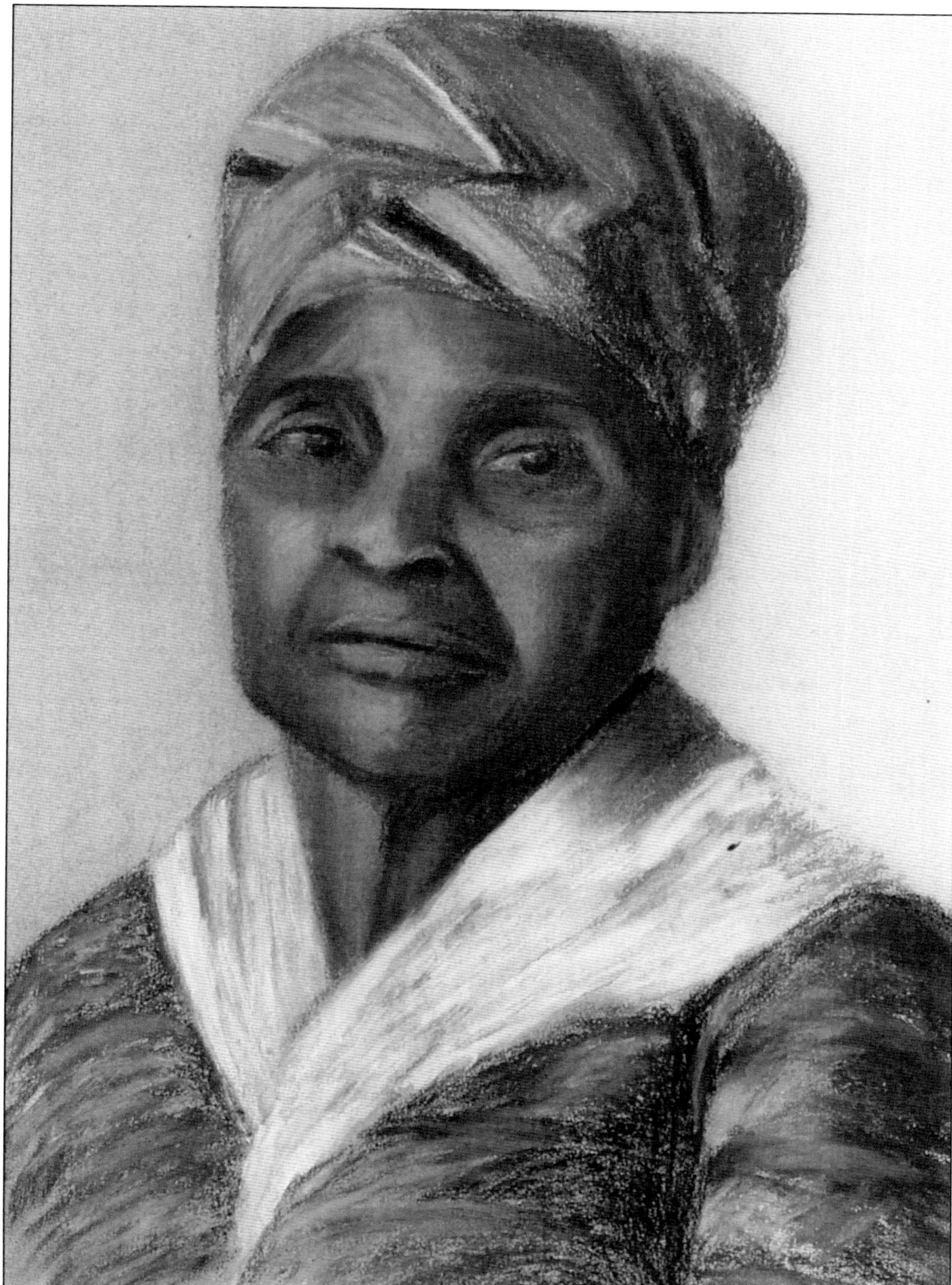

This early painting of Eva Snowden Baker is by Gladys Ligon of Nashville, who was an aunt of Ellen Wemyss of Fairvue. Although Eva and her husband, Mark Baker, lived at Fairvue, she worked for Adelicia Hayes Franklin Acklen Cheatham (former Fairvue owner) at her Belmont Mansion in Nashville.

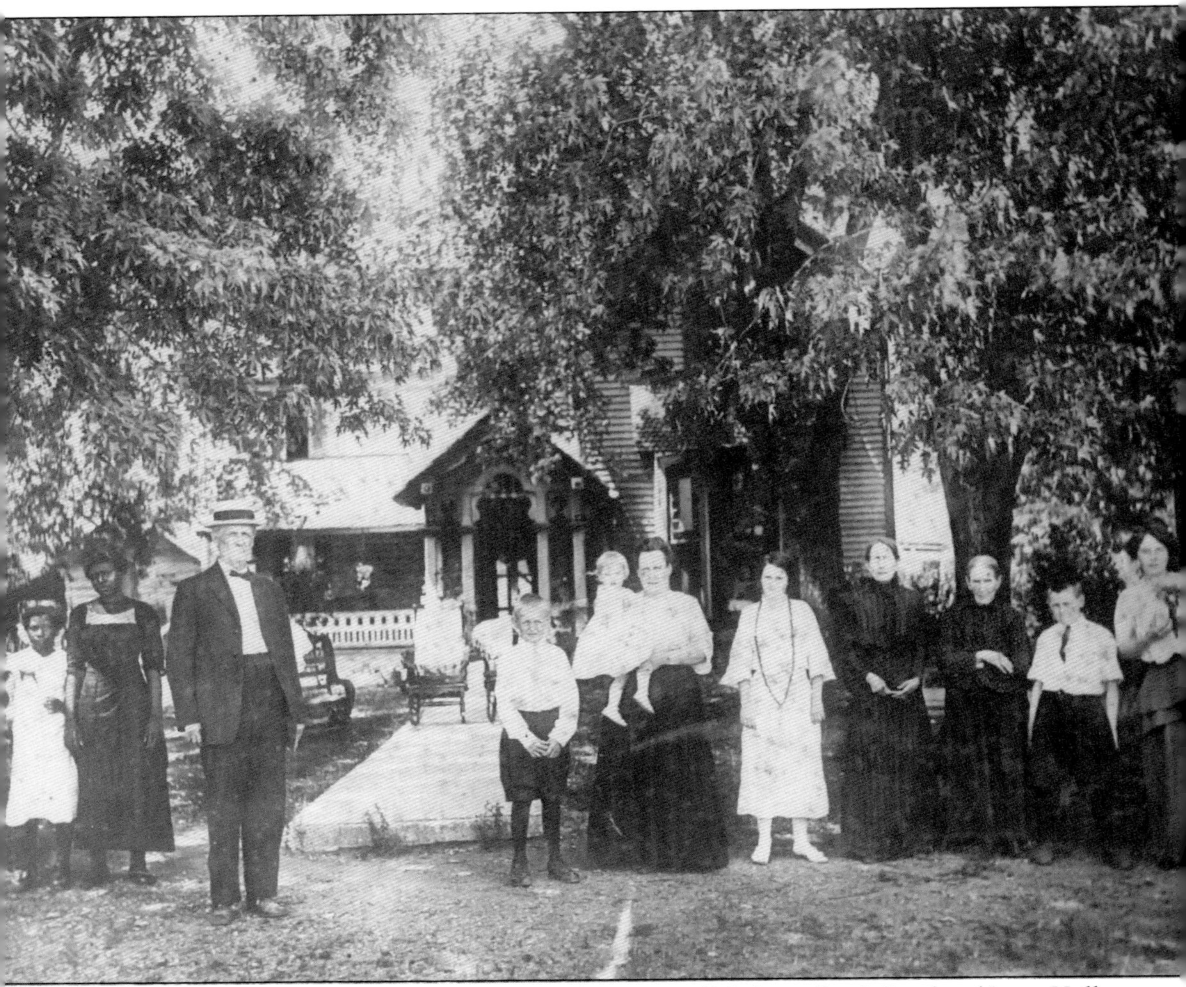

The Old Dr. Joyner homeplace, located at the corner of Madison Creek Road and Long Hollow Pike, was built around 1905. The hill just beyond the house was called "Cantrell Hill" to indicate the area in which the colored families lived. This picture, taken around 1912, shows Dr. Joyner's son-in-law, James H. Shreeve, and his family. At the far left is Laura Cantrell, nurse to the two babies, and Ella Cantrell, the cook.

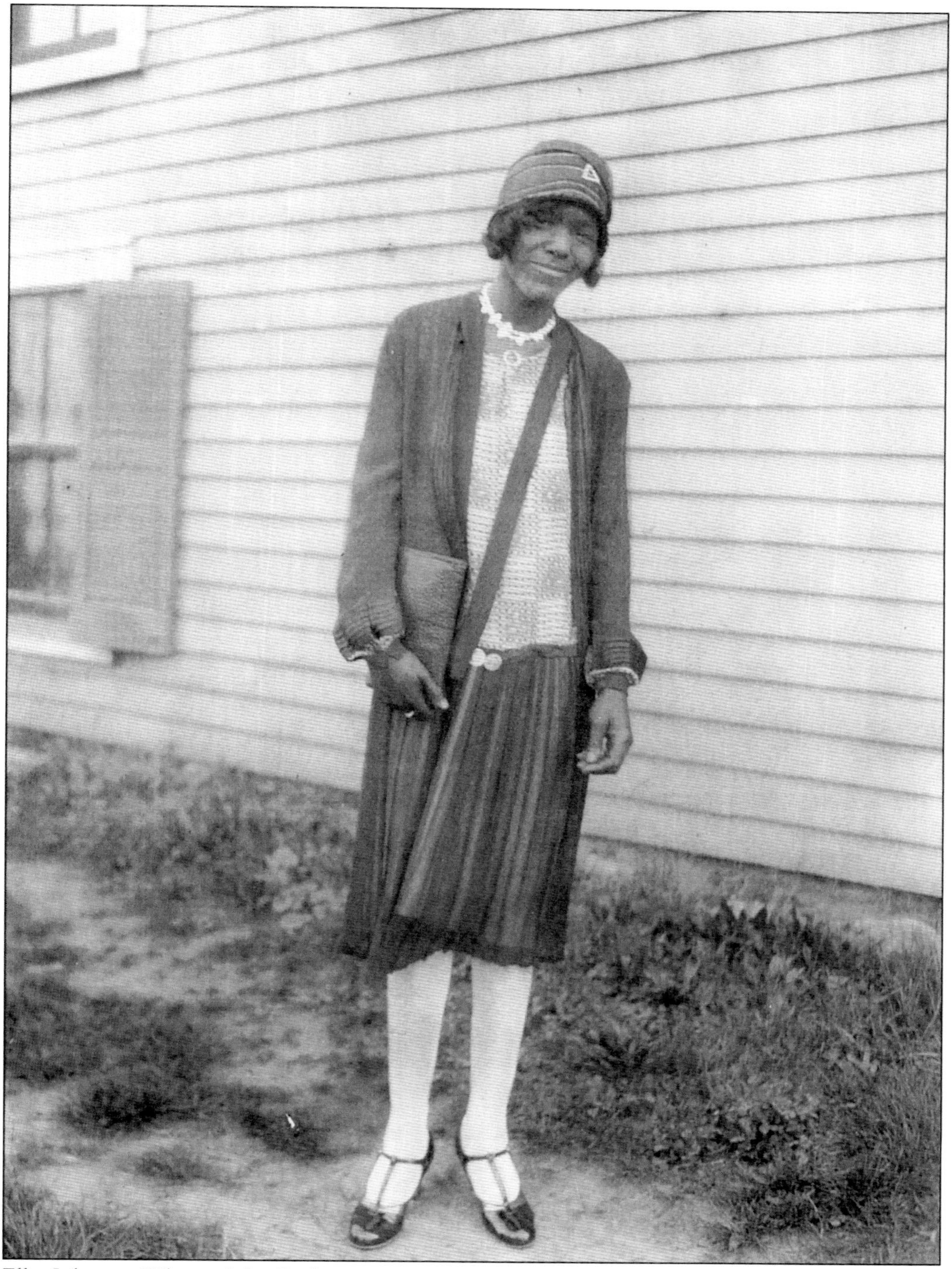

Elba Johnson White of the Bethpage community married John White, a Bethpage farmer, and together they had two daughters, Lady Beatrice White Grizzard Dotson and Willie Mai White Senter Bass. Elba died shortly after Lady Beatrice was born, leaving her parents, Viola and Ben Johnson, to care for the girls. The maternal grandparents reared the girls in Bledsoe Chapel Baptist Church, where Ben was a deacon.

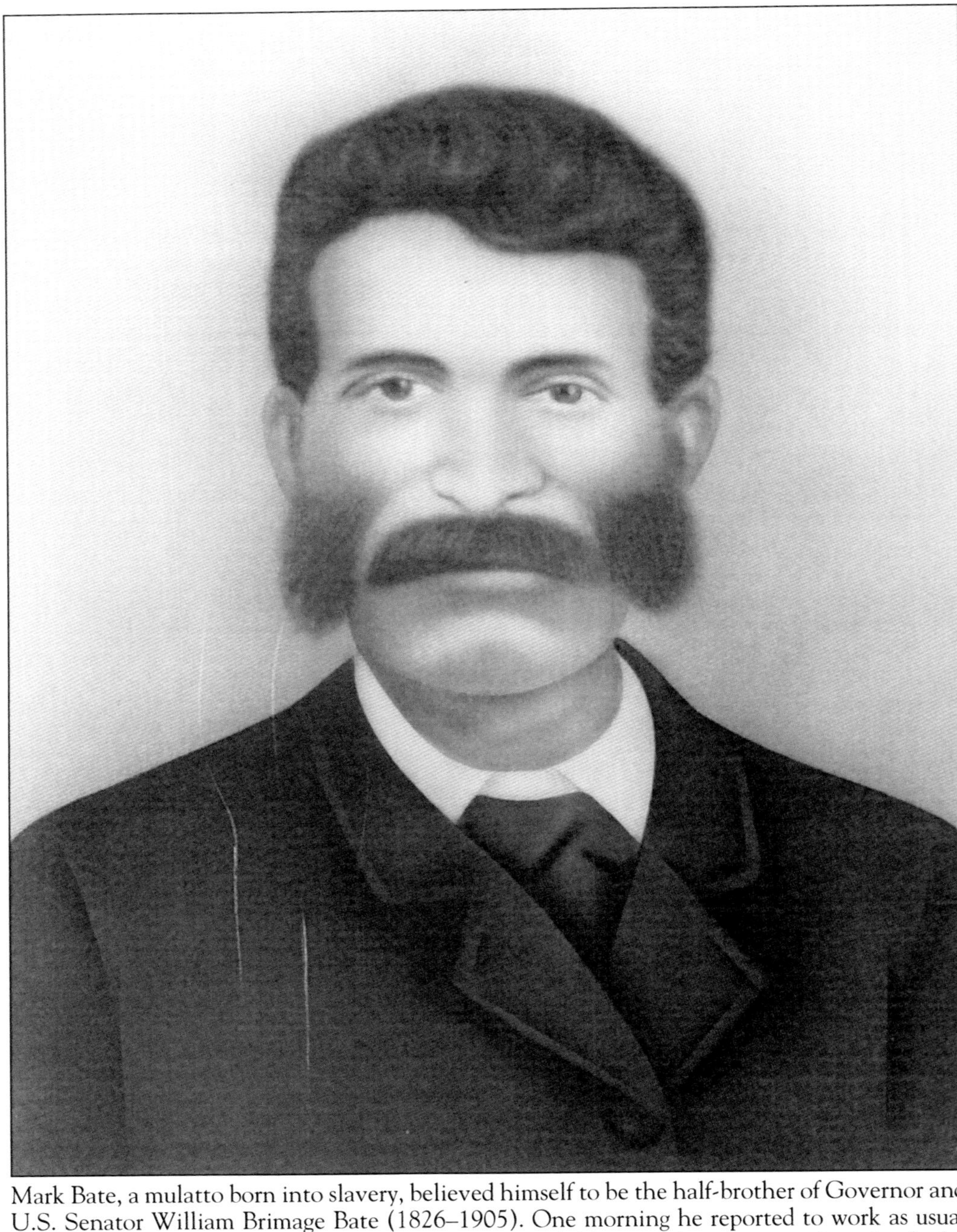

Mark Bate, a mulatto born into slavery, believed himself to be the half-brother of Governor and U.S. Senator William Brimage Bate (1826–1905). One morning he reported to work as usual on the Bate farm, leaving behind his wife and three children on the adjoining farm. Little did he know, he would never see his family again. While Mark worked, his wife and children were sold. After many years of grieving the loss of his family, he married a woman named Mariah and remained on the Bate farm after emancipation.

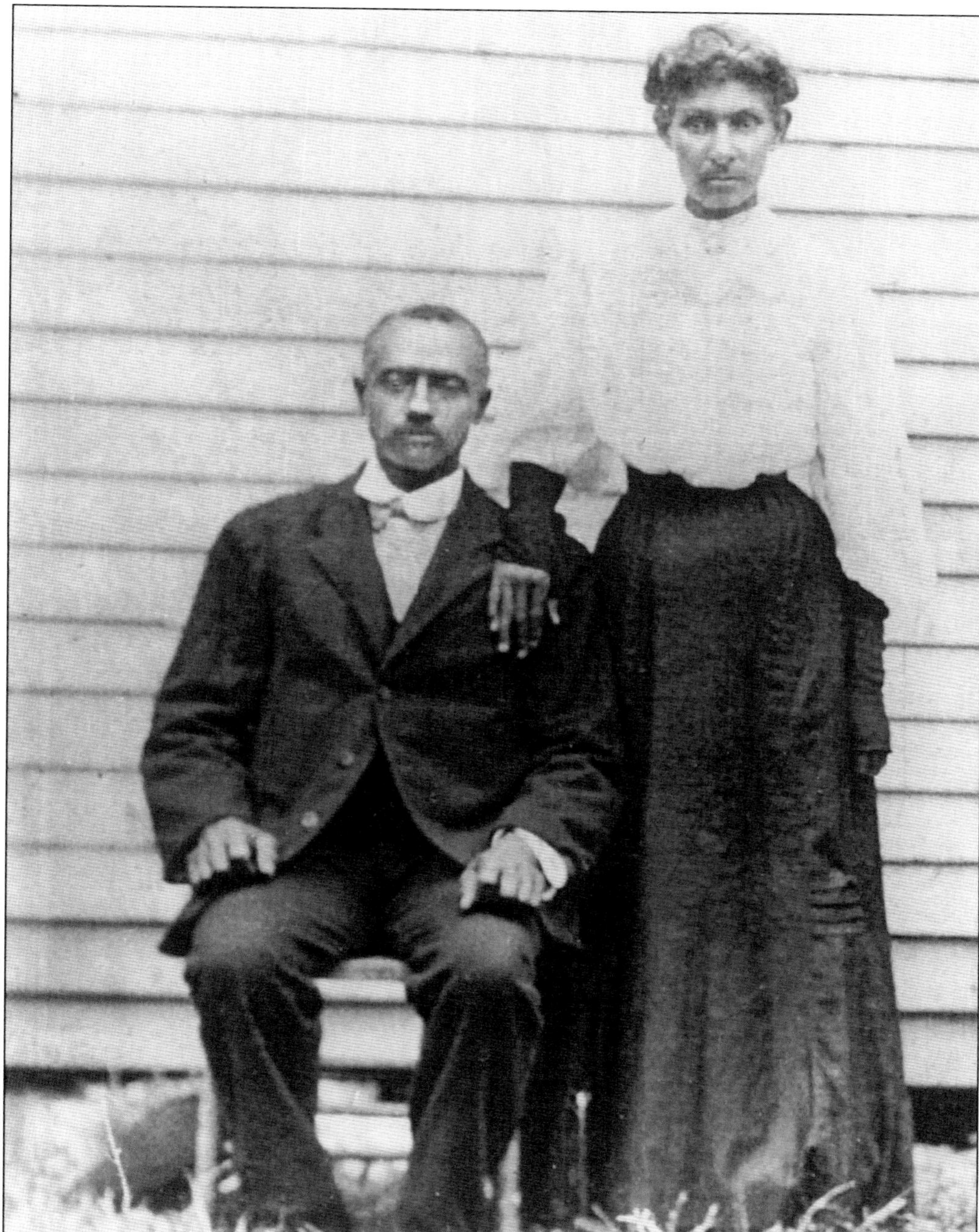

James Ellis Valentine (1865–1934) and his wife, Bettie Elizabeth Thompson Valentine (1862–1949), were the parents of four children: Prince William Valentine, Nellie Valentine Walker, Cora Valentine Epperson, and Fannie Valentine Stewart. Bettie's first husband, Odell Thompson, died after the birth of their two children, Annie Thompson and Odell Thompson Jr. Although James was born in the Goose Creek community in Trousdale County, he and Bettie settled in his hometown of Gravel Hill. The Valentines are the great, great, great-grandparents of Brandon Epperson.

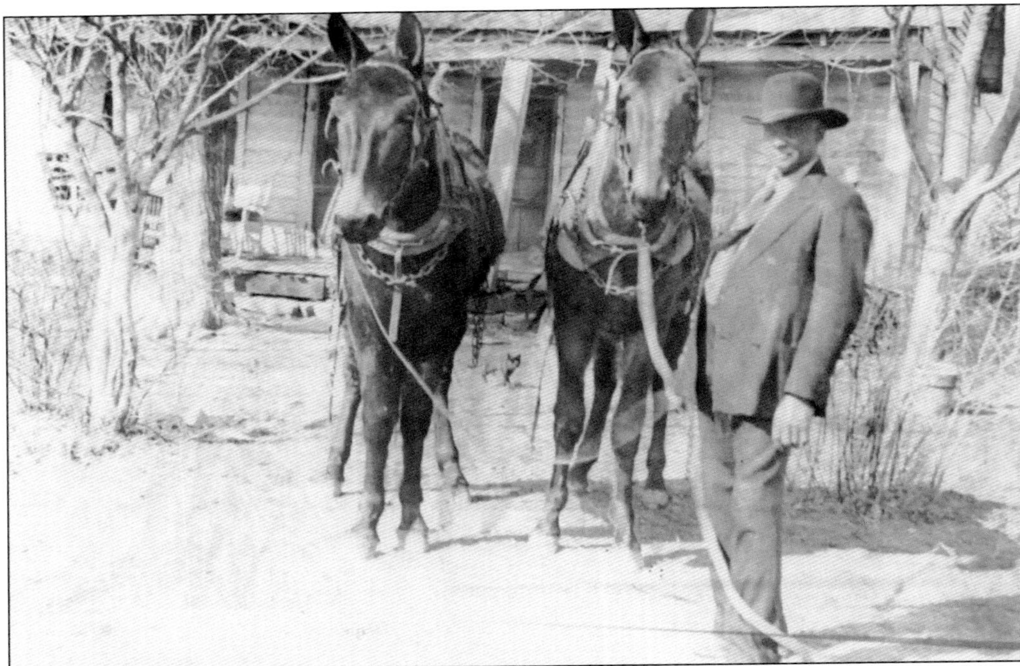

Luther Coakley (1884–1960) is standing with his favorite horses in front of his Portland home. As a blacksmith, he traveled throughout Middle Tennessee practicing his trade. He was married to Lula Rippy and had four children: Virgil, Vernon, Molly Coakley McClain, and Geneva Coakley.

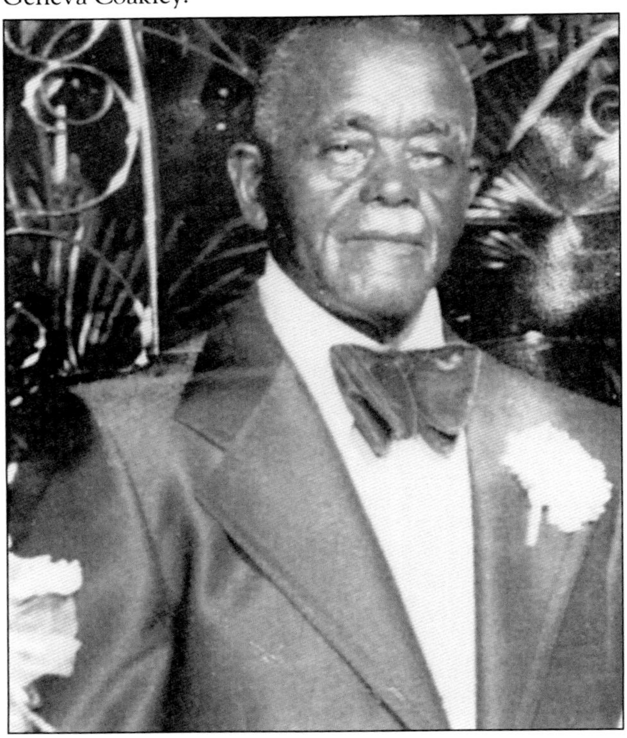

Fred Hamilton (1900–1982) was the son of Edward Gaston and Lou Ella Hamilton of Cairo. He married Susie Johnson of Franklin on February 3, 1924, and they were blessed with nine children. Fred was a great stone mason who lived and conducted business with honesty and integrity in Franklin.

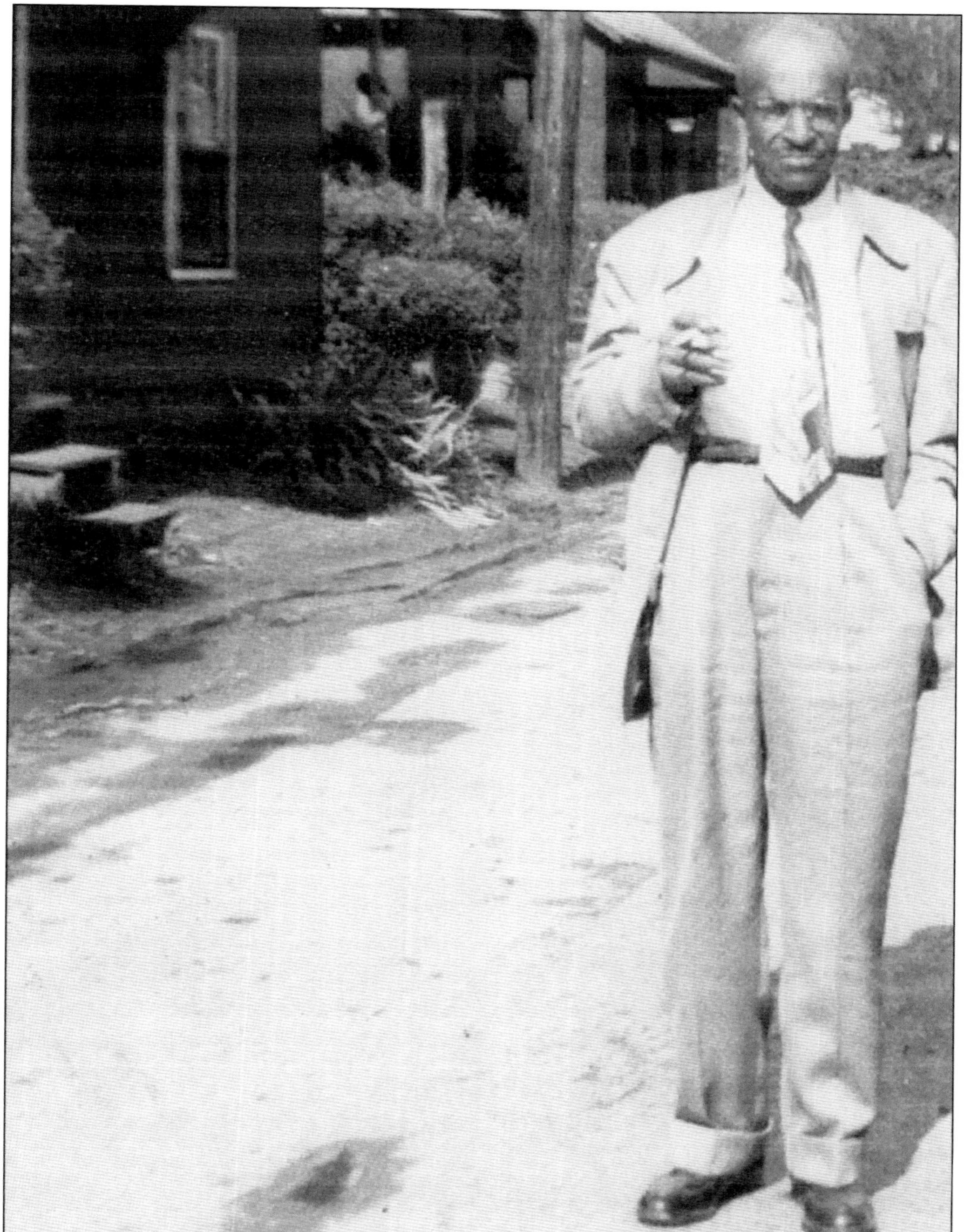

Joseph Cornelius Coakley (1891–1962) was a gifted and industrious Christian man. He was president of the Sunday school department of the East Fork Association, as well as chairman of the Board of Deacons at Parker's Chapel Church for many years. He and his brother Gil were master builders who erected the second edifice for Parker's Chapel Church in 1918. As a tailor, he made clothing for his children, and he also made and sold tombstones. He was married to Idell Merritt of Logan County, Kentucky.

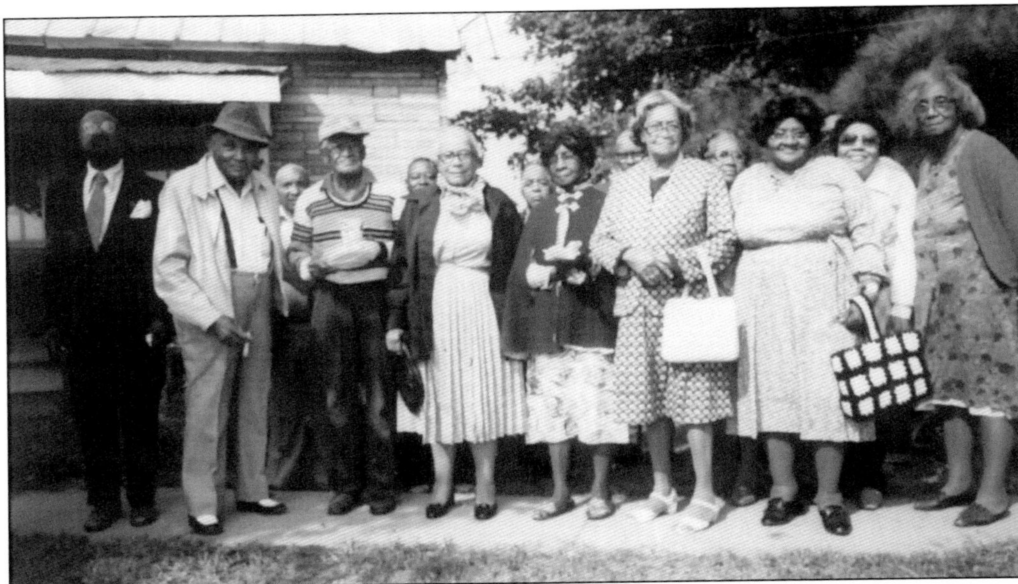

Ella Rippy (1888–1987) is being honored with a birthday celebration at her Parker's Chapel Road residence. Family members and friends in attendance, from left to right, are as follows: (front row) Clifton Hollins, unidentified, Odell Lightfoot, unidentified, Ella Rippy, Idell Coakley, and Maggie Williams; (second row) James Epperson, William Williams, E.A. Gray, unidentified, Effie Coakley, Minnie Coakley, and Vester Rogan.

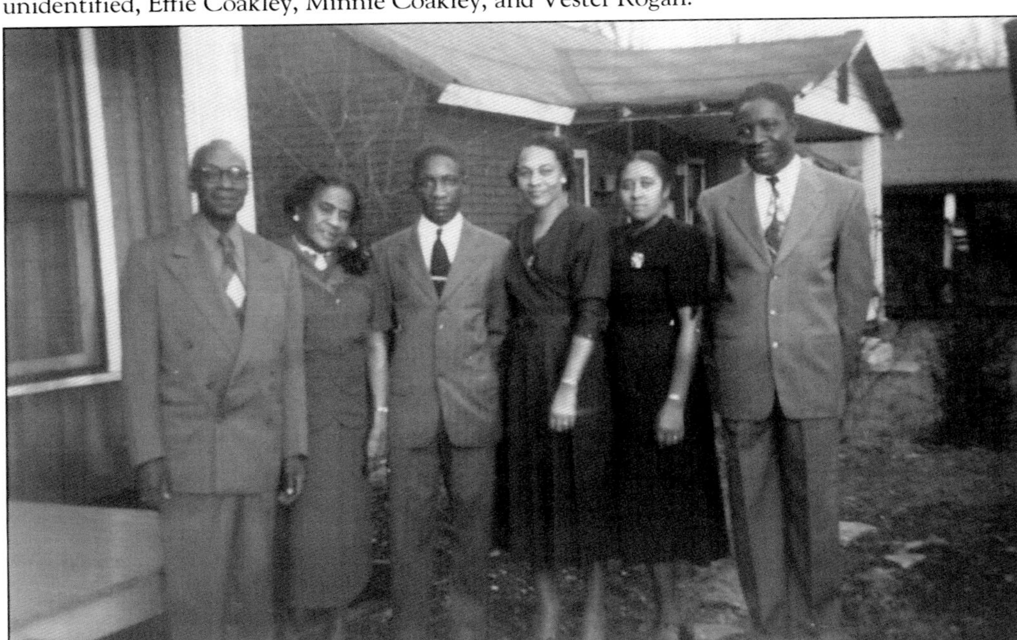

This picture was made in 1951 at the 344 West Gray Street residence of James and Sallie Dobbins. The home in the background belonged to Minnie Sluter and has since been razed. The family members, from left to right, are as follows: Lewis Watkins, Lady Watkins, John Dobbins, Mary Dobbins, Ella Lee Dobbins, and Charles Dobbins. Lewis's sister, Sallie Watkins Dobbins, is the mother of John and Charles Dobbins.

Clara Seay Ballard Baker was married to Robert Benjamin Baker, and they had five children: Harriett "Hattie" Offitt Baker, Robert "Chuck" Benjamin Baker Jr., Edward Baker, Annie Randolph Baker, and Abigail "Shea" Clara Baker. Clara Seay worked for James E. Caldwell at Longview in Nashville.

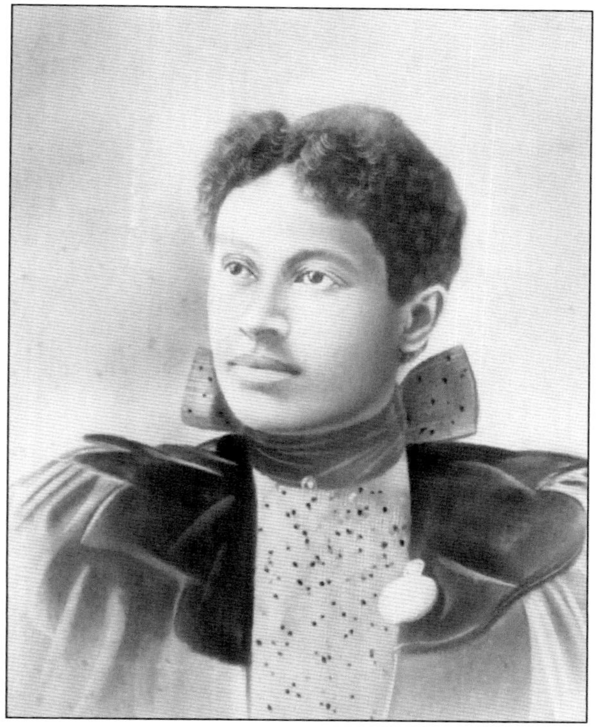

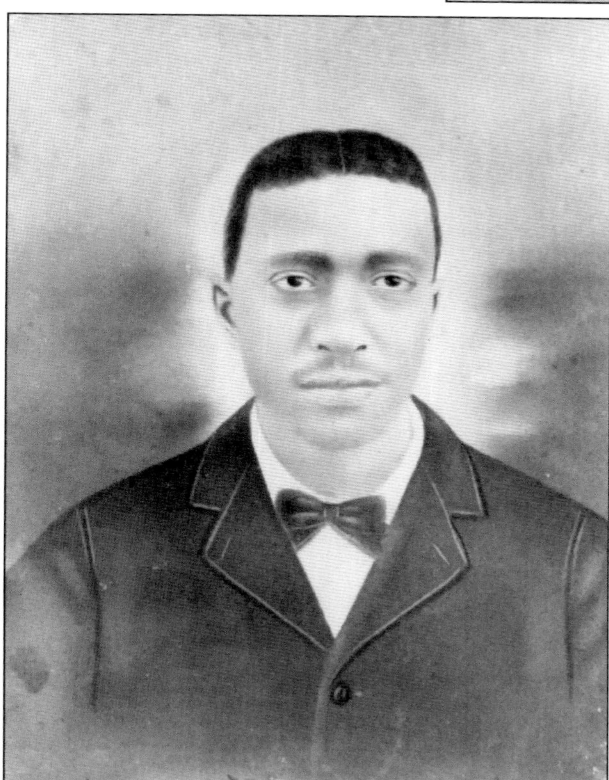

Robert Benjamin Baker Sr. (1872–1940) moved to Sumner County from Mississippi. Robert was known to have worked for the railroad company and was a Methodist preacher.

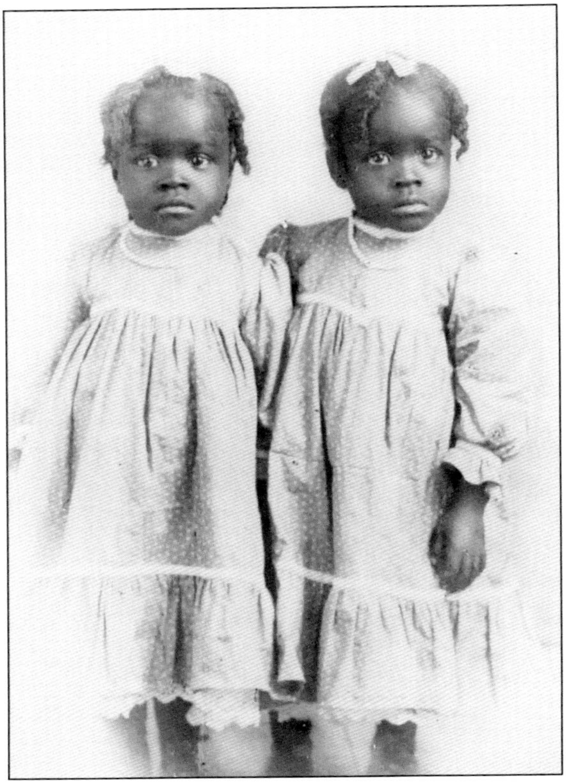

These lassies from Bethpage are Lady Beatrice White (1919) and her sister, Willie Mai White (1918). They are better known as Mrs. Beatrice Dotson and Mrs. Willie Mai Bass.

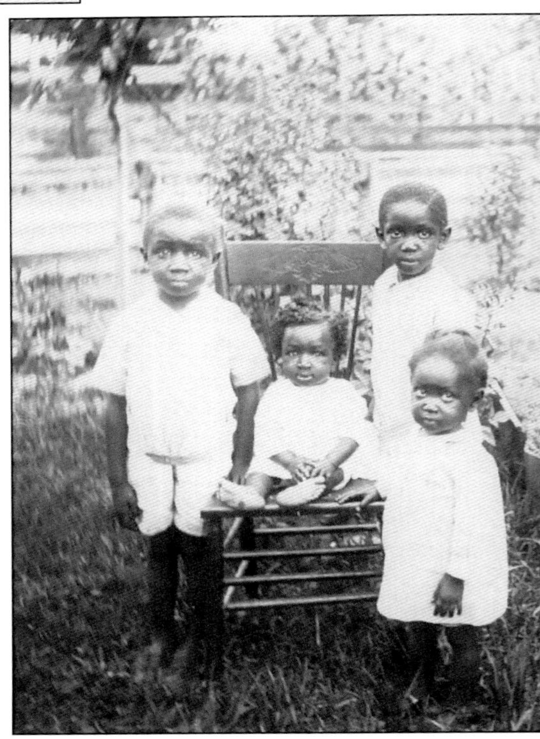

The Dobbins children posed at their Enlow Street address in 1923. They are the children of James and Sallie Watkins Dobbins. The children are, from left to right, as follows: Charles, James, John, and Sarah Dobbins.

Vir Caressa Patterson Jamerson (1904–1952) is pictured standing behind her three daughters. They are, from left to right, as follows: Belulah, Mildred, and Rosie (1923–1998). Vir and her husband, Charlie Jamerson (1897–1981), lived in the Hickory Grove community. Her parents were Sim and Rosie Hibbett Patterson.

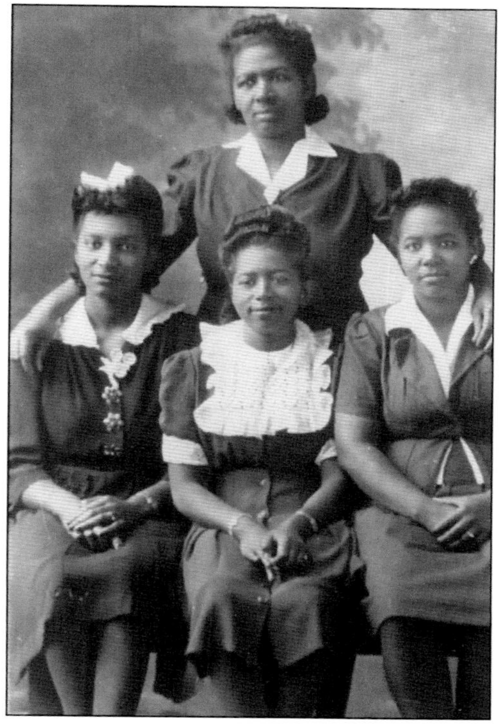

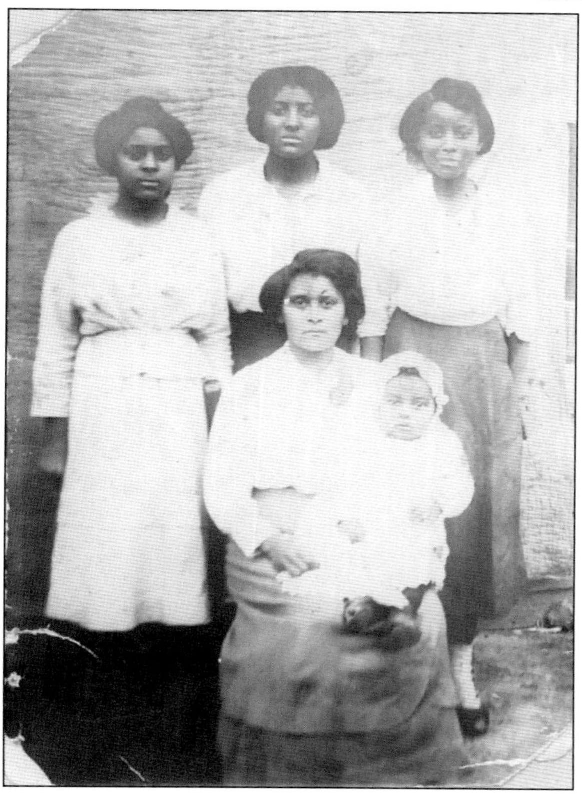

Onie Robinson Coakley is holding her oldest son, Daniel. Her husband, Arthur, was an accomplished bricklayer, and Lousiend Robinson (1856–1943) was her birth mother. Her daughters, pictured here from left to right, are as follows: Allene Coakley Merriett, Anna Mae Coakley, and Ruby Coakley Flippen (c. 1912).

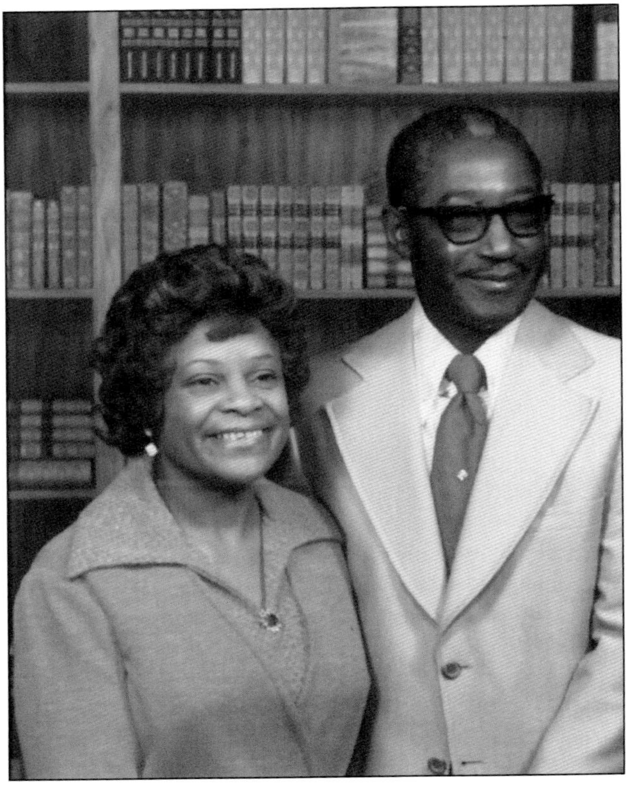

Cortez Dotson (1912–1997) and his wife, Beatrice, were married November 25, 1973, at First Baptist Church by Rev. Talmadge Scott. Cortez began his employment at the Main Street First Baptist Church in 1949 and worked until his retirement more than 40 years later. He was a church trustee and a member of both the Male Chorus and the Brotherhood and Freemont Lodge No. 270. Beatrice retired from her position as mail clerk at Volunteer State Bank after more than 50 years of employment.

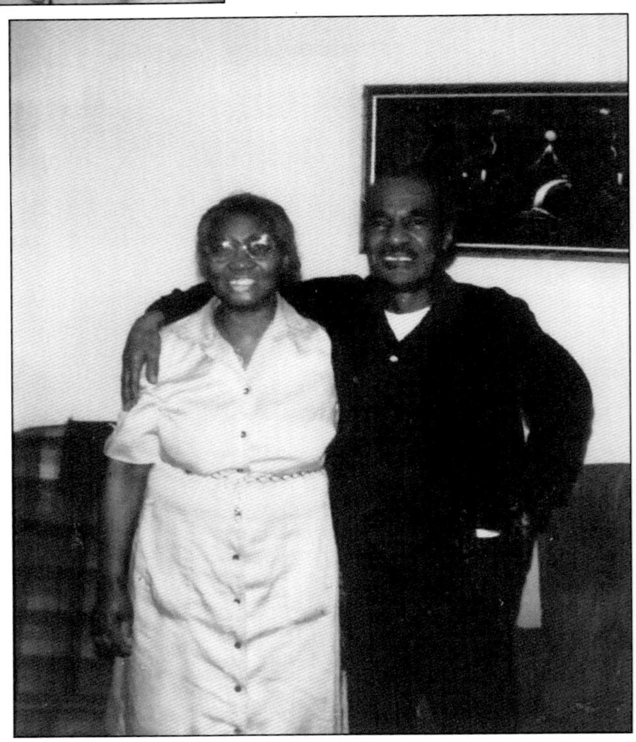

George Douglas Jr. (1911–1984) and his wife, Elaster, became the second generation to occupy the family home on Nashville Pike. In 1948, the young couple moved in and started buying the heir property. The final payment was made December 10, 1965, and their home burned January 8, 1966. They rebuilt the home and continued to raise their children at the home site. Their children are Callie Elnora, Georgia Mai, Vendella, Phillip, William, Arthur, and Marion Douglas.

Pictured here is the McClellan family in front of their Magnolia Avenue home in 1960. The family members, from left to right, are as follows: (front row) Millie Denise, Deloris, and Donald; (back row) Mose Henry Jr., Mamie, Mose Henry III, Kenneth Ray, and Vera Elaine. Donald and Deloris are fraternal twins. Mamie, an accomplished seamstress, made the garments worn by the children. Mose is a 49-year employee at R.C. Owen Tobacco Company, a deacon at First Baptist Church, a plumber, and a friend to all.

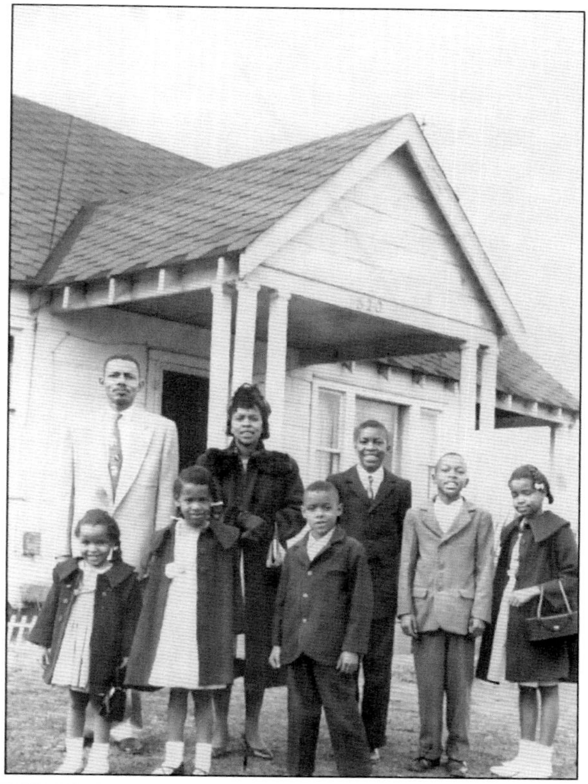

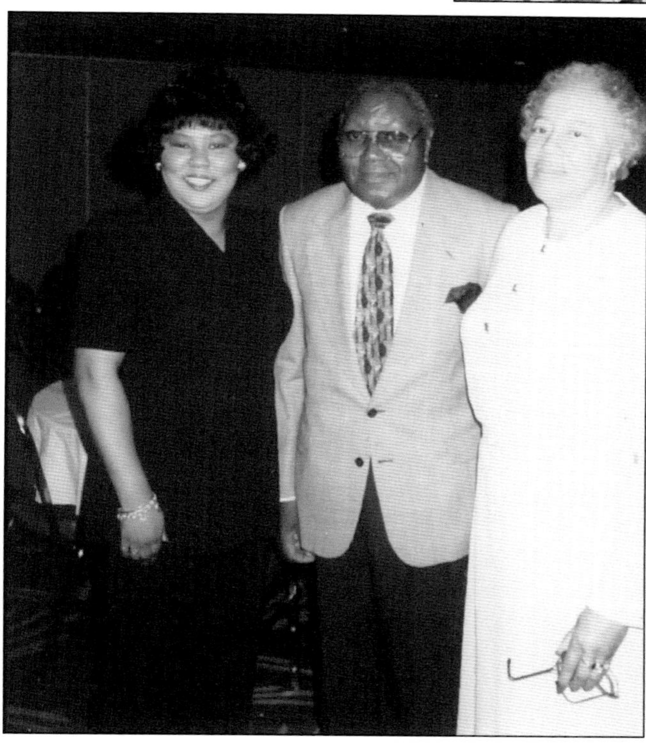

The John Russell Brown family members, from left to right, are as follows: Veronica Lynne (daughter), John Russell Brown, and Maggie Adams Brown. John is a retired electrical engineer associate from Tennessee Valley Authority, a furniture refinisher, and an upholsterer. Maggie is a retired school cafeteria supervisor, and Veronica is employed by Sumner County. From 1958 to 1968, John and Maggie owned and operated Brown's Queen Bee, which was located at 674 Chambers Street.

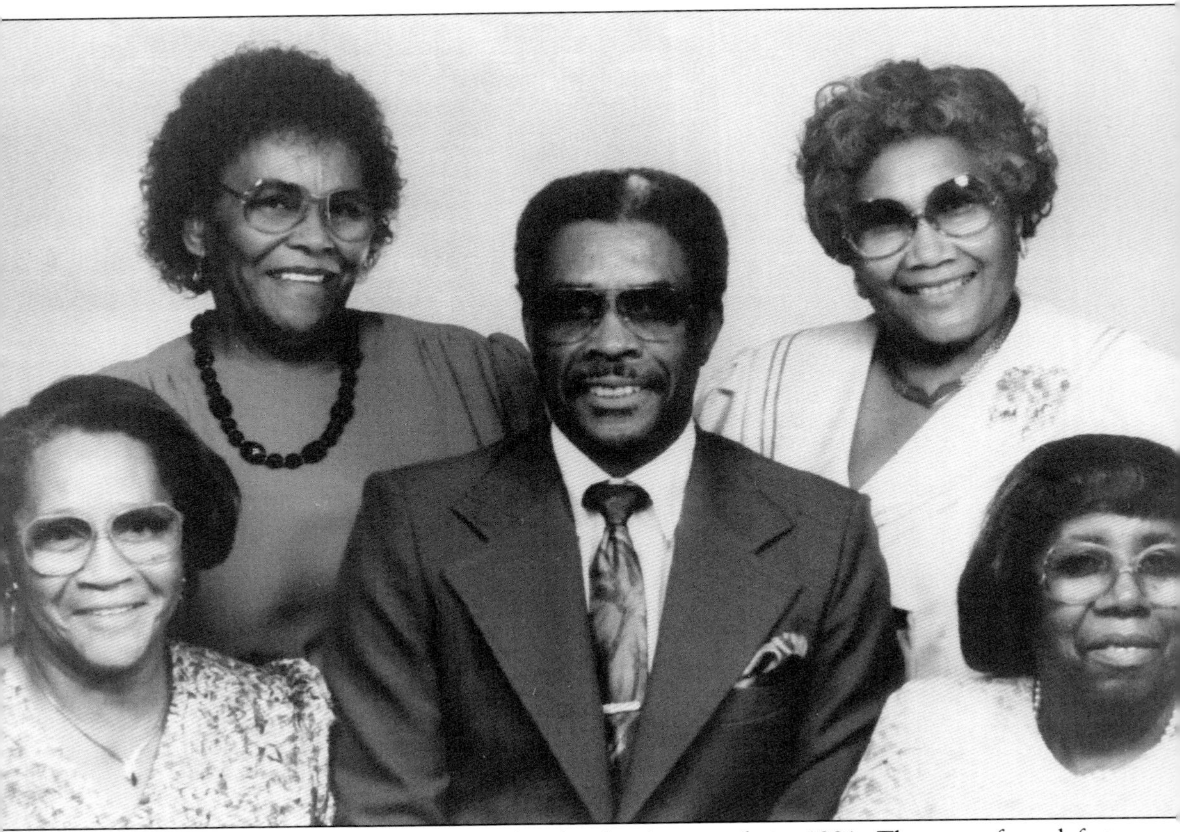

The Watkins siblings gathered for this family photograph in 1991. They are, from left to right, as follows: (front row) Lula Mae Ellen Watkins Brinkley, Rev. Grant Watkins Jr., and Lee Anna Watkins Zirker; (back row) Mable Louise Watkins Shaw (1925–1995) and Mattie Bell Watkins Shaw. Their father's first wife, Martha Adams, died following the birth of her second child. Grant Watkins Sr. married Ida Mai Brinkley and three children were born to this union. Martha Adams Watkins was a sister of Eurika Shaw of Gallatin and Ophelia Brinkley of Mt. Olive.

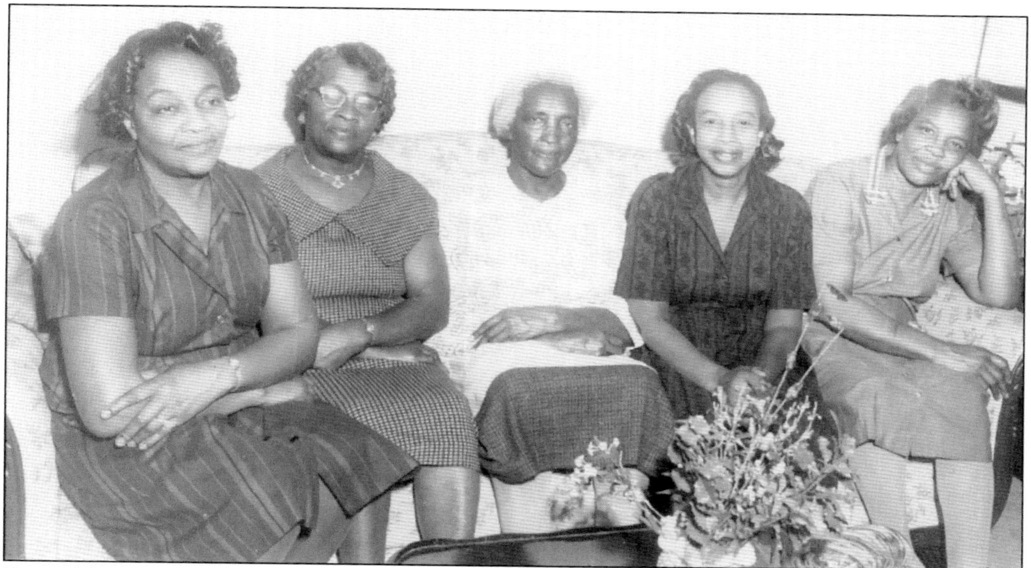

Five of the daughters of Robert and Polly Ann Tyree McMurry were at home visiting the family (c. 1952). They are, from left to right, as follows: Lauretta Young (Sumner County teacher for 43 years), Peggy Samantha Branham (housewife), Maude Lamon Haynes (schoolteacher in Orlinda, Tennessee), Zelma McCord (housewife and esteemed volunteer), and Martha Patterson (beautician at the Blue Bird Beauty Shop for 42 years).

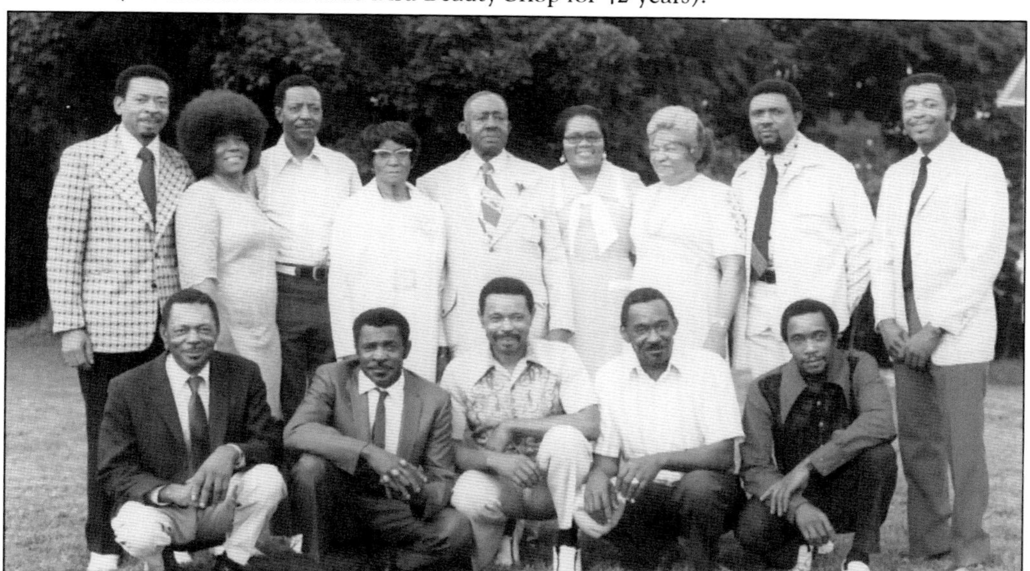

Rev. Willard Martin (1898–1984) and Molly Ophelia Brinkley (1898–1991) of the Mt. Olive community celebrated their 56th wedding anniversary in 1975. Their 12 children in attendance (out of 15 total), from left to right, are as follows: (front row) Benny, Major, Bright, Rufus, and Robert; (second row) Dewey, Elread "Rita" Brinkley Lewis, William, Molly Ophelia, Willard Martin, Eunice Brinkley Shaw, Fannie Brinkley Latimer, Eugene, and Jason Brinkley. Miller Mitch Brinkley was unable to attend the celebration; sisters Lena Brinkley and Marie Brinkley Alexander were deceased.

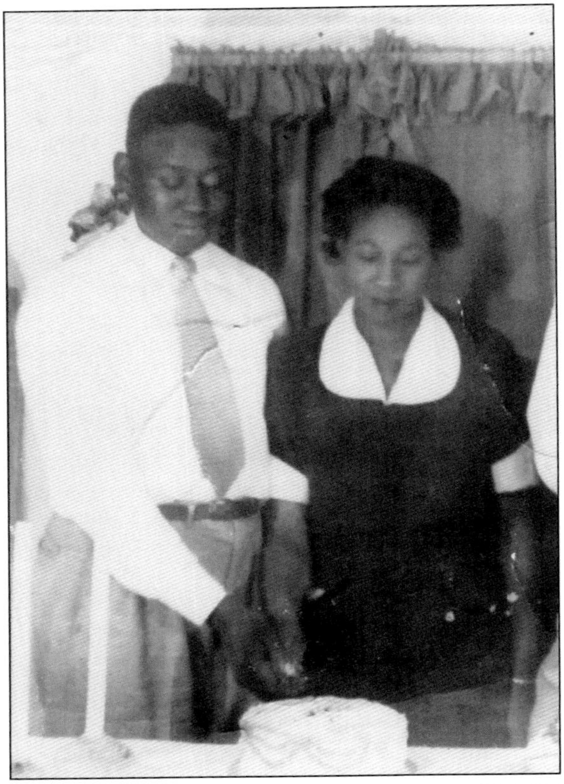

William and Ruby Rippy Williams were wed on July 1, 1949, in Franklin, Kentucky. The reception was held in Portland at the home of Berry and Rosa Nell Smith. Their children are Richard, Betty Carol, Carl Michael (1952–1993), Pamela Annette, James LaFayette, and Linda Bernice Williams. William is originally from Cairo, and Ruby hails from Portland, but Gallatin has been home for the couple since 1954.

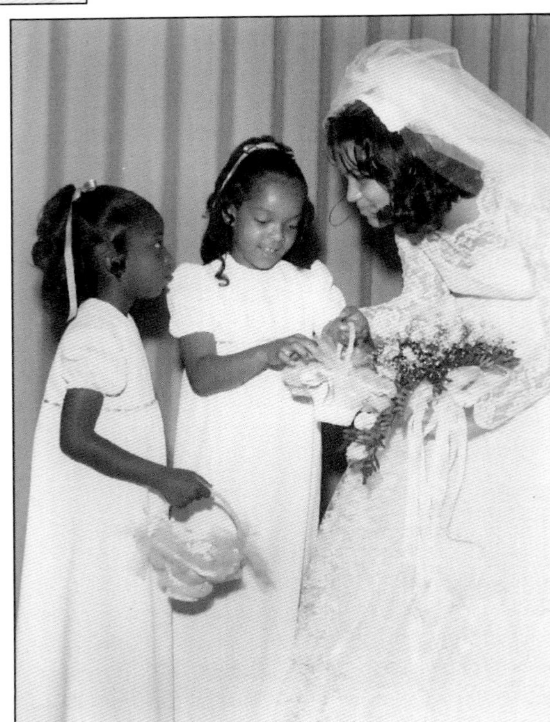

Carlus LaMease Alexander chats with the flower girls just before her wedding ceremony on August 10, 1974. The flower girls are Alicia Laverne Smith (left) and Tonya Sharife Brinkley (right). Carlus was wed to Paul Edward Coakley at First Baptist Church. She is presently a student services coordinator (vice principal) at Vernon School in Portland, Oregon. Tonya graduated from MVSU, and Alicia is employed by the Kroger Company.

Velma Howell Brinkley graduated from the high school department at Coahoma Junior College (1961), MVSU (1964), and TSU (1969). She is a grant proposal writer, a court-appointed special advocate (1994), founder of the First Baptist Church Scholarship Program (1973), yearbook sponsor (1971), speech/drama coach, and public speaker. Career experiences include positions as a teacher at Harris Junior College and a counselor at VSCC, White House High School, and Gallatin Junior High. She was honored for her accomplishments in 1970 and again in 1977 by the Outstanding Young Women of America. She is a published writer.

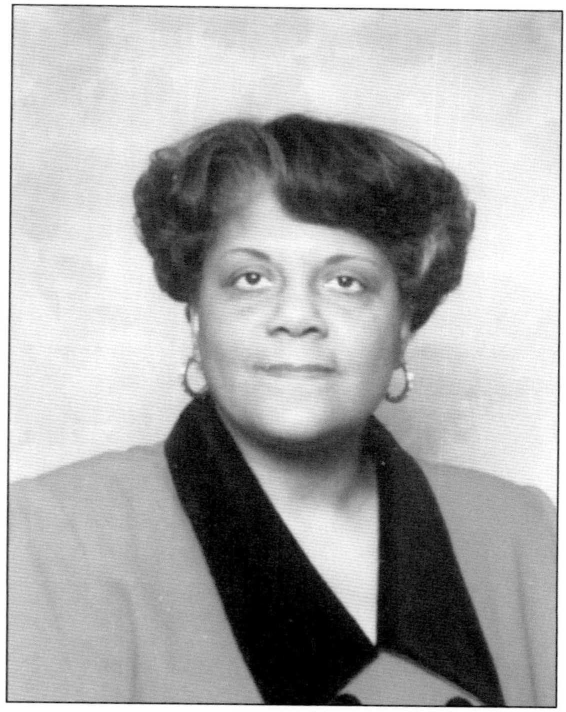

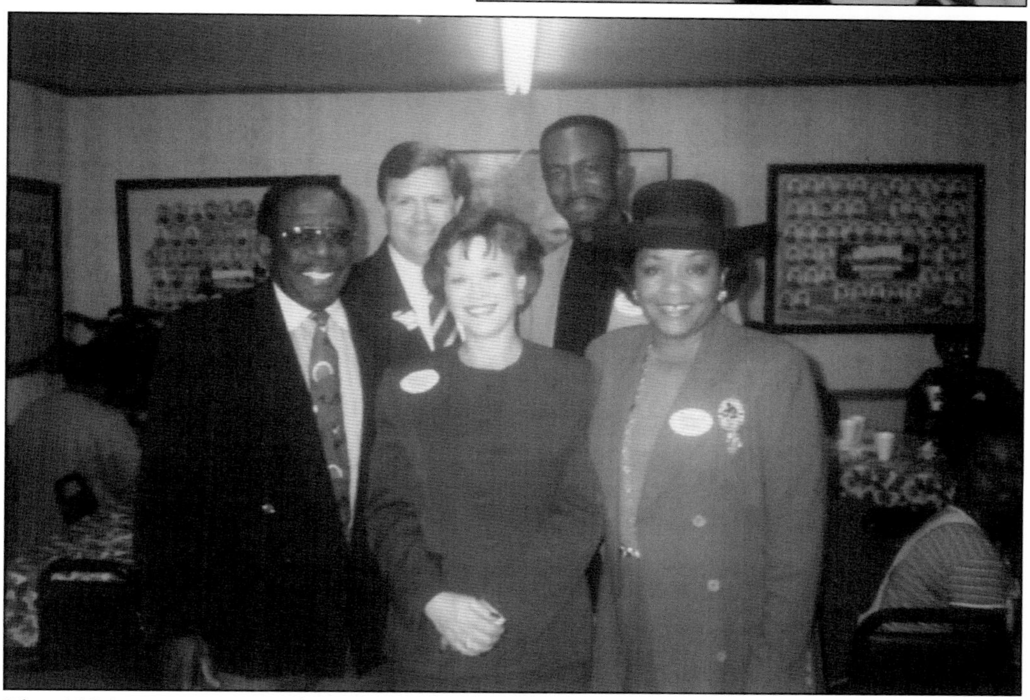

This 1996 picture was made at B and F Diner on Blythe Street while state senator Jo Ann Graves was out campaigning. Pictured, from left to right, are the following: (front row) Frank Brinkley, Sen. Jo Ann Graves (18th Senate district), and Sen. Thelma Harper (19th Senate district); (back row) Rep. Mike McDonald (44th district) and David Black.

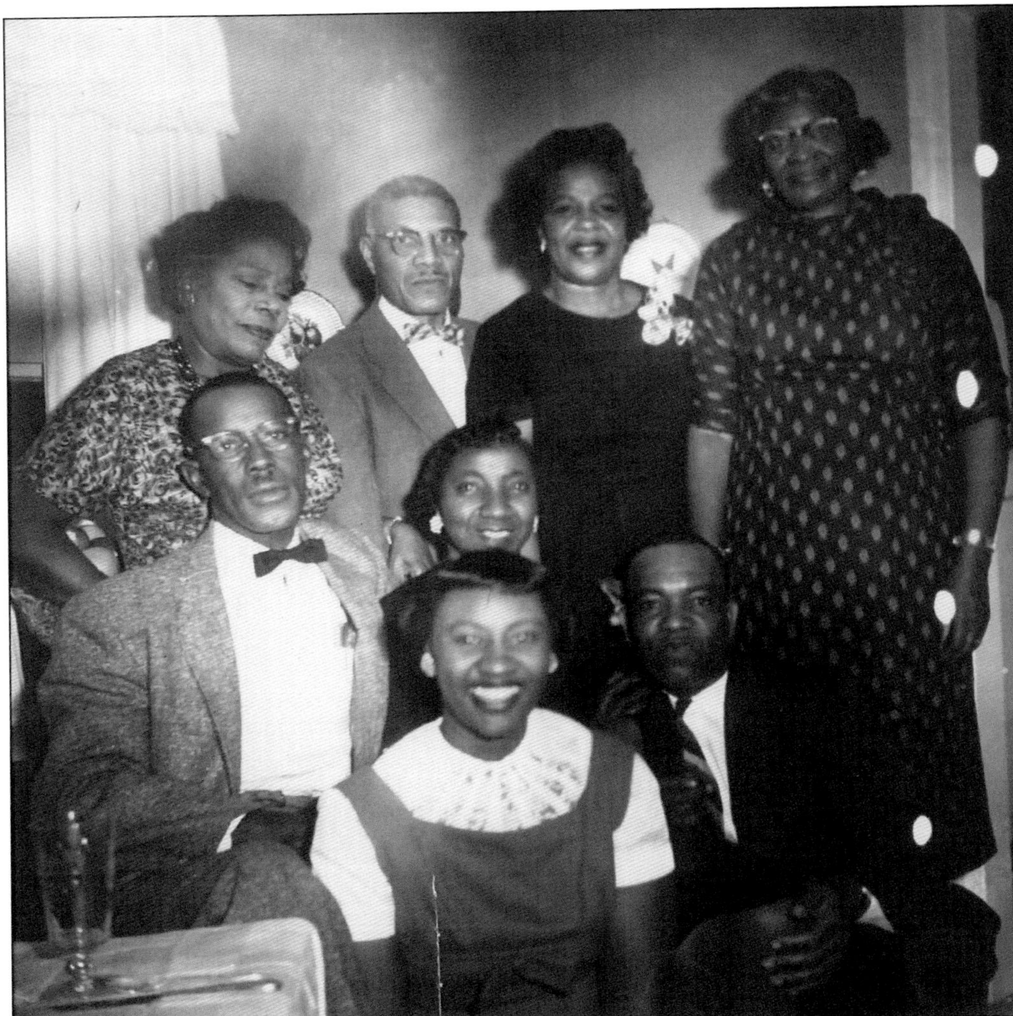

These friends were in attendance at a dinner party given by Herbert Duncan (1906–1992) and Emma Mai Duncan at their Long Hollow Pike residence. Enjoying this event, from left to right, are the following guests: (first row) Dorothy Fitts Hall and Dee Patterson; (second row) Maurice Senter and Annie Mae Brown; (third row) Evelyn Hall, B.J. Hall, Martha Patterson, and Clara Rogan.

Top: John Alexander was appointed to the Gallatin City Council on October 7, 1997, to represent the 5th district. He was re-elected December 4, 1997. John is a recognized lay speaker in the United Methodist Church and is founder of the Alexander and Company Gospel Group (1992). He has studied at VSCC and Louisville Electronic Institute.

Bottom Right: Thurman Vaughn was the youngest of four children born to John and Millie Vaughn Jr. John worked for Zack Allison, owner of the Gallatin Coal Company. The Allison family were neighbors to the Hugh Oliver Love Sr. family, whereby, Hugh Love Jr. and Thurman had become playmates. At age seven or eight, Thurman's parents died, leaving him defenseless. Young Hugh's mother, Mrs. Helen Miller Love, readily took Thurman in. He is pictured wearing an expensive Curlee suit she purchased for him at the Gallatin Dry Goods Store.

Bottom Left: John William Dowell, board member of the Gallatin Housing Authority, associate minister at Zion Upper Room, and advisor of the church's youth department, was elected 4th district constable in 1996. He is presently a meter setter and collector for CEMC at the Gallatin District Office. John is married to Audrey Carey Dowell, and they are the parents of six children (four biological and two foster children).

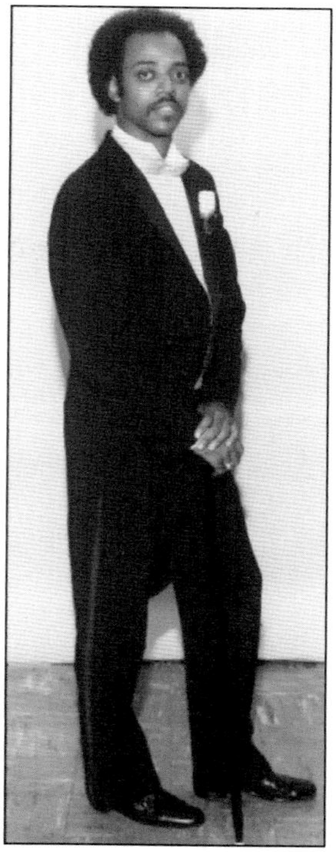

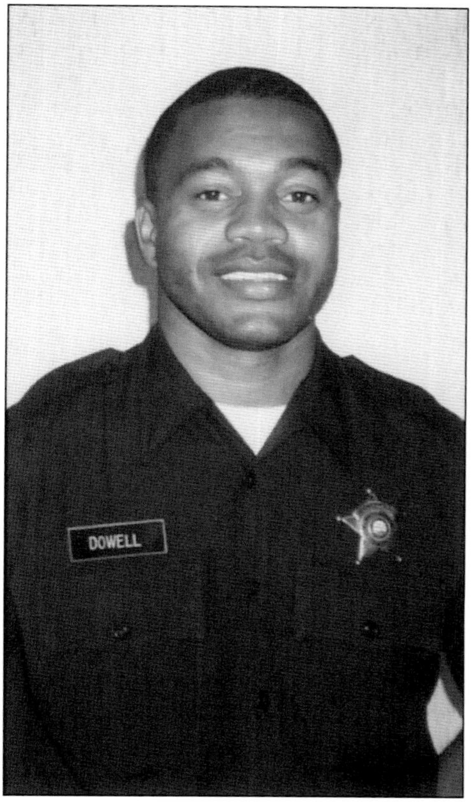

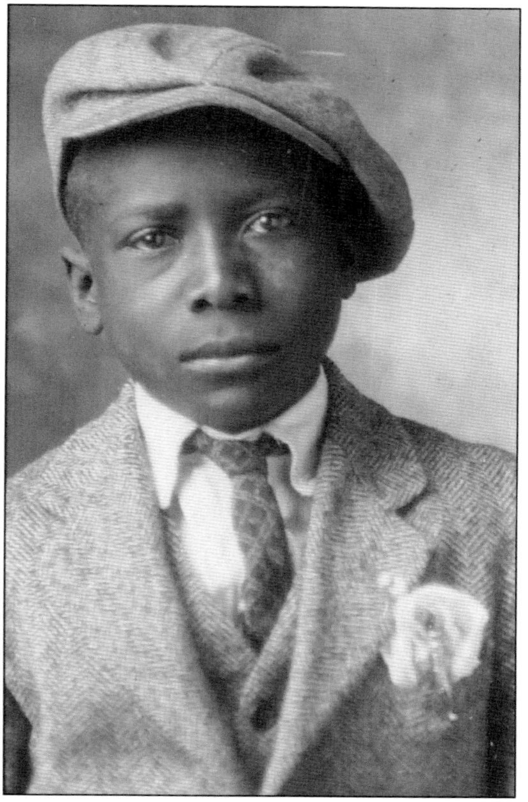

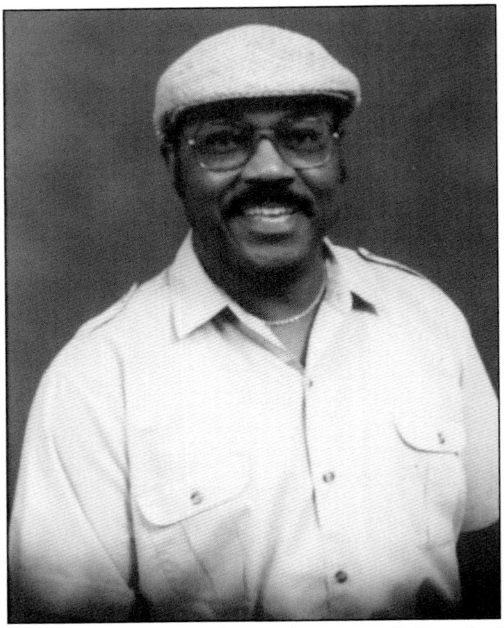

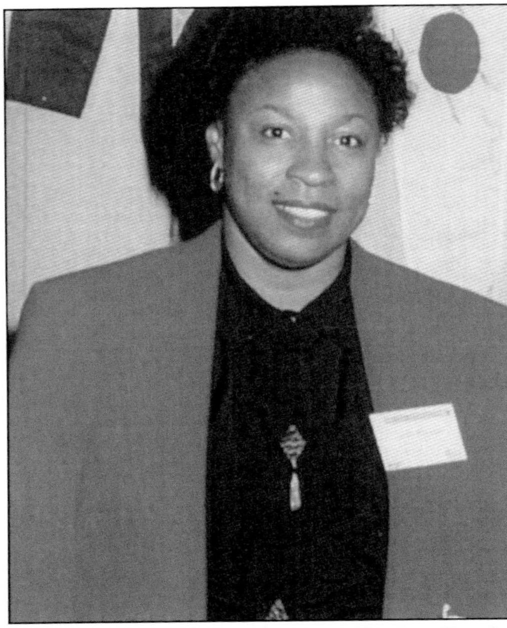

Left: William Bender is the son of Claude Bender (1903–1974) and Emma Taylor Bender (1905–1998), both of whom were natives of Avondale. He retired from the U.S. Air Force after having earned the military rank of major on June 1, 1975. Bender graduated from TSU in 1961 and attended Central Michigan University in 1977. He has completed programs in hospital administration, medical equipment repair, and human/race relations and is presently employed with Chevron USA, Inc.
Right: Betty Williams is a graduate of TSU (1973), graduate school (1975), and was admitted to a doctoral program at MTSU in 1980. She has been teaching for 22 years (with 17 years in higher education). She is presently an associate professor of health and physical education at VSCC.

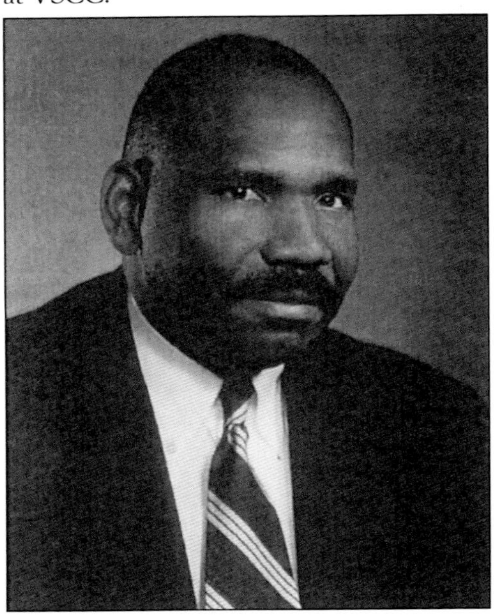

Archie Bransford Jr. was a multinational bank examiner in Charlotte, North Carolina, until his last promotion. In 1995, the office of the comptroller of currency promoted Bransford to district administrator of the Southeastern district, where he supervises approximately 387 national banks in nine Southeastern states. His parents are Archie Sr. and Margaret Sadler Bransford.

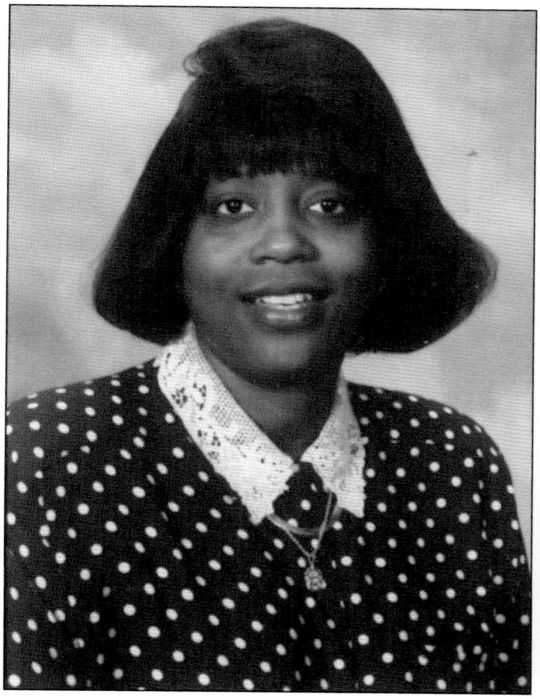

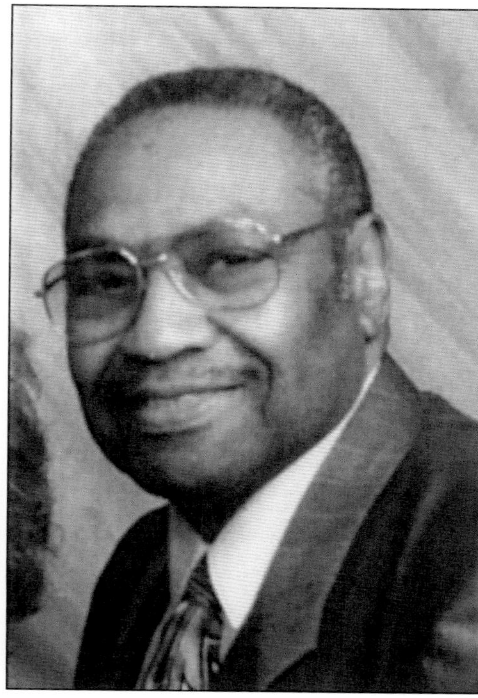

Top Left: Mary Huddleston Malone is a 1968 Union High graduate, and received both a B.S. and M.S. degree from Western Kentucky State University. Her career experiences with the Sumner County Board of Education include elementary teacher/counselor, junior high counselor, high school teacher, and presently, a Beech High School counselor. Mary is co-author of the 1996 book, *Generations*.
Top Right: Robert Leon Fitts (1925–1998) was the son of the late William Fitts and Emma Mai Adams Fitts. He served in the U.S. Army during World War II, graduated from the Wolverine Diesel College of Detroit, Michigan, and finished a training course for the water distribution system personnel. Robert retired as foreman supervisor with the Water and Sewage Department of Detroit after 27 years of distinguished service. He was married to Margaret Turner Fitts.
Bottom Right: Wilbur Bate earned his B.A. degree from TSU and a M.S. degree from Michigan State University. He was the principal of Decatur County Training High School and a teacher at Burt High School, and later taught for 37 years at Florida A and M University before retiring in 1983. His last five years of teaching were devoted to a research project on raising beef cattle. Since retirement, he has become a licensed locksmith and practices the vocation.

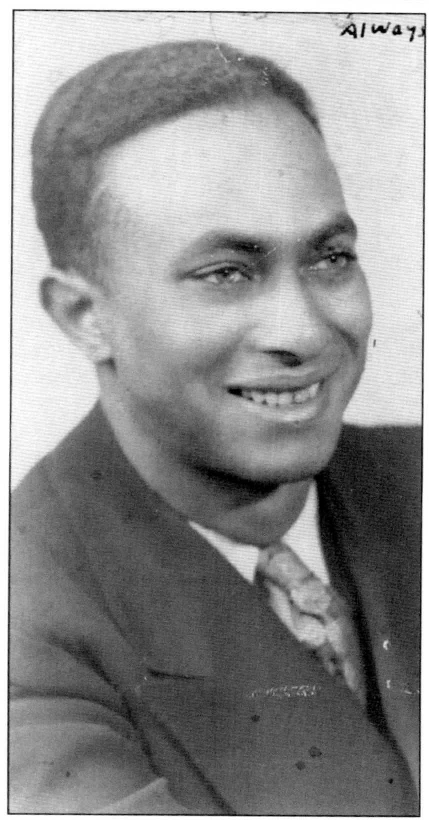

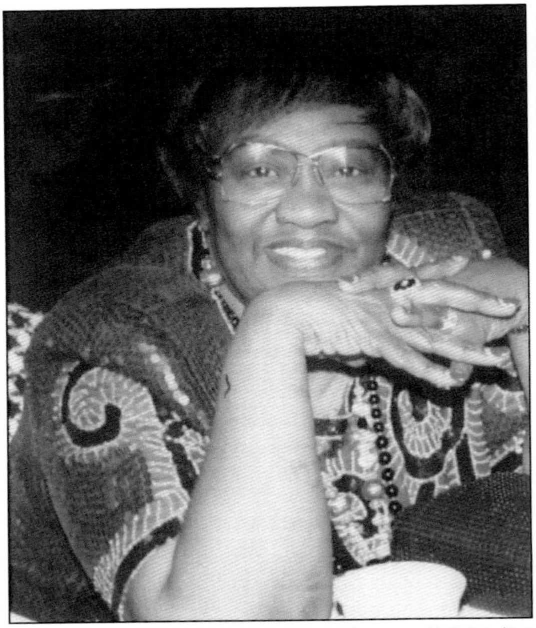

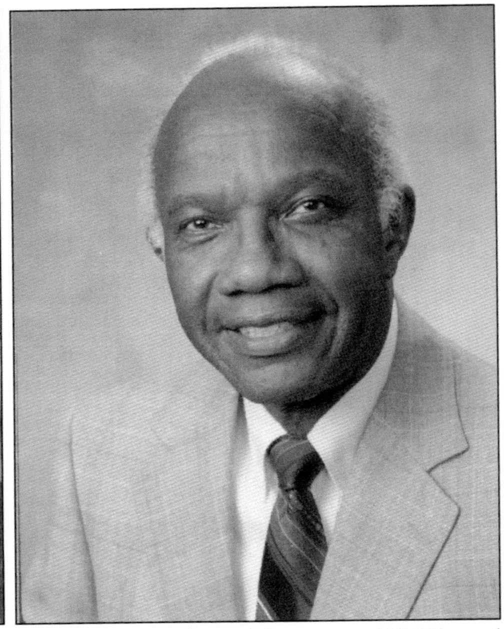

Left: Dorothy Fitts Hall is a graduate of TSU (1951), Eastern Michigan University (1968), and Marygrove College (1980). She taught at Tennessee Swift Junior College and Prince Drive, Benton Harbor, and Newton Elementary Schools. When she retired in 1989, she was the reading coordinator and student teacher advisor. Dorothy spent a ten-year interim with the IRS before returning to teaching.
Right: Roosevelt Haynes, a native of the Macedonia community, is a graduate of Stillman College (1959), Louisville Presbyterian Seminary (1962), and State University of New York at Buffalo (1971). He has worked as a home school coordinator, church pastor, community developer, psychiatric social worker assistant II, family counselor, medical social worker, psychiatric social worker I, and is presently a psychiatric social worker II.

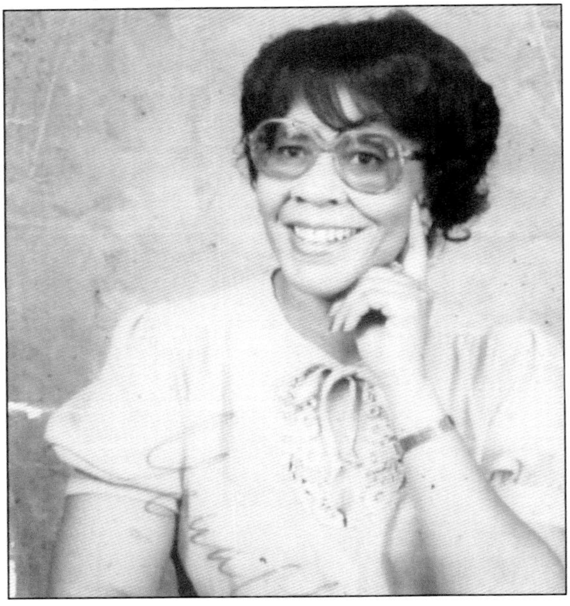

Geraldyne Brinkley North is a graduate of MVSU (1962), University of Tennessee at Chattanooga (1977), and McKenzie Junior College (1983). Her teaching experiences were in Cleveland, Mississippi, and Chattanooga public schools before retiring in 1992. Presently, she is a state probation officer. She has traveled extensively in Israel, Jordan, and Egypt (1996); Korea (1990); Malaysia, Thailand, Singapore, and China (1987); Greece, Corinth, and Holland (1983); Venezuela, Puerto Rico, and St. Thomas (1984); and Venice, London, Paris, Solburg, and Geneva (1985).

Five

Sports, Leisure, and Labor

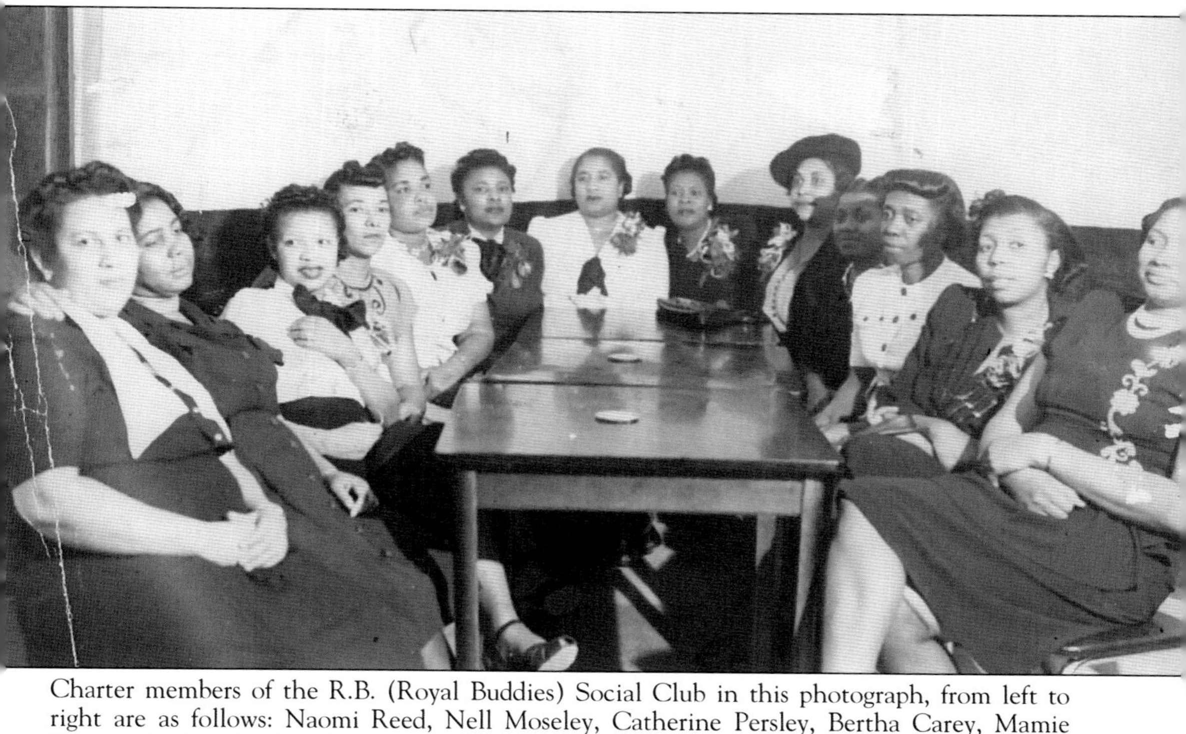

Charter members of the R.B. (Royal Buddies) Social Club in this photograph, from left to right are as follows: Naomi Reed, Nell Moseley, Catherine Persley, Bertha Carey, Mamie Brown, Virginia Persley, R.L. Martin, Louise Seay, Callie Cantrell, Emma C. Barksdale, Louise Baker, Maudell Baker, and Virginia Haynie. Although a social club, these group members prided themselves on their performance of civic and service projects in the Gallatin and surrounding communities.

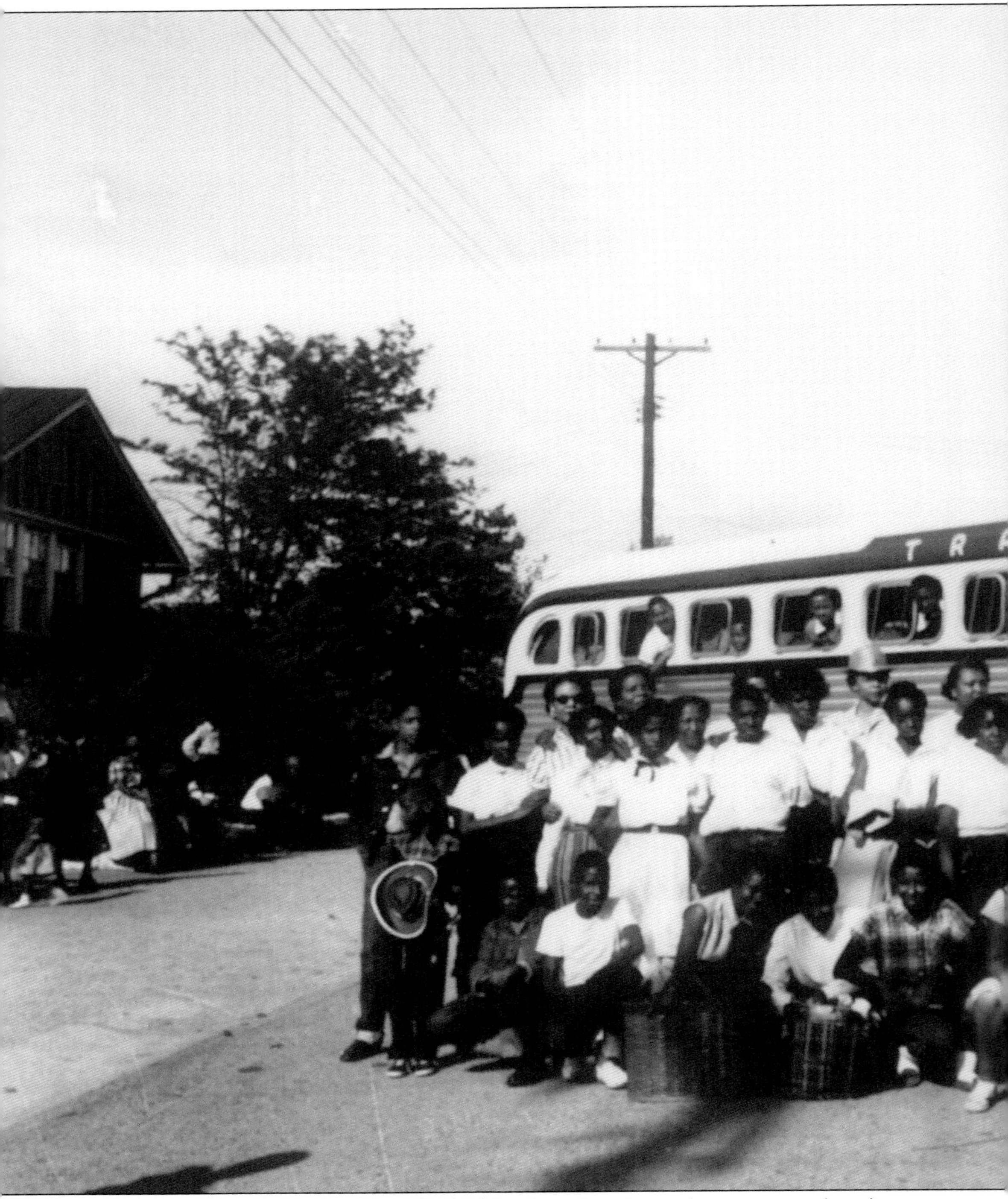

In May 1955, Mrs. Johnnie Gray checked her list of teachers, chaperones, and students more than a dozen times before arriving at this point. On this day, 37 pupils and 7 adults boarded this Trailway Continental bus en route to Washington, D.C., for a two-day tour of the capital. They left Gallatin with an itinerary full of educational things to see and do, including the Senate in

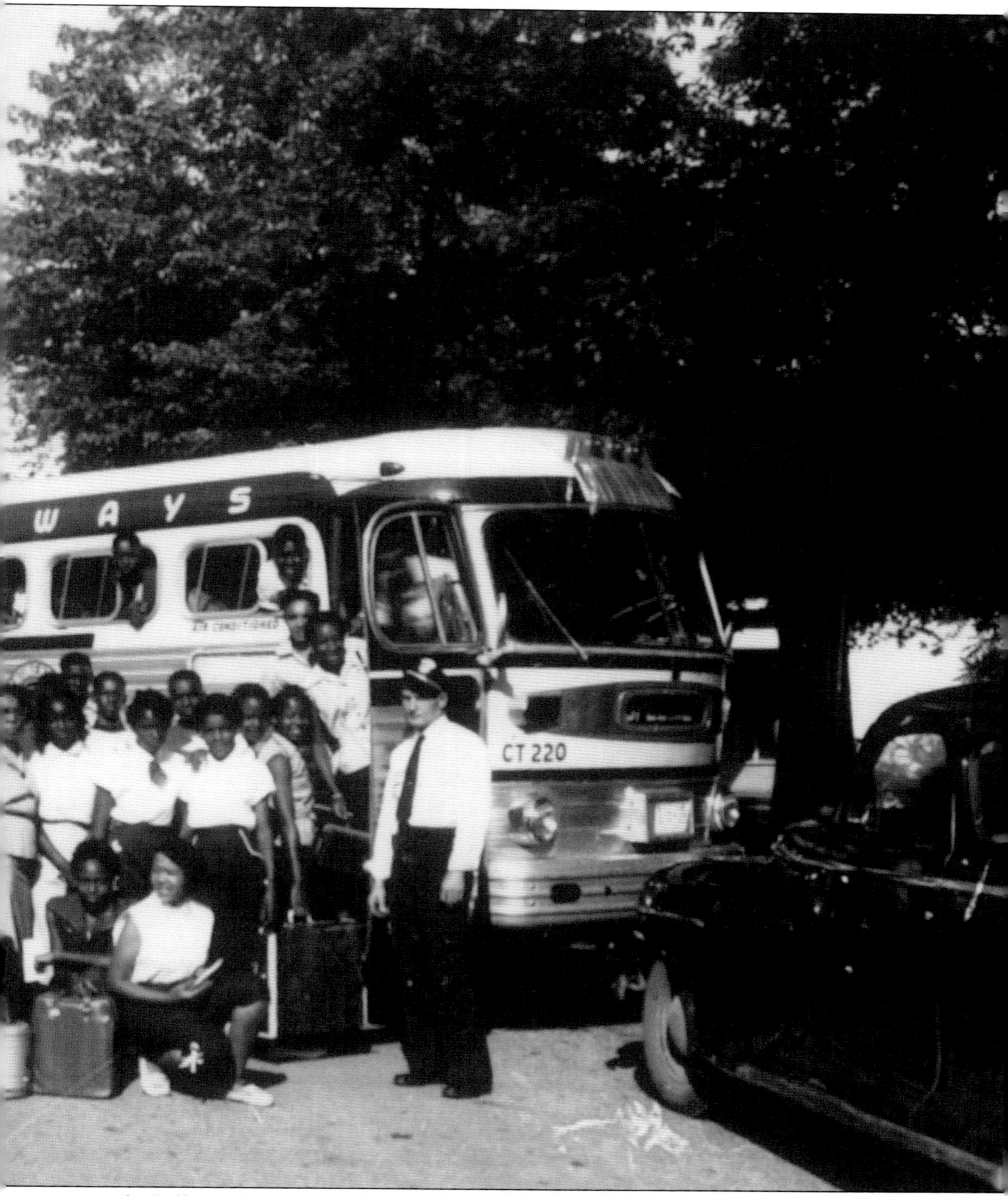

session, the Jefferson Monument, the Smithsonian Institute, the White House, the Bureau of Printing and Engraving, and the Lincoln Memorial. In Arlington, they visited the Tomb of the Unknown Soldier and later took a cruise down the Potomac to Mt. Vernon. The trip organizer, Johnnie Gray, has traveled extensively since retirement.

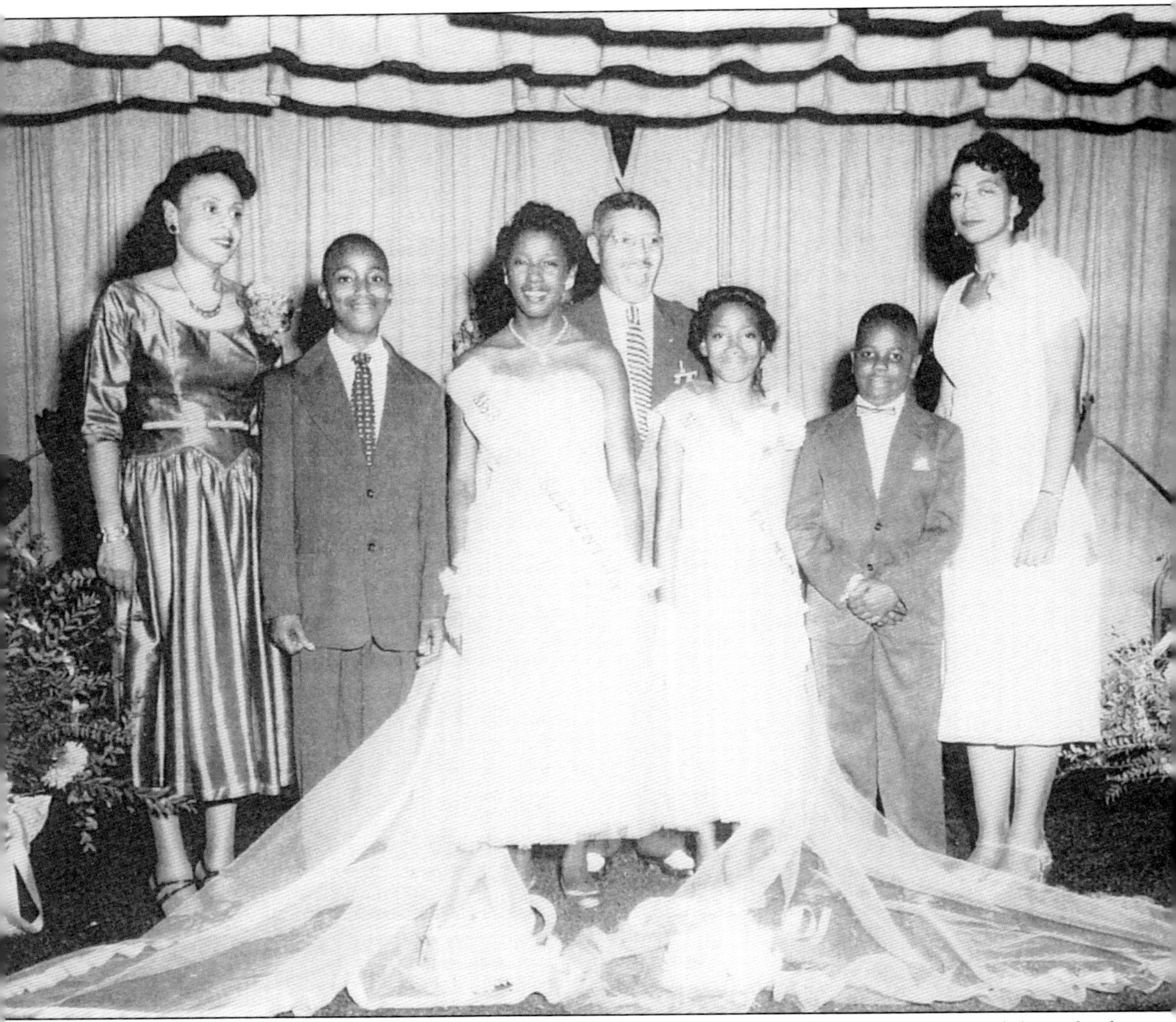

The Miss Union Elementary Contest originated in 1951, in an effort to eradicate debts which the school had incurred. Each class entered contestants, and the pupils reporting the largest sum of money were crowned king and queen. Winners in the upper division (grades five through eight) were James Bransford and Anne Humphrey. The lower division (grades one through four) winners were Willie James Barksdale and Bertha Jones. Coronation participants, from left to right, are as follows: Marvarene Woods (teacher), James Bransford Jr. (king), Anne Ford Humphrey (queen), B.J. Hall (principal), Bertha Jones (queen), Willie James Barksdale (king), and J. Deotha Malone (teacher).

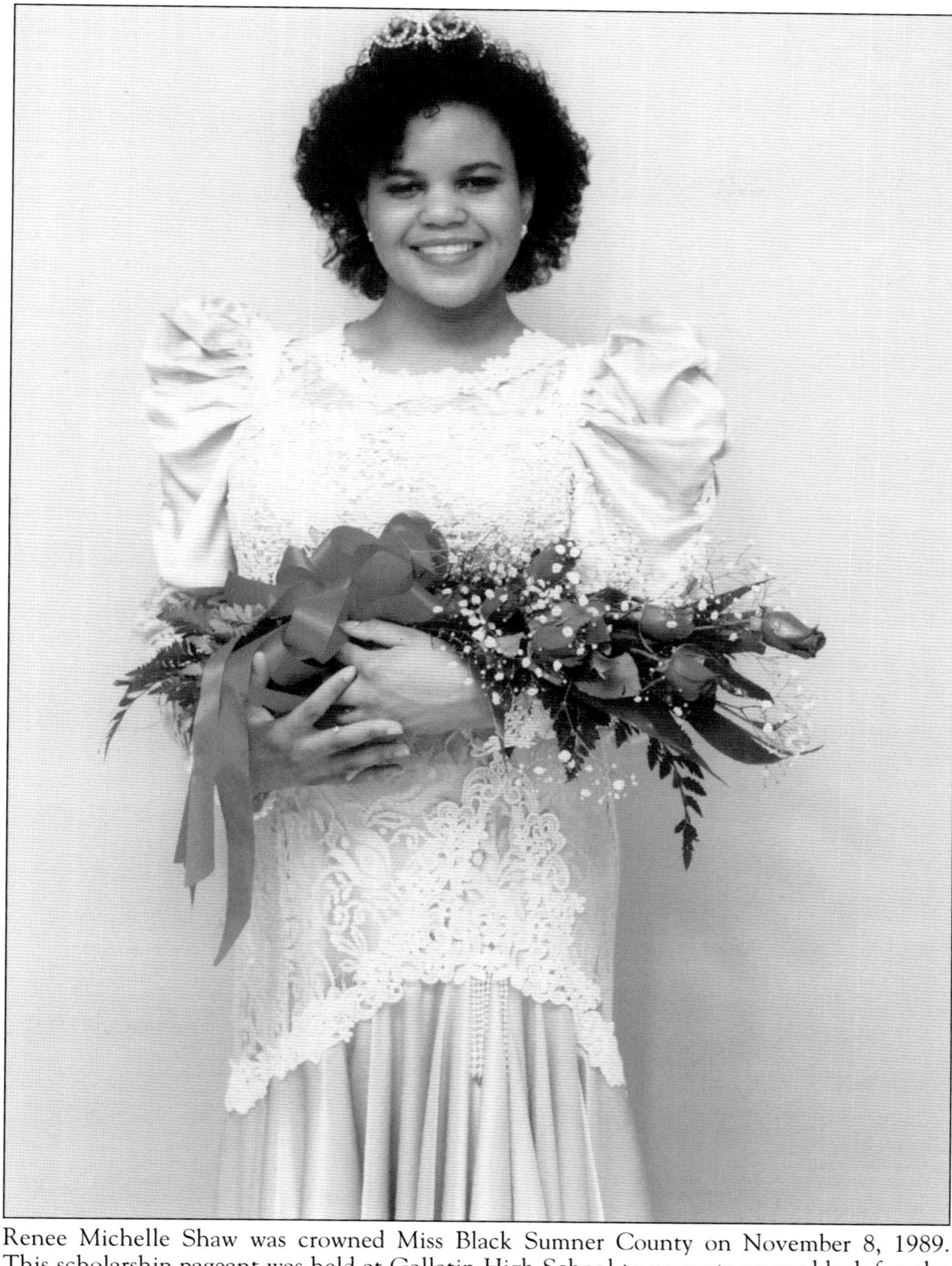

Renee Michelle Shaw was crowned Miss Black Sumner County on November 8, 1989. This scholarship pageant was held at Gallatin High School to promote young black females through the development of education, talent, and beauty. Renee is the daughter of Ferrell and Emma Coakley Shaw of Portland, and is a 1990 graduate of Portland High School. She received her B.A. in 1994 and her M.A. in 1996 from Western Kentucky State University. Renee is presently employed at Kentucky Educational Television in Lexington, Kentucky, as a field producer and reporter.

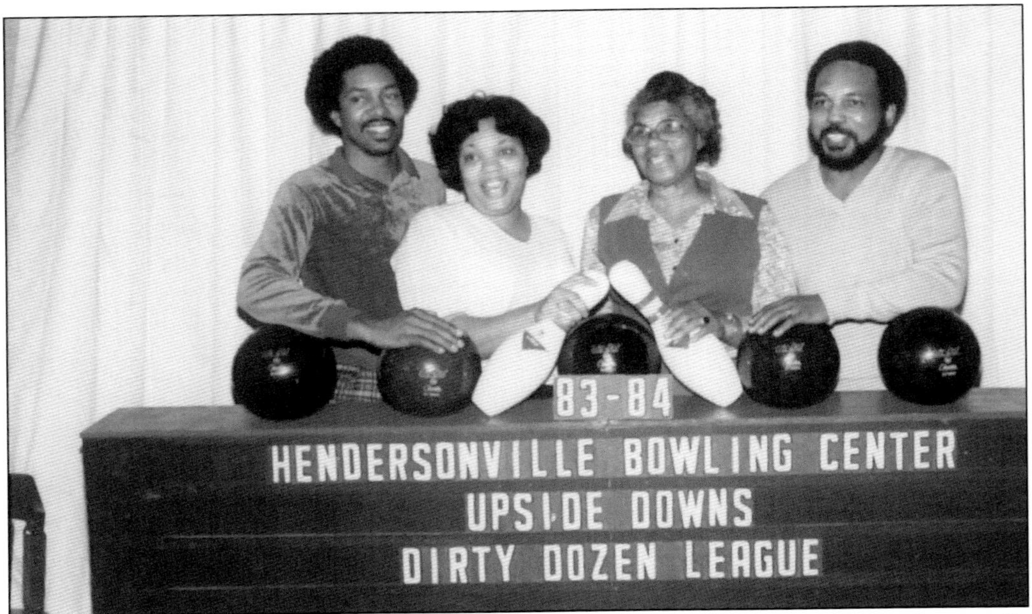

During the late 1970s and early 1980s, various bowling leagues were formed at the Hendersonville Bowling Center. Members of one of the teams participating in the Dirty Dozen League, from left to right, are as follows: Mose McClellan III, Paulette Lyles McClellan, Anna Bransford Ligon, and James Malone.

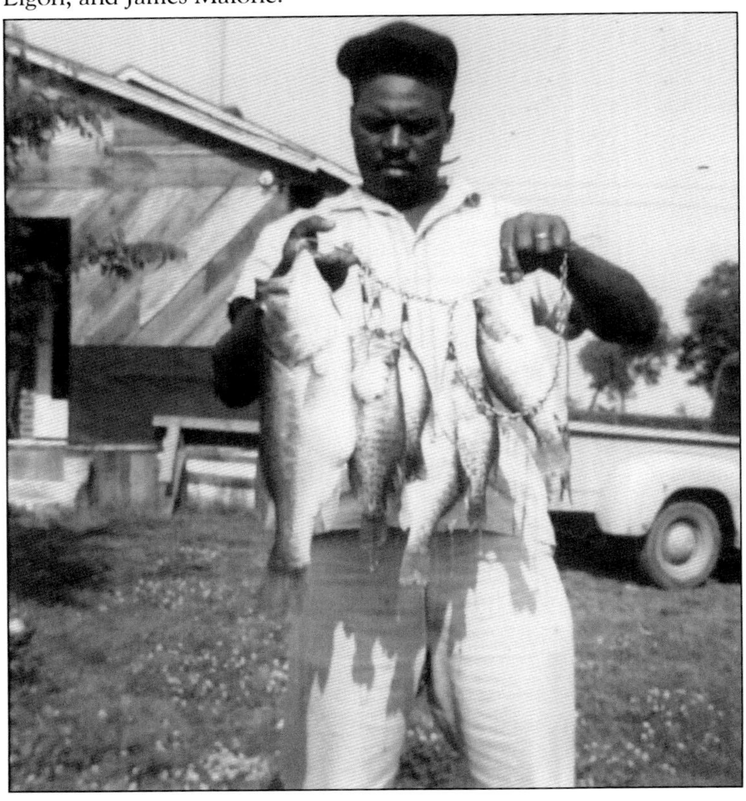

Homer Huddleston Jr. (1924–1991) was the son of Homer Sr. (1903–1984) and Bettie Bennett Huddleston. He was a skilled concrete finisher by trade. In 1975, he was employed by Donnelly Printing Company and retired after 15 years of service. Homer loved fishing and was captured on film in this 1960 photograph, displaying a string of fish he caught from Old Hickory Lake.

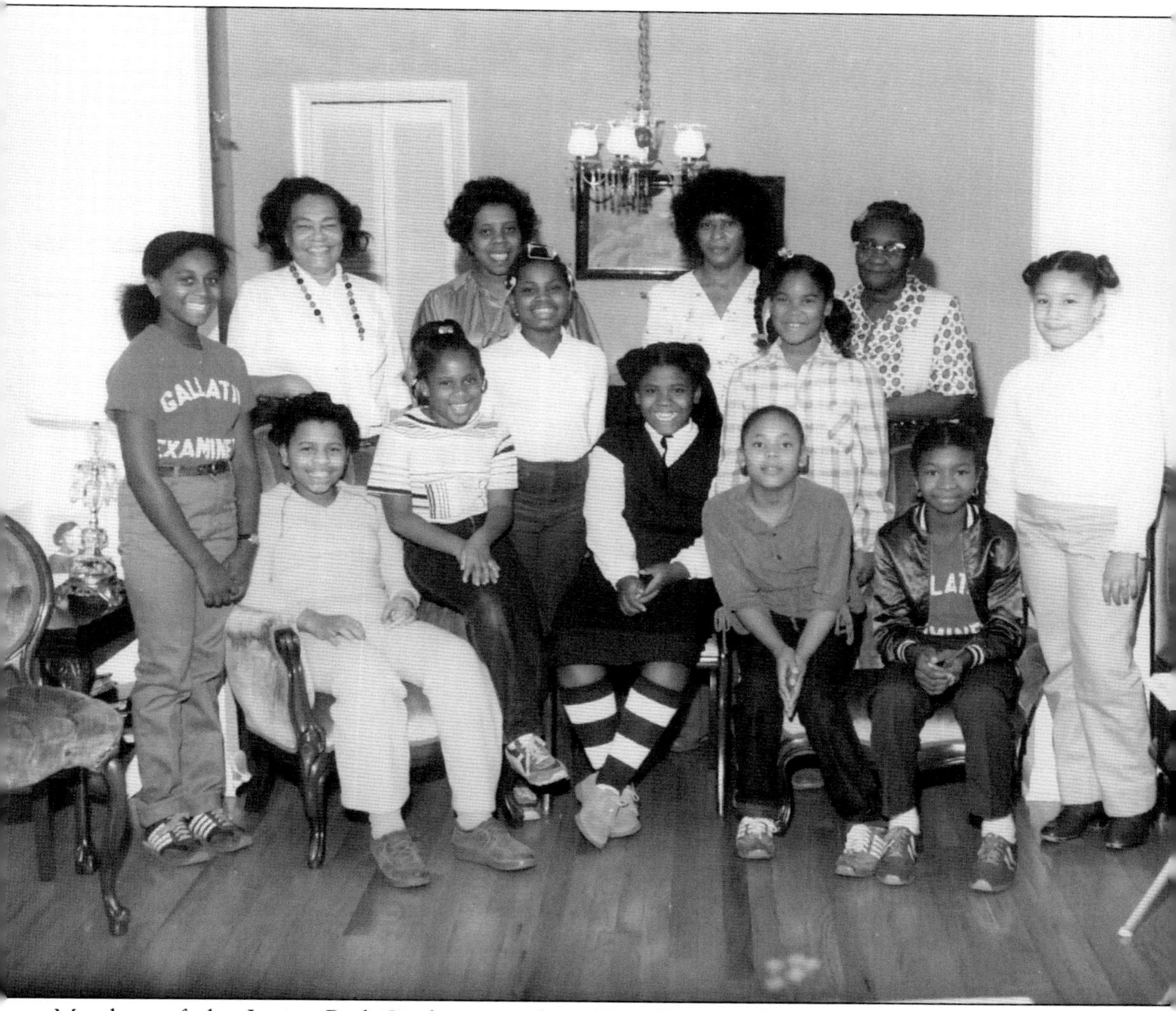

Members of the Junior Red Circle group from First Baptist Church attended a Saturday gathering at the home of Mary Alexander Dobbins. The members pictured, from left to right, are as follows: (first row) Princess Parker, Nikki Oglesby, Angela Rogan, Trina Glover, and Kathy Jenkins; (second row) Shelia Gooch, Tonia Goodall, Pamela Phillips, and Angela Odom; (third row) Mary Dobbins, Betty Sue Goodall Parker, Edith Pearl Fitts Glover, and Emma Adams Duncan.

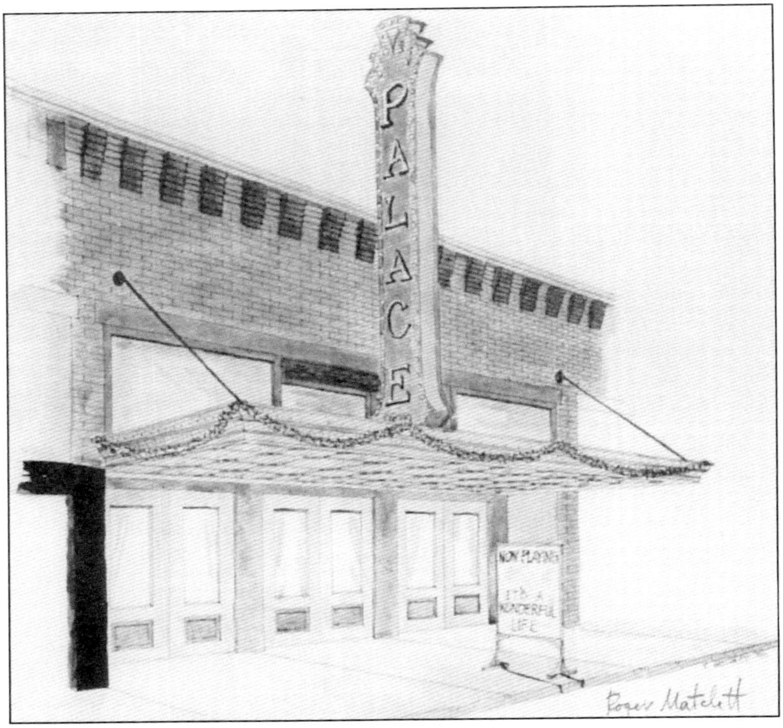

The Palace Theatre, built by William Roth in 1913, had its last movie showing in 1977. This is believed to be the oldest movie house in Tennessee still standing in its original location. Both the Palace Theatre and the adjacent Roth Building were deeded to Greater Gallatin in 1993. Both buildings are now in the process of being restored.

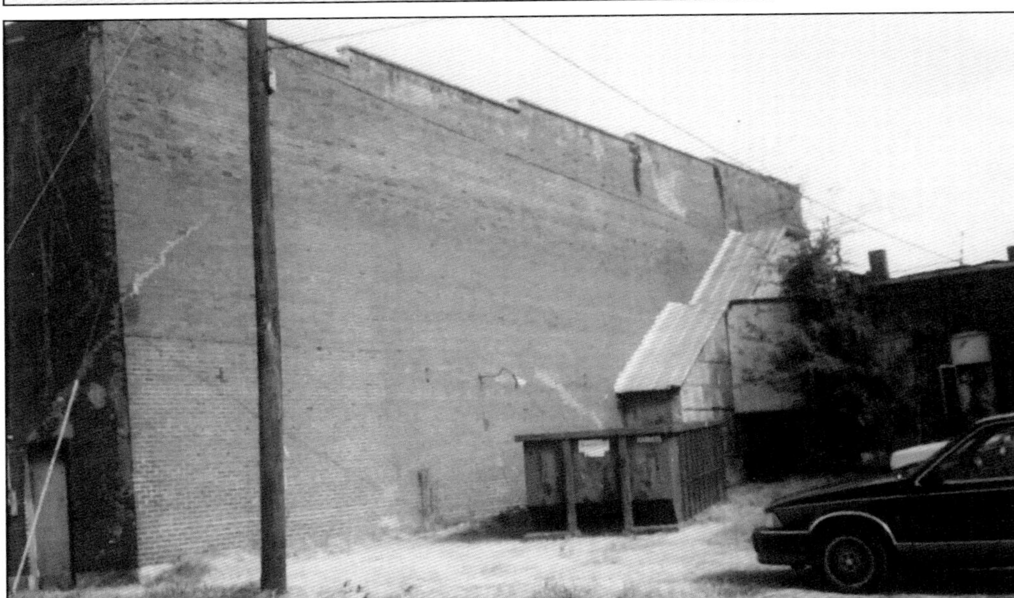

The front entrance, ticket booth, lobby, and main floor of the Palace Theatre were for "Whites only." A small, dimly lit, rodent-infested balcony was reserved for "Colored People." To gain entry, African Americans would come to the rear of the this building and climb the stairs leading to the balcony. At the top of the steps, an African-American man called John "Pig eye" Rogan sat in a cubby hole and sold tickets to African-American patrons. The balcony was enclosed with chicken wire, and the restroom rested on stilts.

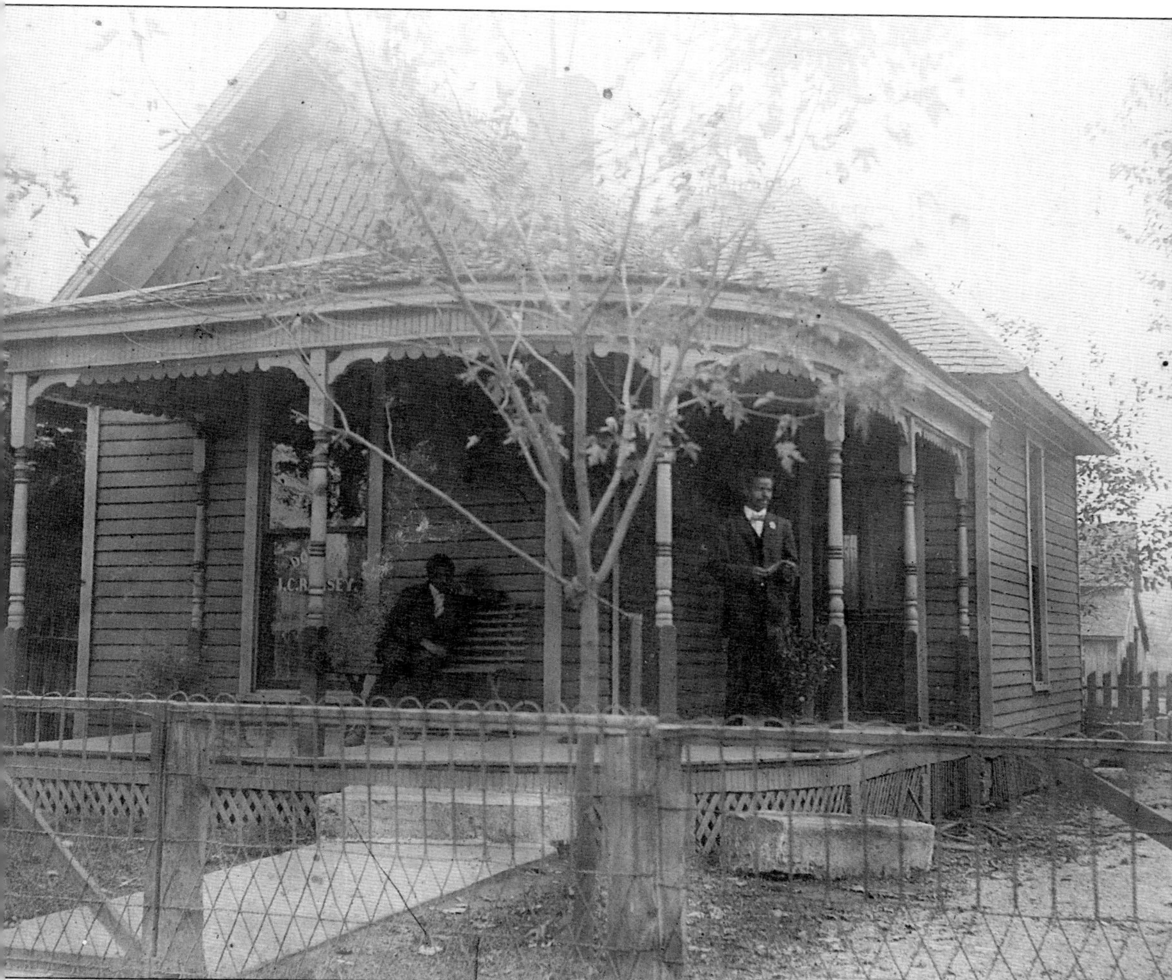

Pictured is the West Eastland Street medical office and residence (Immaculate Hall area) of Dr. I.C. Ramsey. He graduated from Fisk University (1898), Meharry Medical College (1902), and then began his medical practice in Gallatin. Reportedly, he had only one suit and no money when he arrived in Gallatin; he had to walk when making house calls. He later purchased a bicycle to ride, and eventually, made house calls on horseback. He organized the first Union High School PTA in 1919 and served as its first president.

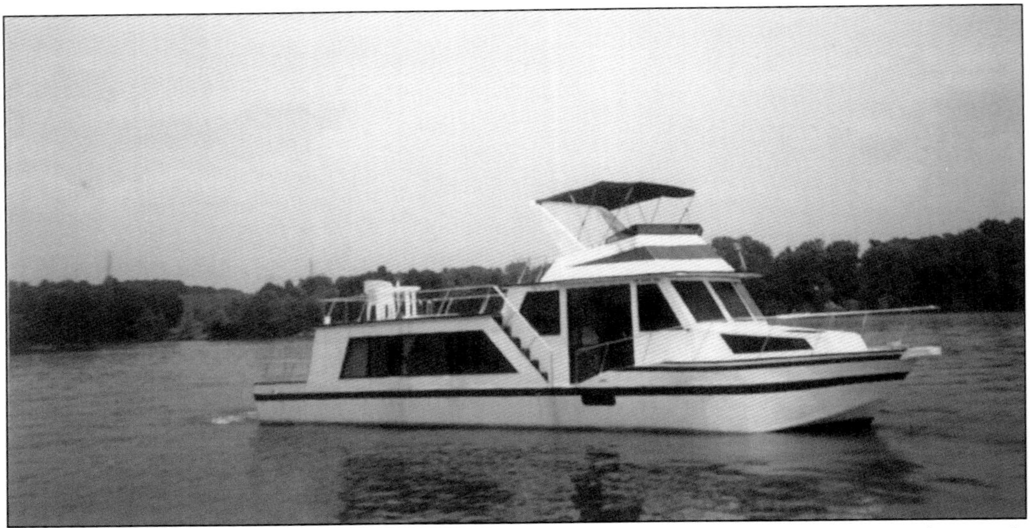

Between February 1993 and January 1994, Clifton Harper Jr. and son Travis Harper, along with Joe Betty and Kevin Vaughn, built this 50-foot houseboat. Previously, he had built two other boats, one of which was 24 feet in length and the other 34 feet. Harper has been the owner of Harper's Aluminum Window Company since 1980. This minority-owned Gallatin business manufactures windows and doors and specializes in houseboat products.

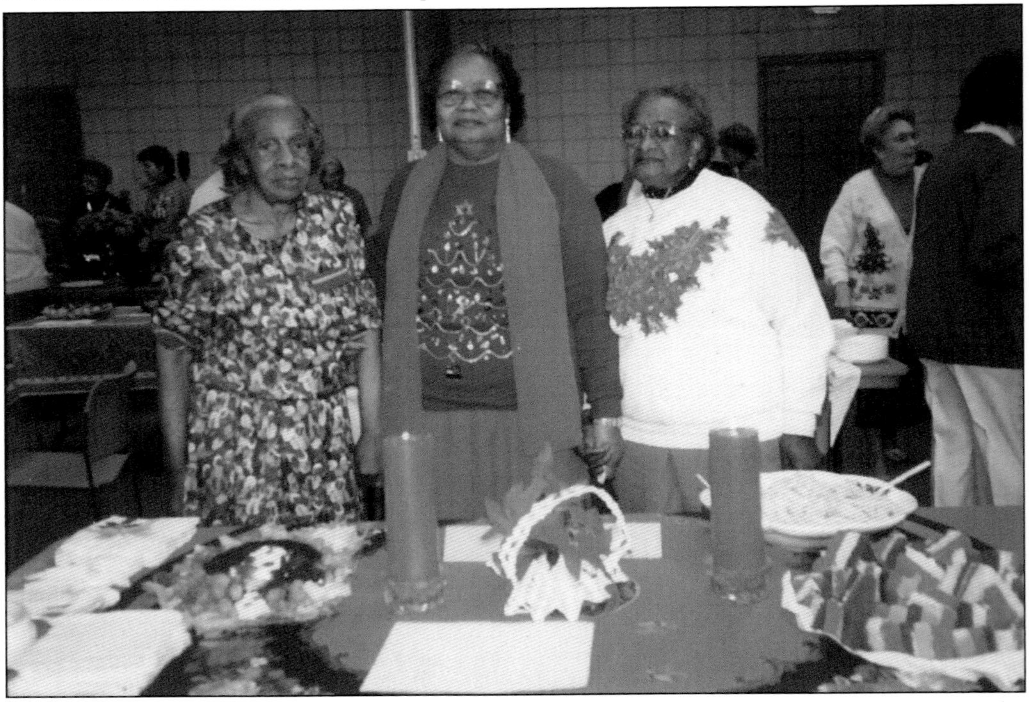

These Family, Community, and Education (FCE) Club members were in attendance at the November 29, 1995 "Holiday Sampler." This event marked the beginning of the annual Christmas celebration, which is spent sharing recipes and Christmas cuisine. Lucille Wynne Barr, Frances Carey Cantrell, and Nell Blakemore Bettis, pictured here, are members of the Gallatin Neighborhood FCE Club.

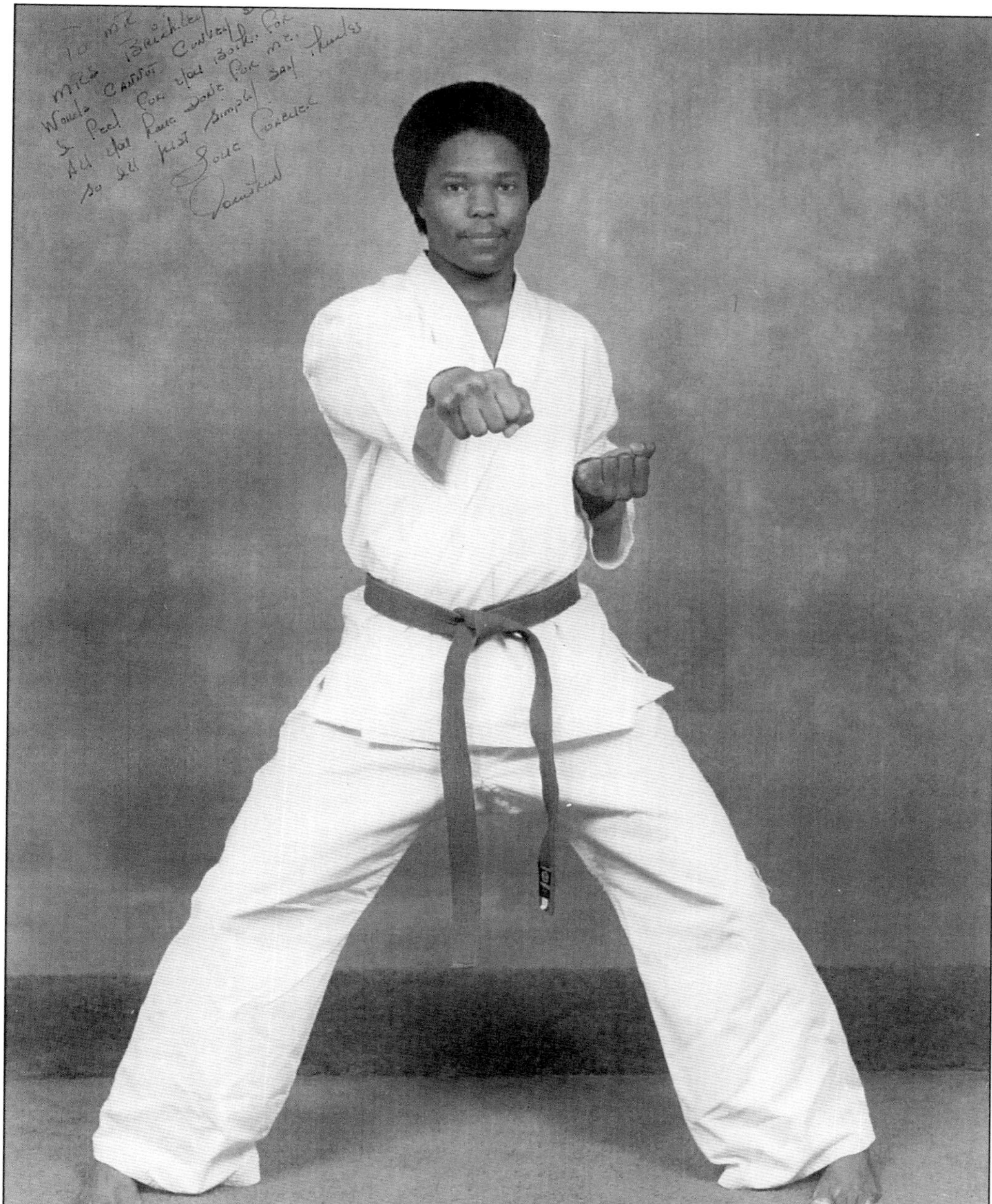

Johnathan S. Kelsey is a fourth-degree black belt in Wado-Ryu Karate, a black belt in Judo, and a master instructor at all levels. He is a graduate of TSU, with B.S. and M.A. degrees. From 1982 to 1988, Kelsey owned and operated the School of Five Rings, and later became a facility training officer for the Davidson County Sheriff's Department. He was program director and senior instructor at David Deaton Karate Studios in Brentwood from 1992 to 1997, and is presently teaching in an alternative school program for the Deole Wallace Center in Nashville.

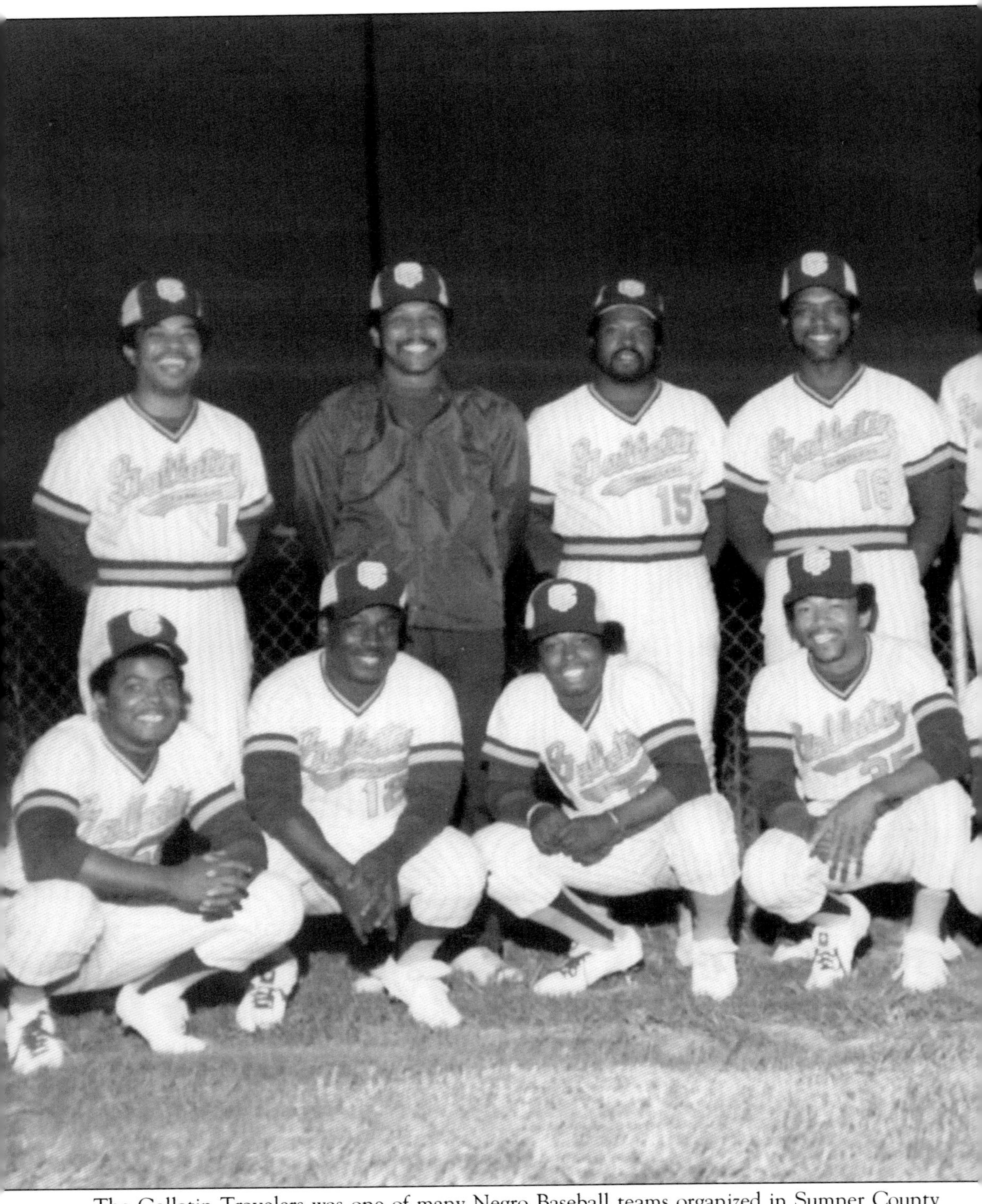

The Gallatin Travelers was one of many Negro Baseball teams organized in Sumner County during the early years. From left to right are as follows: (front row) Charlie Johnson, Rufus Perry, Larry Turner, Robert Alexander, Percy Halcomb Jr., Rufus Burnley, Morris Vance, and

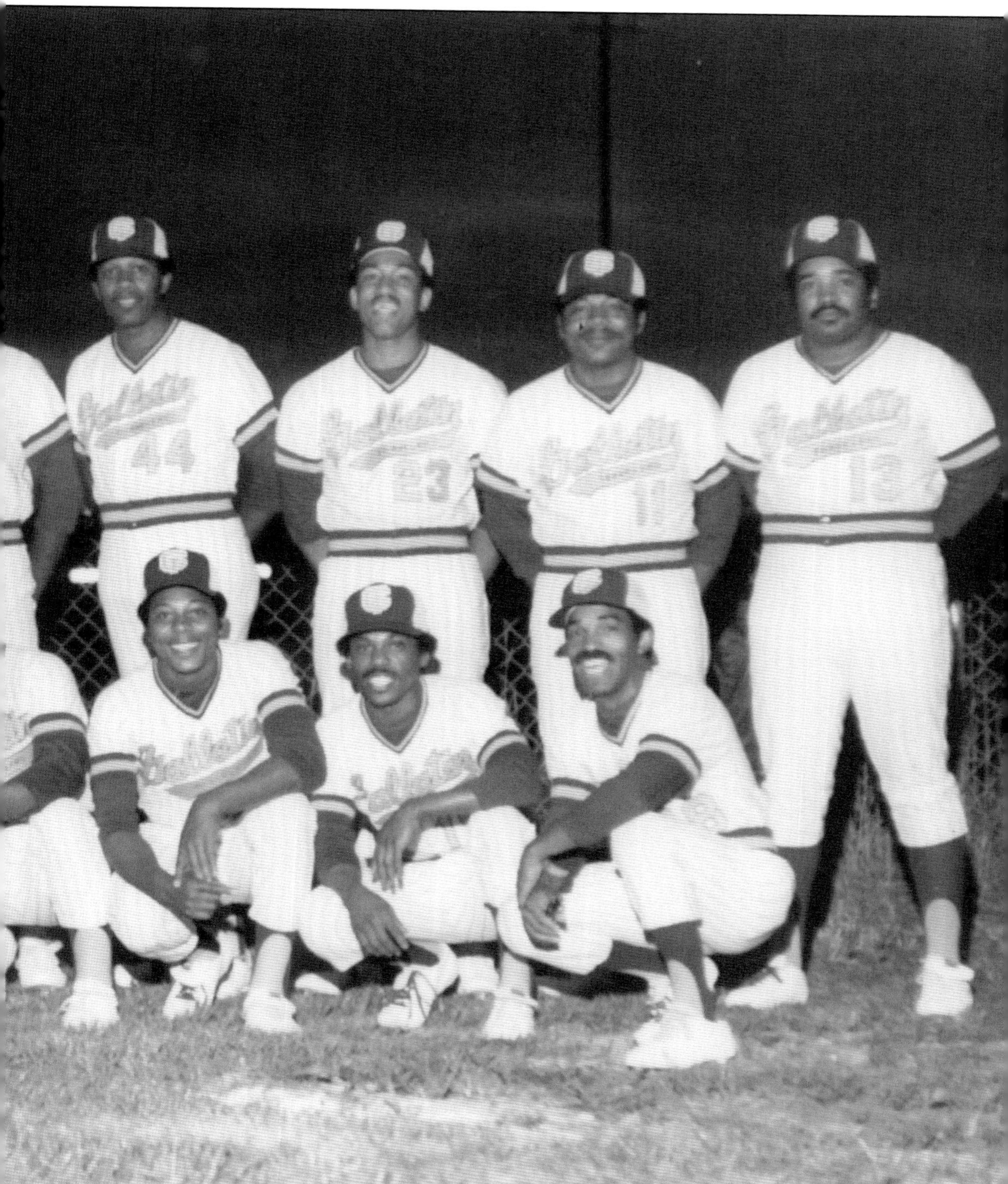

Joe Parker; (back row) William Turner, Tommy Bragg, Robert Walker, Scottie Law, Michael Crenshaw, James Branham, Joe Smith, Richard Burnley, and Robert Rice.

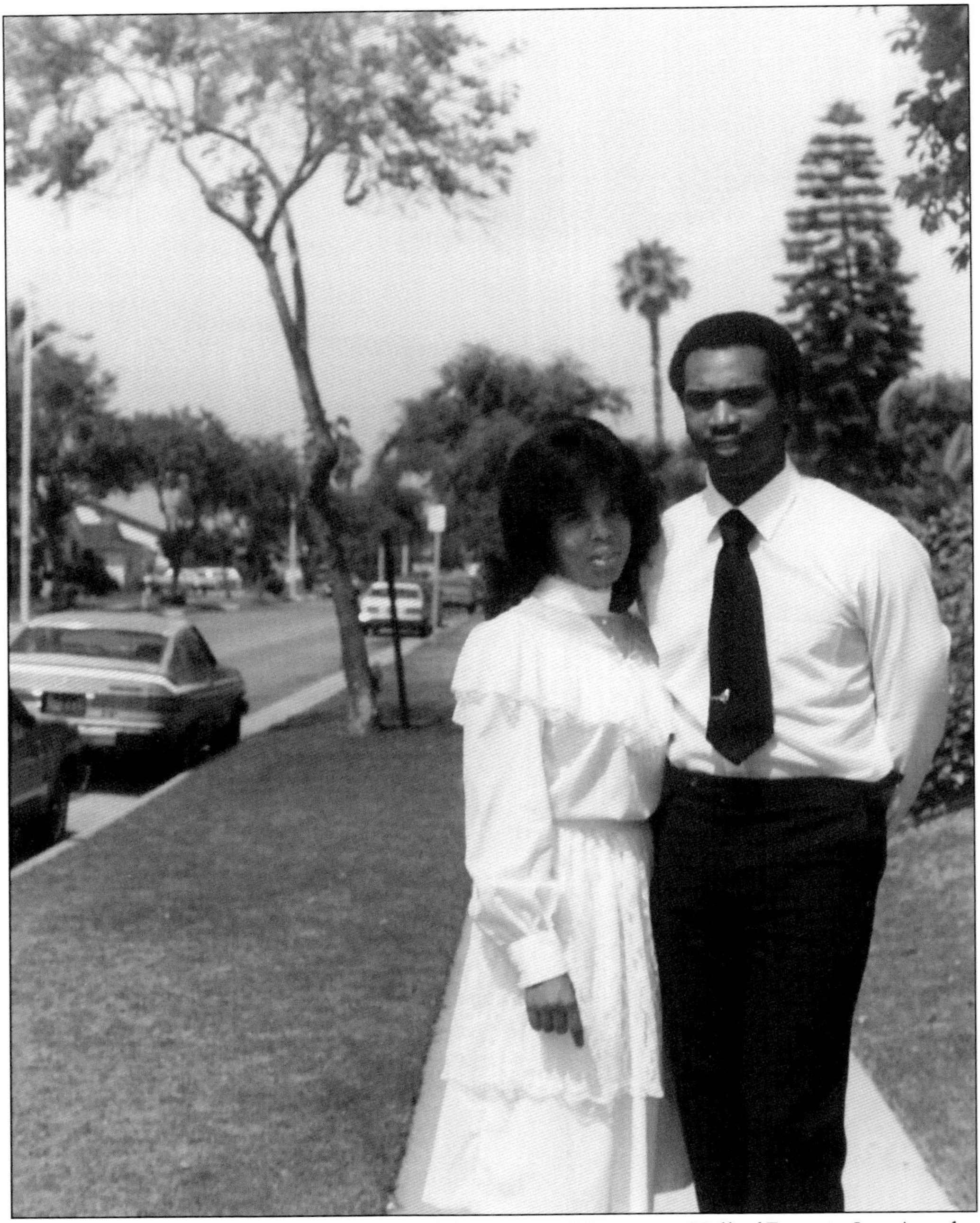

Charles Gwynn was inducted into the California State University Hall of Fame in Los Angeles in 1995. A most prolific offensive performer, he owns the record for most home runs in one season (17), most extra base hits in a career (74), longest hitting streak (22 games), three-time NCAA Division I selection, and ranks in the top five in 11 different offensive categories. Charles, who is the older brother of major league baseball stars Tony and Chris Gwynn, enjoyed a three-year career at Cal State in Los Angeles. Pictured here with his wife, Lavette, he now teaches at 102nd Street School in Los Angeles.

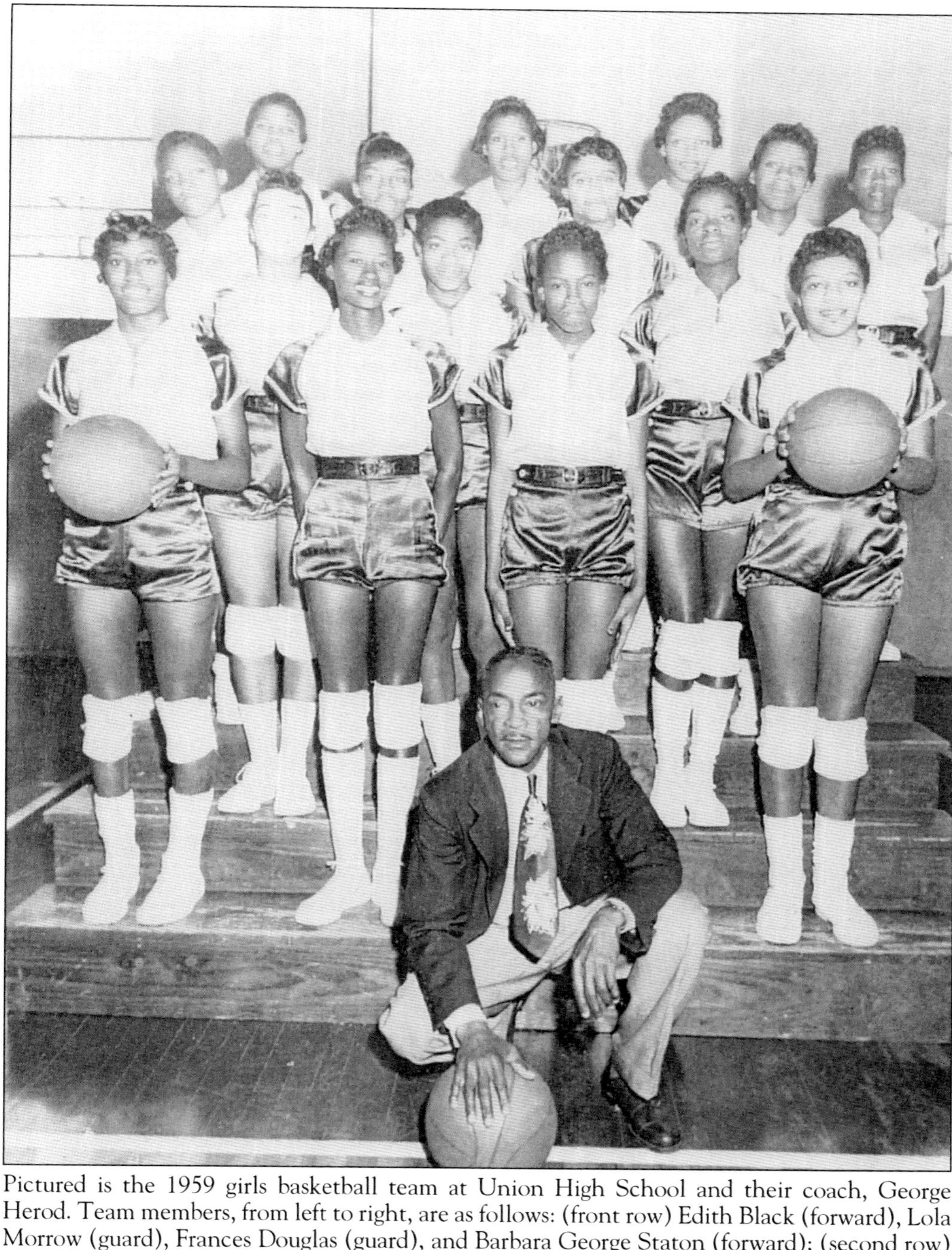

Pictured is the 1959 girls basketball team at Union High School and their coach, George Herod. Team members, from left to right, are as follows: (front row) Edith Black (forward), Lola Morrow (guard), Frances Douglas (guard), and Barbara George Staton (forward); (second row) Shirley Gwynn (guard), Leona Branham (guard), and Mildred Carey (guard); (third row) Laura Douglas (guard), Pervis Barksdale (forward), Nellie Lee Malone (forward), and Bettye Jean Robinson (forward and captain); (fourth row) Leona Douglas (guard), Ann Woods (forward), Barbara Walker (forward and co-captain), and Dorothy Parker (forward).

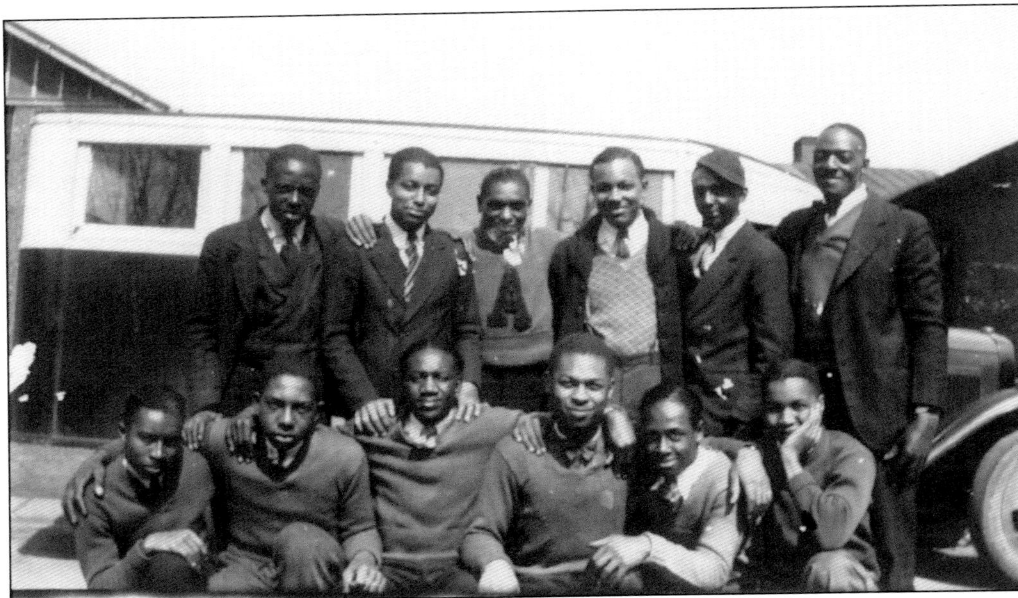

This early Union High School basketball team stopped to pose beside their bus before traveling to an away game. The team members, from left to right, are as follows: (front row) Daniel Coakley, Howard Coleman, Thomas Odom, Joe C. Randle, Joe Wesley Winston, and unidentified; (back row) James Willie Humphrey, David Coakley, Vernon Coakley, Herman Drake, William Bragg, and Rev. Henry L. Tolliver (coach).

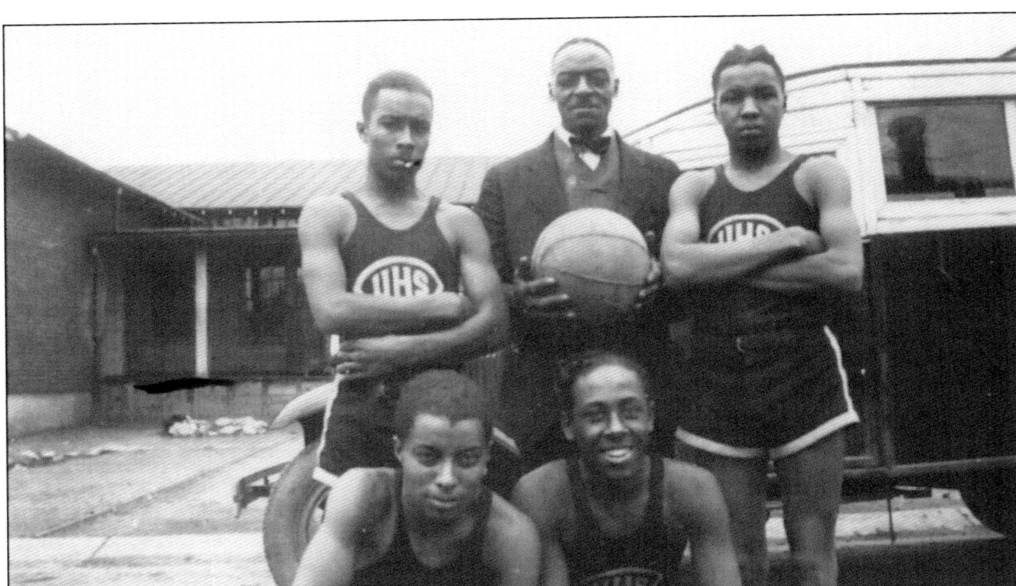

Union High team members, from left to right, are as follows: (kneeling) David Coakley and Joe Wesley Winston; (standing) Daniel Coakley, Rev. H.L. Tolliver (coach), and unidentified.

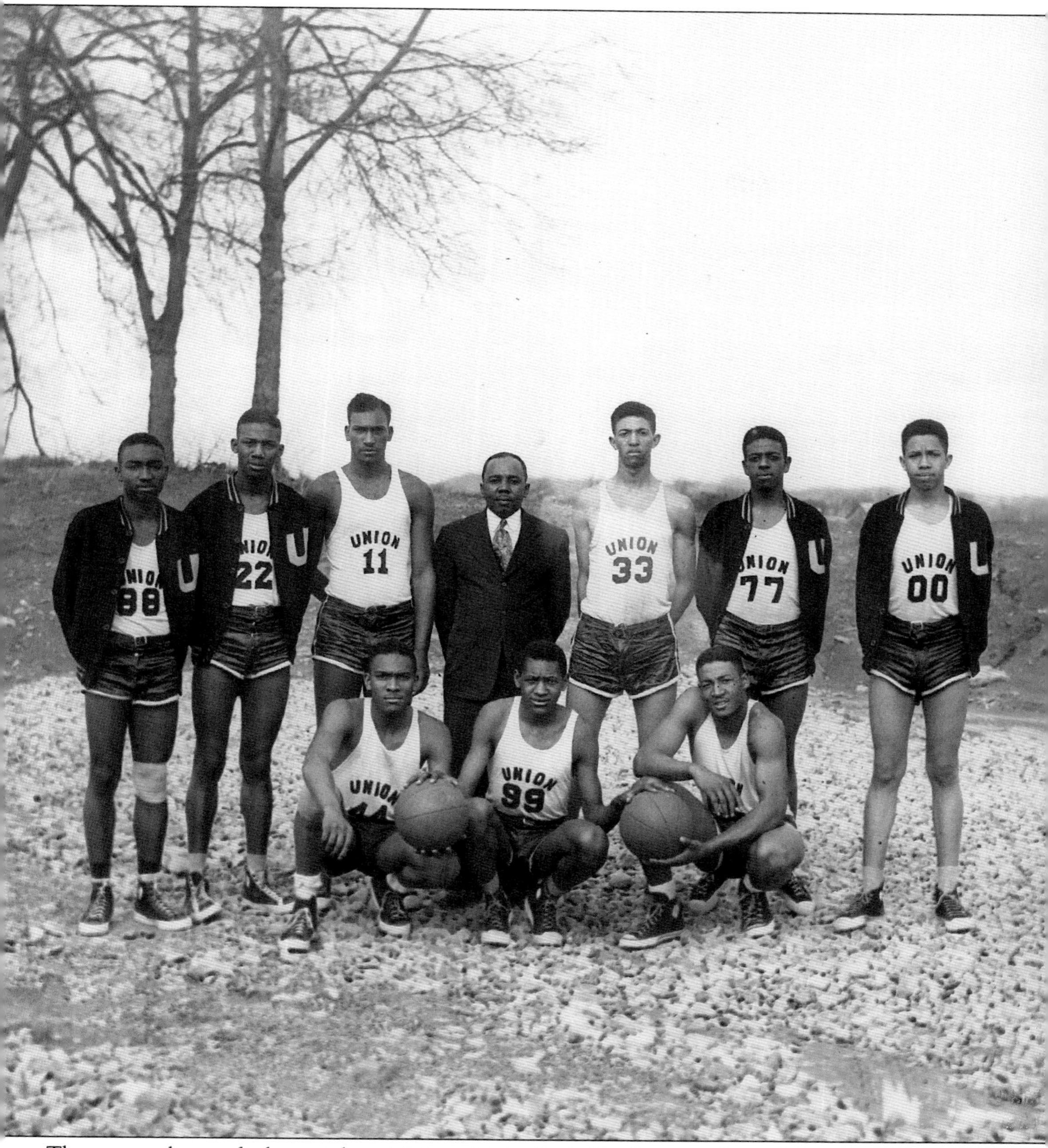

These members of the mighty Union High Red Devils are, from left to right, as follows: (kneeling) Lawson Persley, Freeland Shaw, and Leon Adams; (standing) Charles Gwynn, Cretdell Adams, Richard Sweat, E.A. Gray (coach), Leroy Lyles, Marion Gwynn, and Charles Dalton.

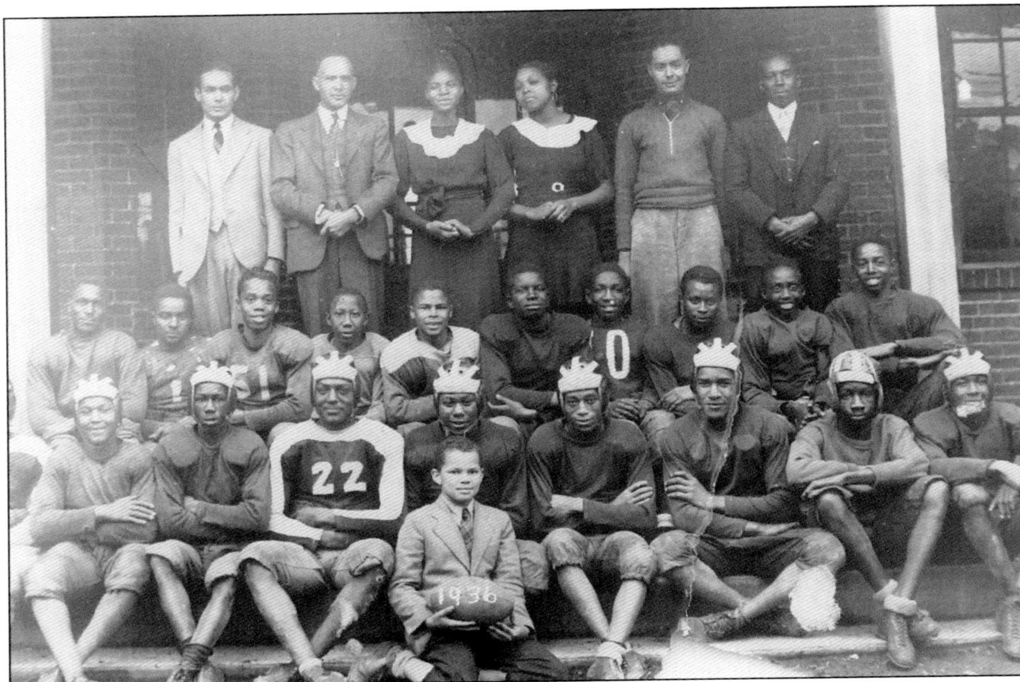

This Union High School football team was undefeated in 1936. Holding the trophy ball is Foster Anthony, and from left to right, are the following team members: (first row) Talmadge Wilks (barely visible), Jack Hamilton, Winfield Scott, Rossie Johnson II, William Fitts, Walter Horsley, Peter Vertress, Charles Dobbins, and John Thompson; (second row) Isaac Robb, Robert Johnson, Julius Scott, Cecil Vaughn, Edward Anthony, Russell Rickman, John Dobbins, Joseph Coakley, Hubert Scott, and James Robinson; (third row) Peter Rucker, Dr. J.N. Rucker, Anna Ligon, Ruth Robinson, Harold Bryant, and E.A. Gray.

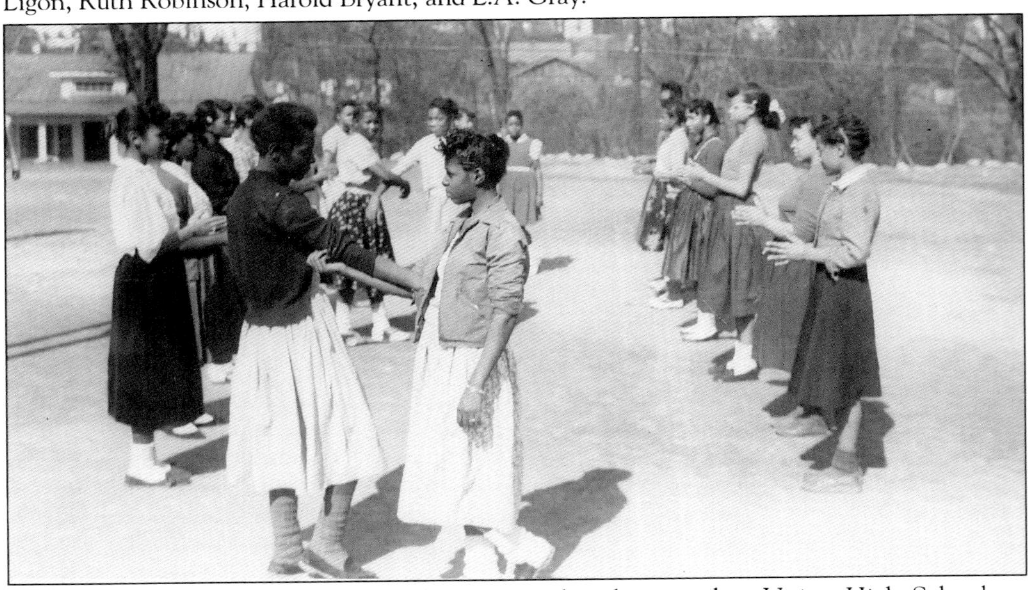

These students appear to be square-dancing on the playground at Union High School on Winchester Street. Note the Roy Everett home (left).

Bobby Lee Turner is an avid sportsman who enjoys both golf and fishing equally. He is pictured holding a 5-pound large mouth bass he caught in March 1979. Since that time, he has pulled in an 8-pound large mouth bass. Bobby is the head produce clerk at Kroger Store #897, where he has been employed for the last 28 years. Prior to this, he worked for three years at the A&P grocery store.

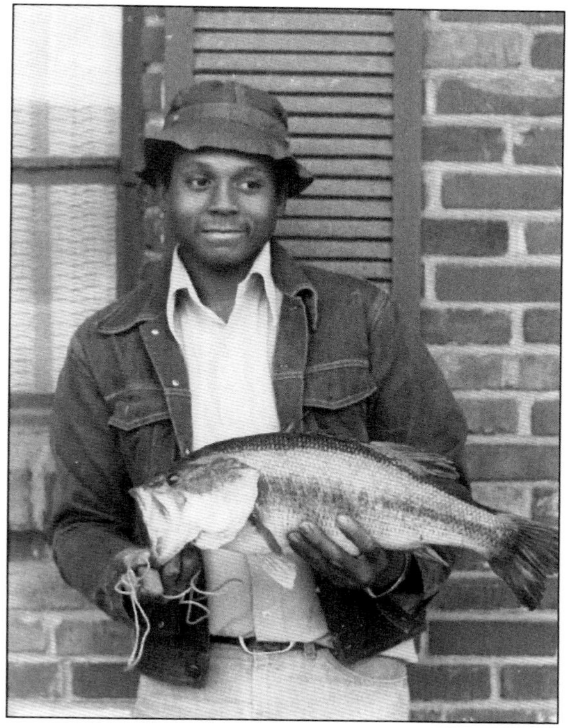

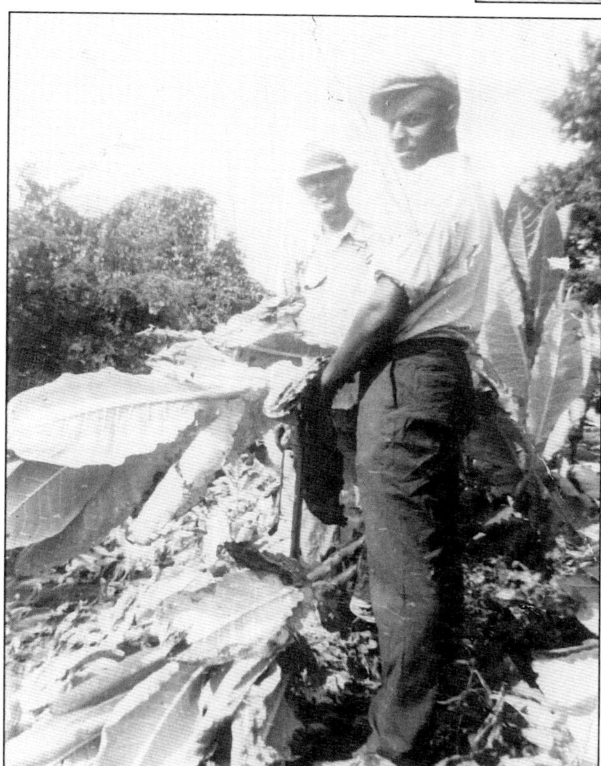

Willie Jeffery Carr (1913–1971) was spiking burley tobacco at the Johnny Dyer farm on Lock Four Road. Johnny Dyer is pictured in the background on the left. Willie and his wife, Maggie Walker Carr (1914–1994), made their home on Magnolia Street in Gallatin.

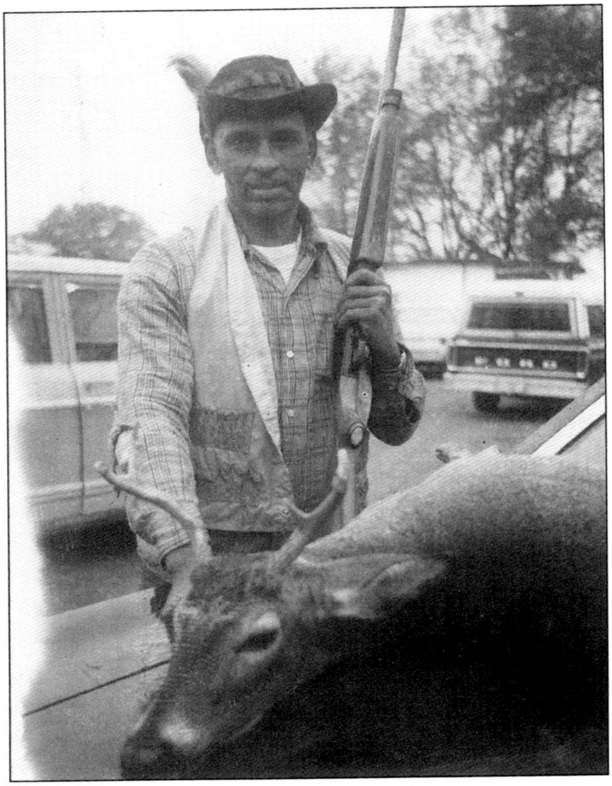

Sportsman W.H. Carr reports that this buck weighed in at 246 pounds, field-dressed, in 1987. He was hunting in the Cairo community. This buck, he believes, is a record holder. Carr is a U.S. Air Force veteran who has spent many years working with youth in the community and at First Baptist Church.

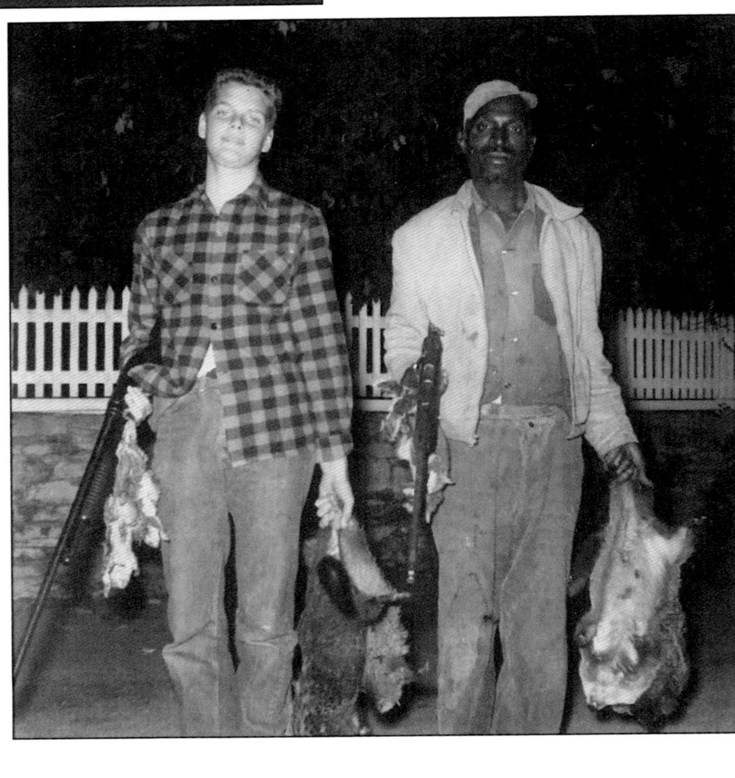

Henry "Snake" Carmon (right) and his hunting partner John Parks have been squirrel and groundhog hunting in Fountainhead. This hunting trip took place in October 1958.

ACKNOWLEDGMENTS

The author would like to thank the many individuals who took time to search attics, dresser drawers, cardboard boxes, and photograph albums for these precious pictures. We reserve a special debt of gratitude for the following people and organizations: Patrick T. Meguiar for writing six captions; Nathan Knight for writing one caption; Tony Utley for fort-drawing; Highland Rim Historical Society for drawing Parker's Chapel Church; Greater Gallatin, Inc. for the Palace Theatre drawing; and the Unionite 1959, 1960, and 1965.

We appreciate the loan of pictures from the following: John Alexander, Curtis Barr, Allie Bell, William Bender, James Branham, Margaret Bransford, John Brown, W.H. Carr, Julia Carter, Clarence Coakley, Irene Coakley, Ella Lee Dobbins, Beatrice Dotson, Elaster Douglas, Michael Douglas, Beulah Dowell, John Dowell, Emma Mai Duncan, James Epperson, E.A. Gray, Johnnie Gray, John Hanna, Clifton Harper, Roosevelt Haynes, Harold Herod, Lester Mae Hill, Kay Hurt, Alice Malone Lauderdale, Anna Ligon, Hugh Love Jr., Katherine Lowe, Deotha Malone, Yvonne Malone, Zelma McCord, Lillie Odom, Allen Parks, Alva Ray, Odessa Rice, James Robb Sr., Ola Roberson, Clara Rogan, Lucy Rush, Emma Shaw, Henry Shaw, Mattie Bell Shaw, Thomas Staten, Kenneth Thomson, Bobby Turner, Ellen Wemyss, Betty Williams, Ruby Williams, and all the others who contributed.

BIBLIOGRAPHY

Brinkley, Velma Howell and Mary Huddleston Malone. *Generations: A Pictorial Journey into the Lives of African Americans in Sumner County*. Nashville: Morgan Publications, 1996.

History of Tennessee: Sumner, Smith, Macon, and Trousdale Counties. Greenville, SC: Southern Historical Press, 1995.

Hoffschwelle, Mary Sara. *Rebuilding the Rural Southern Community: Reformers, Schools, and Homes in Tennessee, 1914–1929*. Ph.D. diss., Vanderbilt University, 1991.

Scates, S.E. *A School History of Tennessee*. Yonkers on Hudson, New York: World Book Company, 1936.

A Study of the Negroes in Sumner County. Ed. by the Jeanes Teacher from materials compiled by African-American teachers in Sumner County, 1944–1945.

Index